Challenging the State?
The Socialist and Feminist
Educational Experience
1900–1930

Hilda Kean

 The Falmer Press
(A Member of the Taylor & Francis Group)
London • New York • Philadelphia

UK   The Falmer Press, Rankine Road, Basingstoke, Hampshire RG24 0PR

USA   The Falmer Press, Taylor & Francis Inc., 1900 Frost Road, Suite 101, Bristol, PA 19007

First published 1990

British Library Cataloguing in Publication Data
Kean Hilda
   Challenging the state?: the socialist and feminist
   educational experience 1900–1930.
   1. England. Education, history
   I. Title
   370.942

   ISBN 1–85000–775–6
   ISBN 1–85000–776–4

Library of Congress Cataloguing-in-Publication Data
Kean, Hilda.
   Challenging the state?: the socialist and feminist educational
   experience, 1900–1930/Hilda Kean
   p.   cm.
   Based on author's thesis (Ph. D.) — King's College, London.
   Includes bibliographical references (p.13).
   ISBN 1–85000–775–6: — ISBN 1–85000–776–4
   1. Education and state — England — History — 20th century.
   2. Education and state — Wales — History — 20th century. 3. Politics
   and education — England — History — 20th century. 4. Politics and
   education — Wales — History — 20th century. I. Title.
   LC93.G7K43 1990
   379.42‡04–dc20

Jacket design by Caroline Archer

Typeset in 10½/12 California by
Chapterhouse, The Cloisters, Formby L37 3PX
Printed in Great Britain by
Taylor & Francis (Printers) Ltd, Basingstoke
*on paper which has a specified pH value on final paper manufacture of not
less than 7.5 and is therefore 'acid free'.*

Contents

Acknowledgments

I wish to acknowledge the help I have received from many people in writing the Ph.D. thesis which led to this book. In the preparation of the thesis I obtained support and guidance from my two supervisors, Professor Stephen Ball, of King's College, London, and Professor Geoff Whitty, now of Goldsmiths' College, London. I wish to thank the librarians and archivists at the following libraries: Public Record Office, Kew, British, Marx Memorial, Fawcett, South Wales Miners', Institute of Education, Labour Party and TUC. My particular thanks are due to Janet Friedlander at the NUT library for her support and lively interest over a number of years. I wish to thank Paul Foley especially for suggesting particular approaches towards the state, Peter Chowney for his careful typing of illegible scrawl, and Felicity Harvest for her patient unravelling of the mysteries of computer technology. My particular thanks are due to Ken Jones, who has given intellectual support, discussed ideas and directions, and provided practical assistance over the many years of research leading to this publication. Needless to say, no one mentioned here is responsible for my interpretation or errors. I should like to dedicate this book to the memory of those socialists and feminists who campaigned so optimistically for their educational ideals and beliefs.

Challenging the State?
The Socialist and Feminist Educational Experience 1900–1930

List of Abbreviations

ACE	Advisory Committee for Education (Labour Party)
AEC	Association of Education Committees
AMSH	Association for Moral and Social Hygiene
BSP	British Socialist Party
CCG	Communist Children's Groups
CP	Communist Party
ELFS	East London Federation of Suffragettes
EWI	Educational Workers' International
EPL	Equal Pay League
HMIs	His Majesty's Inspectors
ILP	Independent Labour Party
LP	Labour Party
LRC	Labour Representation Committee
LEA	Local Education Authority
LSA	London Schoolmasters' Association
LTA	London Teachers' Association
NAMT	National Association of Men Teachers
NAS	National Association of Schoolmasters
NFAT	National Federation of Assistant Teachers
NFCT	National Federation of Class Teachers
NFWT	National Federation of Women Teachers
NUSEC	National Union of Societies for Equal Citizenship
NUT	National Union of Teachers
NUWSS	National Union of Women's Suffrage Societies
NUWT	National Union of Women Teachers
PSM	Proletarian Schools' Movement
SDF	Social Democratic Federation
SDP	Social Democratic Party
SLP	Socialist Labour Party
SSS	Socialist Sunday School
TLL	Teachers' Labour League
TRC	Teachers' Registration Council

TSA	Teachers' Socialist Association
TUC	Trades Union Congress
WTFU	Woman Teachers' Franchise Union
WFL	Women's Freedom League
WLL	Women's Labour League
WSPU	Women's Social and Political Union
WSF	Workers' Socialist Federation
YCL	Young Communist League
YSL	Young Socialist League

Introduction

This book is about state education in England and Wales over sixty years ago, and the ways in which Marxist and left wing socialists and feminist and socialist teacher trade unionists sought to change it. Their deeds and aspirations have not previously been recorded. Clive Griggs, Rodney Barker and Asher Tropp have documented with clarity the respective educational policies of the Trade Union Congress, the Labour Party and the National Union of Teachers at this time.[1] But the individuals and groups I am concerned with here, are not those who reached the heights of the trade union or Labour Party bureaucracy. They are the women and men who taught, often through their whole working lives, in elementary schools, and who campaigned for their beliefs in the local branches and national conferences of a hostile union. The groups I describe are those who wanted to change society for the better, and saw little hope of achieving this through the politics of the Labour Party. They spent their time campaigning for the type of change in state education which would find little support inside the mainstream of the Labour Party; or else in providing alternative educational and cultural recreation for the socialist movement's own children, within the Socialist Sunday Schools, communist children's groups, or proletarian schools.

I have great empathy with these early 'pioneers'; I believe that their political lives deserve to be introduced to a wider audience. They demonstrated a commitment to often unpopular ideas and exhibited tenacity in pursuing them. This book, however, is not an uncritical eulogy of these activists' politics, strategies or tactics. Rather, I hope to show that despite their enthusiasm and ideals, they were unable to defeat politically (or organizationally) the state's own strategies for education.

So, although the bulk of the pages that follow describe the work of socialists, feminists and teacher unionists, my starting point is not any oppositional group, but the state itself. To understand why the left had such little impact in education, compared to union struggles in the industrial sector, one needs to analyze the particular strategies the state itself developed within and without the educational state apparatus. For, by the late 1920s, it was plain that not only had the left's challenge to state education failed, but that the state had succeeded in achieving broad consent for the framework of its politics. To ignore the achievement of the state in any discussion of educational strategies in this period is to misestimate the relationship between socialists and the state.

When I started to be interested in this field I was attracted by Brian Simon's studies which acknowledge the contribution of socialists to educational debate.[2] However, in due course, I have come to question his conclusions and approach. He has argued that the labour movement was able to achieve qualitative gains from the state because of its own strategies and action. This argument is enhanced by the absence of Simon's work of detailed analysis of the *state's* educational strategies. Such an omission suggests both that the labour movement's ideas were autonomous from those of the state and that the state was pressed into adopting progressive educational reforms by the force of oppositional perspectives. I reject this argument, for reasons stated in my first chapter.

Apart from Simon's studies there is a dearth of publications on the educational views of left socialist activists. Correspondingly, there is little published on the function of state education policy within broader state policy. Stuart Macintyre's excellent study of Marzist autodidacticism makes scant reference to the protagonists' interest in the education of their own children either in state schools or in their own groups.[3] Likewise, the recent feminist writings of Sarah King and of Pat Owen on the National Union of Women Teachers see this group simply within an educational context and ignore the roots of its politics outside the educational arena, in the suffrage movement.[4] The separation of education and broader state policy has led to a distortion of the dynamic role of the state and, ironically, an overestimation of the achievements of oppositional forces. The socialists in, say, the British Socialist Party, or the teachers in the Teachers' Labour League were always small in number. Nevertheless they did attempt to develop what they saw as opposition to the state's educational practices. To ignore the fact that such forces existed and yet were largely unsuccessful is to underestimate the power of the state in achieving consent for its strategies.

I have resisted the temptation merely to comment on the conclusions of others and have turned instead to an extensive range of sources. In so doing I have discovered a series of political debates and disagreements hidden from anodyne conference reports. Any reader keen to discover for themselves a taste of the times would find the letters pages of teacher journals, the arguments on the nature of socialist education in the papers of youth organizations, and the hysterical reports of secret agents to the Cabinet, fascinating reading.

In a similar way, I have tried to explore not only the broad sweep of the state's educational strategies, but their finer detail. Tensions, caused by the delegation of functions to the local state while retaining centrally much financial control of education, are revealed particularly in detailed discussions on the nature of teachers' status of employment, or the sacking of married women.

Some may question whether such a study can be of value other than to historians. I am more confident. Gerald Grace has recently argued that socio-historical inquiry can be a powerful and illuminating mode of educational policy analysis. A sense of history can provide understanding of past principles and dominant practice so that 'we become more keenly aware of the correlates of contemporary change'.[5]

Some supporters of this position, possibly in an attempt to provide encouragement to those seeking contemporary educational change, have invested teachers of the post-war period, for instance, with a political consciousness which bears little resemblance to their practice.[6] Such well meaning attempts disarm contemporary forces by distorting past socialist failures. Teachers and activists need to learn of the past political failures of the socialist movement — as well as its successes in building oppositional cultural activities — in order to challenge the state in education. I hope my account of the fortitude and inventiveness of feminist and socialist teachers and activists will provide some insight for their modern-day counterparts.

Notes and References

1   Rodney Barker, *Education and Politics 1900–51: A study of the Labour Party*, Oxford, Clarendon Press, 1972, Clive Griggs, *The Trades Union Congress and the Struggle for Education 1868–1925*, Lewes, Falmer Press, 1983; Asher Tropp, *The Schoolteachers*, London, Heinemann, 1957.

2   Brian Simon, *Education and the Labour Movement 1870–1920*, Lawrence and Wishart, 1974 (1); *The Politics of Educational Reform 1920–40*, Lawrence and Wishart, 1974 (2).

3   Stuart Macintyre, *A Proletarian Science. Marxism in Britain 1917–1933*, Cambridge, Cambridge University Press, 1980.

4   Sarah King, 'Feminists in teaching: The National Union of Women Teachers 1920–1940', in Martin Lawn and Gerald Grace, *Teachers: the Culture and Politics of Work*, Lewes, Falmer Press, 1987; Pat Owen, 'Who would be free herself must strike the blow', *History of Education Review*, 17, 1, March 1988, pp. 83–100.

5   Gerald Grace, 'Teachers and the State in Britain: A changing relation', in Lawn and Grace, *op. cit.*, p. 194.

6   Jenny Ozga and Martin Lawn, *Teachers, Professionalism, and Class — a study of Organised Teachers*, Lewes, Falmer Press, 1981; Martin Lawn, 'Deeply tainted with socialism: The activities of the Teachers' Labour League in England and Wales in the 1920s', *History of Education Review*, 14, 2, 1985, pp. 25–35; Martin Lawn and Jenny Ozga, 'Unequal partners: Teachers under direct rule', *British Journal of Sociology of Education*, 7, 2, 1986, pp. 225–37; Martin Lawn, *Servants of the State. The Contested Control of Teaching 1900–1930*, Lewes, Falmer Press, 1987.

Chapter 1

State Strategies for Education

In analyzing the responses of socialists and teacher trades unionists towards state education policy in England and Wales during the first decades of this century, my starting point is the state itself. During this period state activity occurred in various sites: Parliament, its bureaucratic apparatus, the civil service, the courts, the armed forces, police force and secret service bodies, the national insurance scheme, welfare services, including public health services, and the education system. The broad function of these institutions was to maintain capitalism through the use of both coercive and hegemonic strategies to counter class interests inimical to capitalism.[1]

Parliament was particularly important in state education and social welfare policy. The social welfare programme passed through Parliament in the 1880s — and extended considerably in subsequent decades on a centralized and localized basis — was described by Lord Randolph Churchill, then Chancellor of the Exchequer, as 'a scheme of social progress and reform ... a social revolution which pass[ed] by and divert[ed] attention from wild longings for organic change'.[2] Parliament could claim to 'represent' all classes. By 1885 the franchise was extended so that for the first time male manual workers constituted a majority of the electorate. By 1928 when all women finally achieved the franchise, Parliament could be seen as the 'sovereign expression of popular will'.[3]

Through educational legislation and social welfare reforms, passed by Parliament, the state was able to represent the unequal positions of classes in society as equal within the state. Even the revolt of the working class against the domination of the ruling class took place within the framework of dominant legitimacy. It was to Parliament that working-class organizations addressed their demands: campaigns in the factories and workplaces played little part in their own strategy. The incorporation of the working class into the representative state had the effect, as Perry Anderson has put it, of depriving 'the working class of the idea of socialism as a different type of state'. Parliament, he argues, 'reflects the fictive unity of the nation back to the masses as if it were their own self government'.[4]

The Nature of the 1902 Act

For the first time, in the 1902 Education Act, the education system was defined and organized as a national state institution. Centralized controls were instituted, facilitated by the establishment three years earlier of the Board of Education, set up to intervene in the ideological and financial domain.[5] The Act was a break from the state's dominant practices both in respect of local government and education. Legislation governing the provision of state education has been more closely linked with industrial legislation than with that governing local councils.[6] In the nineteenth century public services had been established to contain the urban problems of insanitation and destitution under the administration of local councils.[7] Schooling had been organized under the aegis of local school boards set up to administer the 1870 Education Act. They were financed by central grants and a local rate but were not part of the structure of the local state as constituted by councils.[8]

Even the democratic basis of election to the school boards and the method of voting, a cumulative vote, was different to that used in local council elections. This method had the effect of increasing the chances of election of labour movement candidates who would have been prevented from standing for local councils.[9] The schools boards were, above all, local bodies relating to the elementary educational needs of a specific geographical area. Although they relied on the central state for most revenue funding the school boards appeared relatively free from central state controls. This changed when the London School Board attempted to use its relative autonomy to finance education for students over the age of fifteen. Its decision was quashed by reference to the procedures of local government. The ruling of Cockerton, the district auditor, was to set a precedent for the future organization of education.[10] Henceforth, the central state was to exercise greater control of education by incorporating it within the parameters of local government.

The 1902 Education Act served to bring education firmly within the structures of the central and local state. The operation and organization of the Act had three important aspects in respect of the state's interventionist role in education. The first was the shift of functions to central state control, creating a national institution. The second aspect was the alteration of the electoral basis which diminished the possibility of the election of socialist candidates.[11] The school boards had provided an arena for the political involvement of progressive and socialist representatives in education. However, the local council structures which now administered education ensured fewer opportunities for working-class involvement. The Act laid down regulations for education committees. The committees had to contain a majority of councillors. They were allowed to include teachers employed by other education authorities. The committees were obliged to include women. The property and sex disqualifications which applied to candidates standing for direct election to councils ensured that women could not be elected to education committees in a political capacity but only on the basis of their sex. In addition, working-class and socialist candidates were unlikely to qualify for cooption to the committees on the professionalist grounds implied by the Act of 'expertise in the needs of education and knowledge of the needs of various kinds of school'.[12] Parental and socialist involvement in the running of school boards had been replaced by 'professional expertise'. Such initial moves to encourage teachers to see their interests as being aligned with those of the state were later developed in the Burnham pay restructuring after the First World War, to create a specific 'alliance' of the central and local state and organized teachers.

A third important aspect of the Act was the creation of a close financial relationship between the central and local state in respect of education. Significantly, the statutory education committees, although invested with 'all powers pertaining to the implementation of the 1902 Act', had no powers to levy rates or borrow money.[13] These powers lay with the existing structures of local government.

A national system of financing education, which ensured a national uniformity of approach and prevented local councils lobbying for their own financial needs on an individual basis, was set up on the basis of formula and allocated grants related to rateable value.[14] Such arrangements were crucial to the establishment of the 'organic relationship'[15] between the central and local state which tied local education authorities more closely to the centre while allowing for apparent local autonomy.

The 1902 Education Act displays the clear interventionist role for the state: the creation of a national system, financed in part centrally by non-negotiable formula grants, with the remainder raised through rate-based finance administered locally. Ironically, it was this financial relationship which, in time, would draw increasing attention to the central state's own responsibility in financing an education service of its own making, rather than focusing on local authorities' financial 'excesses'.

The Role of Financial Structures in Strengthening State Control

The financing of education within the local government structure relying on revenue from local taxation in the form of rates to complement income from the national taxation systems gave rise to conflict between the central and local state.[16] Such conflict, however, was to strengthen the central state's influence on the local state in that it was increasingly approached to finance educational initiatives arising from particular local circumstances. The rating system, based on the collection of rates locally according to a nationally determined rateable value, was one which gave rise to disputes between the local and central state. This was particularly the case when the main method of allocating revenue monies was based on fixed rather than percentage grants. There was an inevitable mismatch between a national grant formula and a local variable rate income. This resulted in constant friction which drew increased attention to the role of the *central* state in financing — and controlling — education.

The initial cost to the exchequer of the 1902 Act was considerable.[17] In addition, the overall expenditure of local authorities increased in successive years, particularly due to the implementation of enabling legislation such as the Education (Provision of Meals) Act 1906 and Education (Administrative Provisions) Act 1907 which attracted no grants from the central exchequer.[18] The proportions of central to local expenditure were neither constant not nationally uniform through the following years. By 1907 the Association of Education Committees demanded increased central expenditure to the extent of advocating that the whole cost of education be met from the Imperial Exchequer to ensure that a uniform system of elementary and secondary education was available to all classes nationally.[19]

The problem was not simply the lack of revenue forthcoming from the central exchequer. The remedy of inadequate financing, revenue from local rates, was no simple solution. In theory the local councils, rather than the Board of Education, were now responsible for being the financial watch-dogs of education. In practice this was rather more complicated. The determination of rate levels lay with local councils composed of ratepayers and local businessmen, rather than with central government (or the members of the education committee). However, the central state was in-extricably and explicitly drawn into these questions as the body determining the rateable value of the area. Many of the local education authorities' diffi-culties in financing education related to the income derived from the rateable value of the area. The famous West Ham case highlighted the problem of insufficient rate income from the penny rate coupled with a large school population.[20] Even the capital city itself was heavily penalized under this arrangement.[21]

The financial difficulties of local councils became increasingly acute after the local implementation of the Provision of Meals Act and the legis-lation permitting medical inspection in schools. The Association of Education Committees catalogued the financial strain Local Education Authorities (LEAs) felt as a result of the state's imposition of new and onerous duties, the continued growth in ordinary items of expenditure, and the failure of Whithall to contribute its fair share to the increased burden of the increased costs.[22] A deputation representing nearly every education authority in England and Wales pressed their point with Asquith, the Prime Minister. His response was to hide behind the structures of the 1902 Act, re-iterating that education was a national service administered locally.[23]

However, it was not just difficulties over the revenue situation which highlighted the financial tension between the central and local state in respect of education. As part of local government, education became subject to the Local Government Act of 1888, concerning the power of local

7

authorities to raise capital finance through borrowing. An integral feature of the legislation was the power invested in Parliament to control the amount and period of loans, when the loan in question exceeded one tenth of the rateable value of a county council. Strict limits were placed on the time for repayment: thirty years in the case of county councils.[24] The power of the Public Works Loans Commissioners to determine the timescale of repayment of loans caused great concern amongst local authorities. The stipulation that capital loans had to be repaid over the relatively short period of thirty years affected adversely the rates burden of local authorities and led to various calls for the extension of the repayment period.[25] When they were agreed, loans were advanced through the Public Works Loans Commissioners set up for the purpose of advancing sums obtained on national credit. The rate of interest was fixed by the Treasury. This ensured both that no loss was caused to the central state and that the long-term spending of councils was incorporated into a national financial system.

The relationship between the central and local state here was one which provided finance for local authorities' schemes, while ensuring central state financial and political control. It also has the effect of ensuring that locally initiated borrowing had beneficial knock-on effects for the central state.[26] Thus, although the operation of capital loans was different to the organization of revenue finances it still had the same effect of increasing local rates and consequently pressurizing the central state to come to the financial assistance of local authorities.

The Role of Welfare Reforms within the Educational State Apparatus

In his *Evolution of National Insurance in Great Britain*, Bentley Gilbert has argued that school meals legislation marked the beginning of the construction of the welfare state.[27] Yet the precondition of the building of this welfare state had been the institution of a national education service which highlighted the poverty of children and young people. The nation's money from the Imperial Exchequer, so the argument went in Parliament, was being spent on children unable to benefit from the schooling provided by the state: 'Education could not be grafted onto starvation.'[28]

Parliament and Board of Education alike recognized the importance of the physical condition of children. The sentiments of Robert Morant, permanent secretary at the Board of Education, were widespread:

> I have for some time past come to feel that for the good of the children and the public, what subjects are taught and how they are taught *do not matter anything like so much nowadays* as attention (a) to the *physical* condition of the scholars and the teacher and (b) to the physiological aspects of the schools [original emphases].[29]

A consequence was the introduction of the Education (Administrative Provisions) Act which established the medical department of the Board of Education.

Another impetus for the feeding and medical inspection of children had come from the findings of the Committee on Physical Deterioration (1904), set up in the wake of public concern at the poor physical condition of working-class recruits to the armed forces in the Boer War. Their poor physical condition had the effect, it was argued, of undermining the physical force of the imperial power and the very notion of Empire.[30] One of the first legislative actions the Liberal government of 1906 enacted was the Education (Provison of Meals) Act in response to the recommendations of the Interdepartmental Committee for a sponsored system of feeding necessitous children. This would ensure that children could take advantage of their time in school. Power was invested in the Board of Education, rather than the Local Government Board. This was an important decision. In return for obtaining forms of 'relief', the poor had to relinquish any rights of franchise to which they were entitled.[31] Placing this authority with the Board of Education meant that parents would not suffer the stigma of the Poor Law. More importantly, it also meant that the educational state apparatus was able to influence the lives of children (and their parents) more extensively.[32]

Subsequently, legislation was passed compelling local education authorities to provide medical inspection of school children. Local education authorities were also empowerd to follow up this inspection with treatment. The primary object of such inspection, said Sir George Newman, Chief Medical Officer at the Board of Education, 'was not to create a healthy people but to enable every school child to take advantage of the education provided for it by the state'. Such Acts were, he argued, 'strictly and properly Education Acts'.[33]

Schools, then, became increasingly the focus for areas of social welfare previously regarded as the proper responsibility of parents — or of charitable institutions. The strategy adopted was one which sought to align parental duties with those of the central and local state, rather than to appropriate them totally. Local education authorities were not compelled to provide meals or medical treatment. When they chose to exercise their rights under the legislation, the cost was borne locally through the rates or through attempts to claw back costs from parents.

In the first decades of this century the state extended and developed its control through an organic relationship between the central and local state which rested upon a financial burden shared disproportionately between the two. A central feature was the contribution of individual local ratepayers towards a national educational system. The state had moved away from nineteenth-century *laissez-faire* notions of individual responsibility only to replace them with a strategy aimed at a national structure of education with the individual ratepayers and the individual 'consumer' at its core. Such an ideology was to emerge later in the form of individual equality of opportunity.

The Nature of the Financial Reforms Proposed before the 1914–18 War.

By the financial year 1910–11 the proportion of total government revenue spending on elementary education was less than 10 per cent. However, the proportion of *local* government revenue expenditure on education was more than double this.[34] This had the effect of making education of greater material significance in local, than in central, expenditure and thus ensured that local government directed its attention to the central state to relieve its own rate-borne expenditure.

However, it was not simply the case that local government was seeking more resources from the central state. Local education authorities themselves made a significant financial contribution to the economy. By 1905 already more than one half of government expenditure had been undertaken by local authorities. Further, the funds of local authorities had been used by the Bank of England to back up its policies, helping it to be the world's chief lender by 1914.[35]

The Departmental Committee on Local Taxation, which reported in 1914, recognized the shift in the balance of elementary education funded by Parliamentary grants and local rates. The bulk of evidence reflected both the growing discontent with the financial constraints of the 1902 Act and the state's refusal to alter fundamentally its strategy. The Committee recommended the redefinition of education as a semi-national service in which the central and local state both had an interest. It further recommended amendments in the allocation of central exchequer finance to education, although this continued to be dependent on (variable) rateable values.[36]

Thus the structural relationship between the central and local state remained intact, strengthened by an increased subvention from the central exchequer.[37] The formulae used to effect such allocation also ensured the maintenance of central control. Importantly, the rates system was maintained. This both ensured an inherent element of local control by a local electorate — an apparent degree of local autonomy — and also allowed a focus for the expression of dissent other than that of the central state.[38]

The Background to the 1918 Education Act Outside the Educational State Apparatus

It was the consequences of the war, including massive industrial unrest, which led to the new 1918 Education Act.[39] These factors led to a greater emphasis on the ideological and political function of education. The financial relation between the central and local state was both maintained and strengthened. The problems caused by the inequitable distribution between rate-based and tax-based revenue were recognized. The Act adopted a system of substantive annual grants-in-aid to local education authorities.[40] These ensured that central financial contributions accounted for not less than half of the total expenditure of the local authority on education, as recognized by the Board of Education. This injection of further central funds into the localities strengthened the links between the central and local state.

The 1918 Education Act also widened the concept of education. Local areas were given the powers (and grants) to set up nursery education for 2- to 5-year-olds and the duty to set up continuation schools for school leavers up to the age of 18. Powers and duties were also extended to cover: the provision of school camps for those attending continuation schools; school swimming baths; physical training centres and general recreational facilities for young people. Existing legislation on medical inspection and treatment was incorporated into the Act.[41] Additionally, modifications were made to the Prevention of Cruelty to Children Act (1904) and to legislation covering the employment of children, which were incorporated into this Education Act.[42] State education, then, was to cover the intellectual, social, and physical life of children and young people, extending its remit far wider than had previously been the case.[43]

Education as epitomized by the Education Act 1918 also performed an important role outside the educational state apparatus creating consensus and diluting class conflict. An important development in harnessing education to the broader strategies for maintenance of the state, focused on the fostering of the ideology of nation above separate class interests in postwar reconstruction.

Educational historians such as Selleck have acknowledged that schools were recognized by the state as vehicles for the accomplishment of 'noneducational ends'. However, the main factor contributing to such educational developments as those advocated by the Progressives was, he has argued, the war. Selleck perceives progressive education and changes in state education as antidotes to the world war rather than to the class war which continued to be manifested in intensified industral unrest.[44] Although he acknowledges that educational changes were a response to events outside the educational state apparatus, he does not see the importance of the 1918 Education Act in ideological terms outside the educational state apparatus.[45] In the same way that education had performed a social role in administering welfare reforms, so too, in this period, it performed a different social role, the amelioration of class conflict. Education was seen by the state as providing the nation with a skilled workforce, especially one which could emulate the technical expertise of the Germans. It was also seen as playing a role in diffusing heightened political consciousness, through the ideology of the nation and of individual opportunity.[46]

At the end of the war there was general concern within state institutions about the future of the British state. A Ministry of Labour was established to monitor industrial unrest.[47] It gave regular weekly reports to the Cabinet. An Intelligence Directorate was formed under Basil Thomson. This also presented regular reports to the Cabinet, on pacifist and revolutionary organizations. 'The routine of the "Home section of my staff" ', wrote Basil Thomson, 'was to attend subversive meetings all over the country and to obtain evidence of money passing from Russia to the extremist section of labour'.[48] In similar vein a Commission of Inquiry into National and Regional Unrest was organized.[49] The tone of the report conveys alarm:

> The unrest is real, widespread, and in some directions, extreme, and such as to constitute a national danger unless dealt with promptly and effectively. We are at this moment within view of a possible social upheaval or at least extensive and manifold strikes. No tinkering schemes will meet the requirements of the situation.[50]

Education featured prominently in the reports on industrial unrest, both as a source of industrial unrest and as a solution. The extension of workers' education and the perceived shortcomings of state education were seen as factors which created a more political consciousness in the mining areas of South Wales.[51] The absence of any municipally maintained library within the whole of the central block of the Glamorgan coal field had 'retarded a civic spirit and community sense'.[52] As an alternative, South Wales working-class organizations themselves had organized their own education and libraries, creating a 'spirit of brotherhood'.[53] Class-based solidarity had substituted for civic consciousness:

> They [the mining lodges] have become centres of educational work from which lectures on political and social subjects have been organized and secondly, they have become centres of social and political activity more potent than perhaps any other of the social movements in the community. Indeed it is often within the lodges that the men seek and cultivate the spirit of brotherhood and goodwill which they have failed to find in the world outside.[54]

The miners were not accused of ignorance, but of advocating an alternative type of education (for adults) to that which would be conducive to the harmonious spirit the Commission wished to create. Describing the work of the Central Labour Colleges and Miners' Lodges as a response to the desire for tuition in economics, the report criticized the education given: 'Economics is often degraded into a gross materialist conception of cause and effect and the essential spirituality of education is neglected or forgotten.'[55] Although many of the Commission's findings refer to the economic and industrial sphere, attention is also drawn to ideological and political questions meriting state action. Similar matters were raised in the weekly Cabinet reports of revolutionary organizations. In particular, it was considered a priority to combat the education provided by the Labour Colleges.[56]

It is within *this* context of other state strategies that the 1918 Education Act needs to be situated. The 'architect' of the Act, Fisher, as President of the Board of Education, also saw the wider implications of the legislation:

> There is no item in the government's programme for raising the social condition of the people more immediately necessary than the improvement of our education system ... Ignorance is now the enemy: it is only by education of the democracy that we can hope to lay the foundation of social peace.[57]

However, unlike many of the other state repressive measures intended to stem the influence of socialist organizations, the educational reforms were widely popular. Inside and outside the educational state apparatus, consent was achieved for the proposals advocated by Fisher. Writing some years later, he recalled the popularity of the legislation: 'For the first time in our national history education was a popular subject ... large audiences were attracted to educational meetings.'[58]

He recalled, in particular, a Sunday meeting of Bristol dockers:

> I have never encountered such enthusiasm . . . the prospect of wider opportunities which the new plan might open to the disinherited filled them with enthusiasm. Alas! for these good folk they expected from an Education Bill what no bill on education or anything else can give, a new Heaven and a new Earth.'[59]

For the labour movement, the Bill became a metaphor for its wider hopes and aspirations, summed up wryly by the author of the weekly Cabinet reports as follows: 'This subject continues to attract attention, which is, however, in some certain cases wandering somewhat wide of the Education Bill.'[60]

Equality of Opportunity

The Act itself reflected a spirit of equal opportunity in education as applied to the individual child. Its intentions were to establish 'a national system of public education available for all persons capable of profiting thereby' with the counties 'providing for the progressive development and comprehensive organization of education in respect of their area.'[61] That is, opportunity was raised in the context of the individual child, rather than in relation to the general condition of working-class children. As G. A. N. Lowndes described the Act, 'widening social and educational opportunity operate[d] as a sedative upon class consciousness'.[62]

This attempt at creating consensus through the emphasis on the role of the individual within the nation was consistent with the philosophy underlying the 1902 Act. It was also widely accepted by the leadership of the Labour Party. Adopting a benign attitude to the state, Labour politicians argued that the state had a responsibility to ameliorate the condition of the nation. This was to be effected through a strengthened relationship between the individual and the state: 'The individual is not justified in claiming his national rights unless he fulfils his obligations to his fellow men and to the state: the state must recognise the rights of its citizens if it demands from them a fulfilment of their obligations as citizens.'[63]

Far from rejecting the extension of state activities, the Labour Party welcomed it on the assumption that Parliamentary decisions could control the state and thus promote individual well-being. The establishment of 'democratic control over all the machinery of the state...working along constitutional lines [would put] an end to oligarchical government and the domination of one class by another'.[64] The argument was reinforced by the 1918 Labour Party programme, 'Labour and the New Social Order': 'This is no sense a 'class' proposal...but [rather] social protection of the individual.'[65] Within this context, education was to be 'suffused throughout by art, by culture, by individuality'.[66] Such a position also found resonance with Liberals disillusioned with their party's wartime action and increasingly authoritarian stances.[67]

The state was able to maintain its hegemony by incorporating positions and reflecting them in the ideology of individual opportunity in the 1918 Education Act. A key component of the state's strategy was the strengthening of the ideology of a *neutral* state.

Teachers and the State

Teachers were to play a crucial role in this area of promoting the 'neutrality' of the state: 'The state which values harmony begins by making its teachers happy'.[68]

The problem was how to ensure the loyalty of teachers to the state while at the same time ensuring that teachers were seen to be neutral. Fisher summed up the issue as follows: 'It is better that the teaching body in a country should be ill distributed, unevenly paid and imperfectly qualified than it should be thought to march to the orders of a government in London.'[69]

Consideration had been given to employing teachers as civil servants — and rejected because of the way in which responsibility for paying teachers would fall directly on the central state. This could also cause the Board of Education to be seen as 'an obstacle to educational progress' in that it would be drawn into direct disputes with teachers over salaries and conditions issues.[70]

The provision of sufficient numbers of suitable, well paid teachers underpinned the ideological strategy articulated by Fisher. According to his estimates at least three thousand extra teachers a year for the fifteen following years were necessary to implement the Act fully.[71] Increased expenditure was warranted, Fisher argued, on the grounds that education was in the interests of 'public good'.[72] Yet this aspect of the Act's implementation was thwarted by the prevailing economic climate in general and the state's economic strategies in particular. The Chancellor of the Exchequer castigated expenditure on education, saying 'Education had already been subjected to immense growth, huge liabilities were in prospect, and since the introduction of the Act, expenditure had been breathless'.[73]

The incorporation of teachers into the state's strategy was achieved through a new national structure, the Burnham Committee. This comprised representatives of unionized teachers, and the central and local state. It thus ensured a greater role for the central state while depriving it of a directly interventionist function with respect to teachers. This strategy was successful on ideological grounds; less so on financial ones. Burnham was unable to bring about the doubling, in real terms, of the average wage of teachers which the 1918 Act had envisaged.[74] This was due, in part, to the unwillingness of the education authorities to commit themselves to unsubsidized rate-borne expenditure. For its part the central state was constrained by the relationship from enforcing Burnham salaries agreements on recalcitrant authorities and from intervening on behalf of married women teachers sacked by local authorities in the 1920s in defiance of the Sex Disqualification (Removal) Act.[75]

This structural 'inability' to intervene directly in teachers' pay and conditions of work was highlighted by the feminist teachers' demands for equal pay for equal work. The commitment of unmarried women teachers was the bedrock of the 'neutral' state, yet no direct intervention was forthcoming to reward it. In response to a letter from the feminist Six Point Group in the 1920s, the government stated its 'general sympathy with the idea expressed in the formula equal pay for equal work' but its operation 'would involve the overriding by the state of the views of the local authorities in a matter [the appointment of teachers] which Parliament had entrusted to the Authorities'.[76]

In contrast the state was able to implement financial controls comparatively easily when cuts were demanded in public expenditure, because of the financial relationship which underpinned the relationship between the central and local state. This relationship was made tighter by the powers of the 1918 Act, which tied the payment of percentage grants to the efficient performance of statutory functions.[77] These powers were used to implement public sector cuts in the 1920s. The cuts, as recommended by the Geddes reports, advocated no change in the financial structure of the relationship between the central and local state with respect to education. The same percentage grant system introduced by Fisher as a way of encouraging spending on education was also found to be an effective way of implementing cuts, to the extent that the Board of Education's white paper on finance in 1926 argued for the retention of this system on the grounds that such grants could be a 'powerful engine for restricting expenditure'.[78]

The relationship conceived as a part of the state's ideological strategy of creating social peace in the immediate post-war period had been constructed over and above the detailed aspects of educational legislation. The 1918 reforms in continuation education were not enacted; but the state was successful in incorporating local education authorities and teachers within a common framework for education which remained intact for nearly seventy years.

The Consent Achieved for the State's Strategies

Most of this book will deal with the particular educational strategies of teacher trade unionists and socialists. However, although some of these strategies did seek to oppose the state, it is important to stress the overall success of the state's positions in this period. The ideological and political emphases in the post-war period built upon the financial regulatory structure between the central and local state, first established in 1902. This achievement of the state has not been acknowledged by Brian Simon in his writing on this period. He has analyzed the strategies and activities of working-class organizations without paying much attention to the relationship between these strategies and those of the state. As such he has present the labour movement as entirely autonomous from the state: '. . . the lesson to emerge for the labour movement was that nothing is gained (or retained) without persistent and determined pressure. In an important sense it [the labour movement] made the running . . .'[79]

In noting the growing elision between the policies of the Labour Party and those of the state, Simon has argued that:

> This evolution, and the change in outlook that accompanied it, may in a sense be regarded as the triumph of a more general educational initiative, that which has been consciously directed to training Labour to rule in the interests of the nation rather than the interests of the working class.[80]

The triumph of a more general educational initiative should be ascribed more specifically to the success of the state in incorporating working-class demands within its own framework. This arose both from the state's strength and also from the political weakness of the organizations commanding working-class broad allegiance.[81] David Coates has documented the Labour Party position thus: 'In 1918 it had at least openly talked of a "new social order". By 1925 it talked merely of "National Reconstruction and Reform", and by 1927, simply of "Labour and the Nation".'[82]

Trevelyan as Labour President of the Board of Education enthusiastically supported the existing structural relationship between the central and local state and teachers. Labour made few major changes of any sort on education policy.[83] The 'broad highway of educational opportunity' was entirely consistent with a state emphasis on the role of the individual, as opposed to classes, in the nation. Also untouched in the two short periods of (minority) Labour government in the 1920s was the financial relationship which bound the central and local state.[84]

Conclusion

It is clear from this summary that proactive strategies were adopted for the educational state apparatus itself and for use within other strategies for the maintenance of the capitalist state. The adoption of a strong financial organic link between the central and local state in the 1902 Education Act provided the basis for maintaining and extending state education in the future in a broader form. The welfare reforms transmitted by the nation's schools were part of the state's social imperialist strategies designed to promote economic efficiency.

The structural changes in the post-war years assisted in the state's political and ideological attempts both to reassert its hegemony and to destroy socialist ideas and influence. In order to achieve these goals, two broad and apparently distinct approaches were adopted in the 1920s. The first was to incorporate the labour movement, through its leaders, into the framework of the state. The second was to isolate the labour movement totally, characterizing it as extremist and about to cause socialist revolution. From different perspectives Andrew Gamble and Maurice Cowling analyze these two approaches by highlighting their differences.[85] Yet what united these strategies was the common aim of asserting the power of the nation over and above its constituent parts, with a greater emphasis on the state's own role within the economic, political and social fields.

By definition this chapter has concentrated on the role of the state to the exclusion of those socialist organizations which did attempt in different ways either to achieve significant welfare reforms from the state or to challenge fundamentally its strategies. To assess the extent to which they were able to achieve the success attributed to them by Brian Simon involves discussion both of their own political strategies and those of the state. The extent to which socialists were able to challenge the state's trajectory in any coherent way will be considered in the next chapter.

Notes and References

1   V. I. Lenin, 'The State and revolution', in V. I. Lenin, *Selected Works*, London, Lawrence and Wishart, 1969, Karl Marx and Frederick Engels, 'Critique of the

Gotha programme', in *Selected Works*, London, Lawrence and Wishart, 1968; Manual Castells, *City Class and Power*, London, MacMillan, 1978, especially p. 180.

2 As quoted in Nigel Harris, *Competition and the Corporate Society*, London, Methuen, 1972, p. 26.

3 Perry Anderson, 'The antinomies of Antonio Gramsci', in *New Left Review*, 100, November 1976, p. 28. See also Goran Therborn, 'The rule of capital and the rise of democracy', in *New Left Review*, 103, pp. 3–41.

4 Perry Anderson, *ibid.*

5 *Education 1900–1950*, The Report of the Ministry of Education, Cmnd, 8244, HMSO, 1950, Chapter 1, para. 5. The original brief of the HMI set up in 1839, the year the education committee of the privy council was established, was simply to act as the financial watchdogs of taxpayers' money (Sir William Pile, *The Department of Education and Science*, London, George Allen and Unwin, 1979, p. 31.

6 For example, Poor Law Act 1834; Municipal Corporation Act 1835; Towns Improvement Act 1847. See Clive Martlew, 'The State and local government finance', *Public Administration*, 61, Summer 1983, pp. 132–3.

7 The earliest nineteenth-century legislation on education was the Health and Morals of Apprentices Act 1802, which stipulated the need for instruction in literacy and numeracy. This trend was continued in the subsequent Factory Acts. All the Factory Acts between 1833 and 1867 made employment of young people below 13 conditional on their part-time attendance at school. Factory Acts from 1878 into the twentieth century retained half-time education, with exemptions based on literacy and numeracy tests (Bernard Lawrence, *The Administration of Education in England*, London, Batsford, 1972, p. 11; Frederic Keeling, *Child Labour in the UK*, London, P. S. King, 1914, p. xiii).

8 Asher Tropp, *The Schoolteachers*, London, Heinemann, 1957, p. 8.

9 Gasworkers' candidates in Barking were successful in their election to the school board in their stronghold of West Ham in October 1889; Pearson, a casual labourer at the London Docks, polled 12, 437 votes in the Tower Hamlets school board election of 1897 (Paul Thompson, *Socialists, Liberals, and Labour in the Struggle for London*, London, Routledge and Kegan Paul, 1967, p. 101). See also Angela Gill, 'The Leicestershire School Board 1871–1903', in Brian Simon (Ed.) *Education in Leicestershire 1540–1940, a Regional Study*, Leicester University Press, 1968, p. 164; Gerard Lynch, *Ideology and the Social Organisation of Educational Knowledge in England and Scotland 1840–1920*, unpublished MA thesis, Institute of Education, University of London, 1974, pp. 142–53.

10 Lawrence, *op. cit.*, p. 31; Hilda Kean, *State Education Policy 1900–1930: The Nature of the Socialist and Teacher Trade Unionist Response*, unpublished Ph.D. thesis, King's College, University of London, 1988, pp. 46–7.

11 This shift in control was seen in different ways by different political currents. Yoxall, the Liberal MP and NUT secretary, argued that the progressive work of bodies such as the London School Board would continue: the main change would be 'in respect of control' (J. H. Yoxall MP, 'The demise of the London School Board', in *Cornhill Magazine*, New Series, 16, 1904, p. 665). It was for this very reason that the SDF opposed the Act (Simon (1), *op. cit.*, p. 225). The ILP had opposed the Act in 1901, but altered its position in the following year (David Howells, *British Workers and the ILP 1888–1906*, Manchester, Manchester University Press, 1983, p. 347).

12 *Education Act 1902*, London, HMSO, 1902, section 17.2.

13 *Ibid.*

14 The larger grant, the formula grant, was based on rateable value (*ibid.*, section 10.1). The concept of national financing for a national education service was strengthened further by the findings of the Royal Commission on Local Taxation reporting in 1901. As a result, local services were divided into two categories:

national and onerous or local and beneficial. Education came into the former category (Herman Finer, *English Local Government*, 4th ed., London, Methuen, 1950, pp. 458–74; Brian Keith-Lucas and Peter G. Richards, *A History of Local Government in the Twentieth Century*, London, George Allen and Unwin, 1978, pp. 141ff.).

15 *Cmnd. 8244, op. cit.*, chapter 3, para. 1.

16 Final report on the Royal Commission on Local Taxation, Cmnd. 1221, Appendix, as printed in W. Thornhill (Ed.), *The Growth and Reform of English Local Government*, London, Weidenfeld and Nicolson, 1971, p. 137.

17 *Education 1900–1950, op. cit.*, chapter 3, para 10; Cmnd. 7315, xi, HMSO, 1914, chapter vii, para. 76; Moses Abramovitz and Vera Eliasberg, *The Growth of Public Employment in Great Britain*, New York, Princeton, 1957, p. 76; Kean (1988), *op. cit.*, pp. 48–9.

18 See Annual Abstract of Statistics as printed in Keith-Lucas, *op. cit.*, p. 128.

19 *The Schoolmaster*, 31 August 1907, p. 362.

20 See Chapter 4, n. 154.

21 *London Teacher*, 27 February 1914, pp. 172–3; Kean (1988), *op. cit.*, p. 50.

22 *The Schoolmaster*, 16 January 1909, p. 116.

23 *The Schoolmaster*, 27 March 1909, p. 559.

24 Keith-Lucas and Richards, *op. cit.*, p. 132.

25 The demands of the AEC, NUT and LTA are reported in *The Schoolmaster*, 22 June 1907, pp. 12–14; 11 June 1910, p. 1072; 20 January 1912, p. 135; 20 February 1914, p. 149.

26 Sidney Pollard, *The Development of the British Economy 1914–67*, 2nd ed., London, Edward Arnold, 1969, pp. 14–26.

27 Bentley B. Gilbert, *The Evolution of National Insurance in Great Britain*, London, Michael Joseph, 1966, p. 102.

28 Slack, MP for Hertfordshire, moving a private member's bill to give local education authorities powers for feeding as recommended in the 1904 report on physical deterioration in *Hansard*, fourth series, vol. 145, 18 April 1905, col. 531.

29 Robert Morant as reported in conversation to Margaret McMillan as quoted in Gilbert, *op. cit.*, p. 129.

30 Sir John Gorst in *Hansard*, fourth series, vol. 141, 14 February 1905, col. 146; Dr MacNamara in *Hansard*, fourth series, vol. 143, 22 March 1905, col. 869; debate in *Hansard*, fourth series, vol. 145, 18 April 1905, cols. 531–65; Asquith quoted in Gilbert, *op. cit.*, p. 77; Kean (1988), *op. cit.*, pp. 51–2.

31 *Hansard*, fourth series, 1905, vol. 145, 18 April 1905, col. 554.

32 Kean (1988) *op. cit.*, pp. 51–2.

33 Sir George Newman, *The Building of a Nation's Health*, London, MacMillan, 1949, p. 194.

34 *Education 1900–1950, op. cit.*, table 100, p. 250; *The Schoolmaster*, 7 January 1911, p. 32.

35 Hay, *op. cit.*, p. 40; Pollard, *op. cit.*, p. 14.

36 Cmnd. 7315, xi, 1914, chapter 4, para. 78; chapter 5, paras 18, 45, 79, 82.

37 *Ibid.*, chapter 5, para. 18, and chapter 18, para. 228.

38 The use of rates as a source of finance for social and welfare services received broad consent. Disagreement focused on the level of rates and the specific purposes to which rates were put (Kean (1988), pp. 55–6).

39 Arthur Marwick, *The Deluge — British Society and the First World War*, London, Bodley Head, 1965, p. 91; Pollard, *op. cit.*, p. 77; *Monthy Labour Review* as quoted in Samuel Hurwitz, *State Intervention in Great Britain — A Study of Economic Control and Social Response*, New York, Columbia University Press, 1949, pp. 113–15; R. J. W. Selleck, *Primary Education and the Progressives 1914–1939*, London, Routledge and Kegan Paul, 1972, p. 13.

40   H. A. L. Fisher, *An Unfinished Autobiography*, London, Oxford University Press, 1940, p. 104; *Education Act 1918, op. cit.*, para. 44.
41   *Education Act 1918, ibid.*, paras. 3, 17, 18, 19, 25.
42   *Ibid.*, paras. 13–15.
43   This is also borne out by Fisher's own comment, 'I felt that education (was) the most fundamental of all the *social services*' (my emphasis) (Fisher, *op. cit.*, p. 98).
44   Selleck, *op. cit.*, pp. 13 and 20.
45   No reference is made, however, to the war's disruptive effect on the economy, which resulted in debt repayments totalling approximately 300 per cent of the total government expenditure by the end of the war (Alan Peacock and Jack Wiseman, *Growth of Public Expediture in the UK*, University of York Studies in Economics, rev. ed., London, George Allen and Unwin, 1967, p. 53).
46   David Reeder, 'A recurring debate: Education and industry', in Dale, Esland, Fergusson and MacDonald (Eds), *Schooling and the National Interest*, Lewes, Falmer Press, 1981.
47   PRO: CAB 24/28 GT 2274, 10 October 1917 (and GT 733, 15 May 1917).
48   Sir Basil Thomson, *The Scene Changes*, London, Collins, 1939, p. 387.
49   Cmnd. 8662–8669, xv, I; and Cmnd. 8696, summary 1917–18, xv, 149.
50   *Ibid.*, Cmnd. 8666, xv, 69, no. 5, London and South Eastern Areas, 1917–18.
51   'With the spread of elementary education and the slow development of the desire for the clear understanding of the condition under which the workers live, a change has spread over the lodges' (Cmnd. 8663, xv, 83, Wales and Monmouth, 1917–18); 'Evidence has been brought before us to show that the workers view with alarm the shortage of teachers and the constant failure of the local authorities to provide proper education for their children' (*ibid.*, p. 34).
52   *Ibid.*, p. 12.
53   *Ibid.*, p. 17.
54   *Ibid.*
55   *Ibid.*
56   PRO: CAB 24/69 GT 6201, 4 November 1918: CAB 24/96 Cp 462, A Survey of Revolutionary Feeling during 1919, 15 January 1920; CAB 24/96 CP 491, 22 January 1920; CAB 24/96 CP 500, 26 January 1920; CAB 24/92 CP 70, 6 November 1919; CAB 24/93 CP 168, 20 November 1919; CAB 24/98 CP 686, 19 February 1920.
57   PRO: CAB 24/98 CP 605, Growth of Expenditure on Education, a note by the President of the Board of Education, 10 February 1920.
58   Fisher (1940) *op. cit.*, p. 94.
59   *Ibid.*, p. 106.
60   PRO: CAB 24/47 GT 4147, The Labour Situation for the week ending 3 April 1918.
61   *Education Act 1918, op. cit.*, Chapter 39, para. 1.
62   G. A. N. Lowndes, *The Silent Social Revolution*, London, Oxford University Press, 1937, p. 112; Perry Anderson (1976) *op. cit.*, p. 28.
63   Arthur Henderson, *The Aims of Labour*, London, Headley Brothers, 1917, p. 81.
64   *Ibid.*, p. 62.
65   *Ibid.*, p. 93.
66   Ramsay MacDonald, *A policy for the Labour Party*, London, Leonard Parsons, 1920, p. 45.
67   J. A. Hobson, *Confessions of an Economic Heretic*, London, George Allen and Unwin, 1938, p. 113; Michael Howard, *War and the Liberal Conscience*, London, Oxford University Press, 1981, pp. 75–84; Charles Trevelyan, *From Liberalism to Labour*, London, George Allen and Unwin, 1921, p. 10.
68   Fisher (1940) *op. cit.*, p. 105.
69   *Ibid.*, p. 97.
70   PRO: Ed 24/1736 Memorandum on the Civil Service and Teachers, 31 January 1917, p. 11.

71 PRO: CAB 24/98 CP 605, *op. cit.*
72 PRO: CAB 24/95 CP 329, Memorandum by Fisher on the growth of expenditure on education, 23 December 1919, p. 11.
73 PRO: CAB 24/97 CP 512, 27 January 1920.
74 PRO: CAB 24/98 CP 605, *op. cit.* The 1913–14 expenditure of teachers' salaries accounted for 58 per cent of the total of local education authorities' expenditure. This rose to 64 per cent by 1919–20. The introduction of percentage grants had enabled the Board to double the average remuneration of teachers in nominal terms. Yet this was offset by increases in the cost of living, rising 81 per cent between 1914 and 1924 (L. O. Ward, 'H. A. L. Fisher and the teachers', in *British Journal of Educational Studies*, 23, 2, June 1974, pp. 191–9).
75 Kean (1988) *op. cit.*, pp. 60–61; PRO: Ed 24/1744; Letter from Cpt. Jessel, 17 November 1923, in Ed 24/1757.
76 Emergency Business Committee response to a letter from the Six Point Group, 16 November 1923, in PRO: CAB/162 CP 467.
77 *Education Act 1918, op. cit.*, para. 2.
78 See Pollard, *op. cit.*, pp. 204–5, for details of the £87m cuts contained in the Geddes reports. For a general discussion of this issue see D. W. Thoms, 'The Education Act of 1918 and the development of central government control of education', in *Journal of Educational Administration and History* 6, 2, July 1974, pp. 26–30.
79 Simon (1), *op. cit.*, p. 363.
80 *Ibid.*, p. 361.
81 Perry Anderson, 'Origins of the present crisis' in *New Left Review*, 23, January/February 1964, p. 41; Kean (1988), p. 16.
82 David Coates, *The Labour Party and the Struggle for Socialism*, Cambridge University Press, 1975, p. 18.
83 Trevelyan, speech made in Newcastle, 22 March 1924, as printed in *The Broad High Road in Education*, Labour Party, 1924; Charles Trevelyan, 'Labour's record at the Board of Education', in H. B. Lees-Smith, *Encyclopaedia of the Labour Movement*, vol. 1, 1928, pp. 228–30; *Education 1900–1950, op. cit.*, para. 22.
84 See a memorandum from Snowden, Chancellor of the Exchequer to Trevelyan, president of the Board of Education in PRO: Ed 24/1393, 28 January 1930: 'I think for the present we have made a sufficient advance in educational development, and that a task no less urgent than that of seeking to expand educational facilities is to make certain that we are getting value for our existing expenditure . . .' (quoted in D. W. Thoms, *op. cit.*); see *Education 1900–1950, op. cit.*, para. 26, for details of the National Economy Act 1931, circular 1413.
85 Andrew Gamble, *Britain in Decline*, Macmillan Papermac, 1981; Maurice Cowling, *The Impact of Labour 1920–1924*, Cambridge University Press, 1971, especially Introduction.

Chapter 2

Socialist Organizations' Educational Strategies

In the previous chapter I analyzed the state's educational strategies. In particular, it was suggested that the central state was able to maintain successfully its hegemony both within the educational state apparatus and beyond it by incorporating education within its wider strategies. In this chapter the focus will be on the strategies of organizations to the left of the Labour Party which defined themselves, in various ways, as socialist. The educational policies of the Labour Party, which did not declare itself to be a socialist organization until its reorganization in 1918,[1] were clearly and deliberately constructed within the framework of the state, as I indicated in Chapter 1.

The socialism of the organizations under consideration: the Social Democratic Federation (SDF), later the Social Democratic Party (SDP), the British Socialist Party (BSP), the Socialist Labour Party (SLP), the Workers' Socialist Federation (WSF), and the Communist Party (CP), has been analyzed in various ways.[2] However, the educational strategies of these organizations have been neglected, even though they formed a significant part of their discussions.[3]

In order to assist the reader possibly unfamiliar with the organizations under consideration, a chronological table is presented in Figure 2.1.

In analyzing the strategies of these socialist organizations emphasis will be placed upon the extent to which they were able to provide an opposition to the state's educational policies.

The Educational Strategies of the SDF/SDP

Brian Simon has given a sympathetic account of the educational campaigns of the Socialist Democratic Federation (SDF), the socialist organization founded in the 1880s,[4] arguing that it:

had adopted a Marxist outlook from its inception, if often in the

Figure 2.1 A Chronological Outline of the Socialist Organizations Discussed in Chapter 2

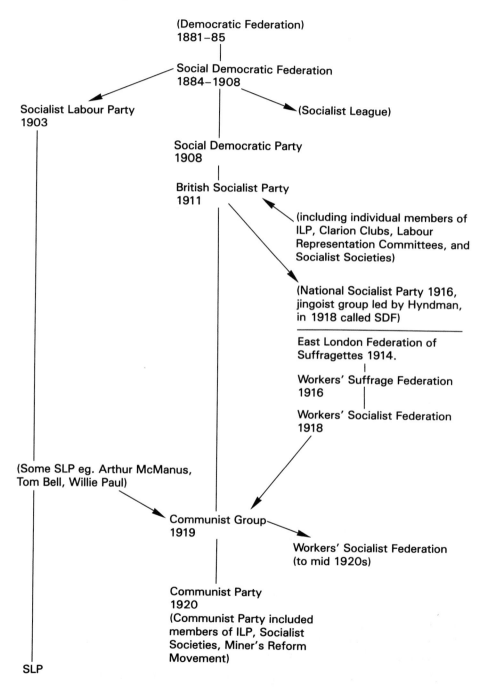

particular and somewhat dogmatic form this was advanced by Hyndman (its founder). This involved the acceptance of the existence of a class struggle, of a fundamental clash of interests, with the resultant need to build up working strength in order to achieve the social revolution.[5]

The SDF's object was 'the establishment of a free society, based upon the principles of political equality, with equal social rights for all and complete emancipation of labour'.[6] This object, as J. T. Murphy argued in a rather more critical account of the Federation's work, 'gave plenty of scope for revolutionary speeches based on a contrast between the conditions of capitalism and the aims of socialism, but nowhere is there evidence of a clear formulation of how the SDF conceived they were going to lead the working class to this goal'.[7] The 'particular' socialism of Hyndman led to sharp disagreements within the organization and frequent castigations from Engels denouncing 'Mr Hyndman' and the SDF as 'an association which poses as the only true church of British socialism'.[8]

This 'particular' position led the organization to distance itself from the Labour Party and to decline to affiliate.[9] It also distanced itself from trade union intervention, despite the prominent trades unionists it numbered in its membership,[10] believing that change would occur by political organization alone and by the education of the masses in socialism.[11]

The positions of the SDF were frequently put forward simply as political propaganda, but occasionally such views were put to the electorate, when SDF members stood for school board positions and obtained some support.[12] However, irrespective of the particular stance adopted towards the state at this time, the rejection of working with broader working-class organizations implicitly meant the adoption of a propagandist approach rather than the evolution of strategies realistically designed to advance and unite working-class aspirations.

A Statist Approach

The educational positions of the SDF were statist. Since its inception in the 1880s it had favoured the state maintenance of children, having been initially inspired by the municipal schemes for the feeding of children which were current in Paris.[13] This demand for state maintenance had featured prominently in the manifestos for candidates standing in school board elections.[14] Although its demands were orientated towards the state maintaining children, the SDF also organized its own attempts to feed hungry children in working-class areas. Writing about his earlier experiences in Canning Town SDF, Will Thorne, the gasworkers' leader, described the regular Saturday evening visits to the butchers, bakers and greengrocers to collect scraps to make into soup to be given to children on Sunday morning from the temperance bar on Barking Road.[15]

The demand for state maintenance was based on the needs of working-class children as future members of the nation. The children's hunger was not described in terms of their class oppression but rather in terms of the future contribution they could make to the nation as a whole. This view permeated the pamphlet 'A Nation's Youth' written by the Countess of Warwick, an energetic member of the SDF and the aristocracy alike: 'Let the children be our first care . . . [There is] no task [which] could more ennoble a nation.'[16] The same position, based on policies to strengthen the nation was also seen in a letter written by Hyndman to the *Morning Post*: 'Lack of good food, good clothes, and good air is the main reason why some 50 % of our urban working class population is unfit to bear arms. Even from the new "imperialist" point of view this is a serious matter.'[17]

There is little in this policy to distinguish the demands for state maintenance from those concurrently discussed in the Board of Education and Parliament. It was not that demands were being placed on the state by a Marxist organization to challenge the state's authority or to 'expose' it for purposes of propaganda to working-class militants. Rather, the very same demands were put forward on the same social imperialist grounds as those used by state bodies themselves. Arguments echoed those made in Parliament about waste and inefficient use of resources. Writing in the *Socialist Annual* of 1906, Rose Jarvis argued that 'To attempt to educate starving and ill clad children is not only a crime, but a waste of energy and public money.'[18] Far from criticizing the role of the state in working-class life, the SDF argued that this intervention should be extended: 'The nation, as well as the parent, is responsible for the upbringing of children.'[19]

Indeed, such intervention was to be positively welcomed: 'It is now the state far more than their parents to whom men and women owe and pay allegiance — to whom they must turn in their hours of need.'[20] Nowhere was there the suggestion that the power of the state should be challenged, nor harnessed in the interests of the working class. Instead it was argued that the needs of the working class should be met by the existing structures of the state. In advocating this approach the SDF consciously aligned itself with those forces endorsing the legitimacy of the state's intervention in social welfare and deliberately rejected socialist positions intended to challenge the state. Thus, in a pamphlet outlining the SDF's position,[21] J. Hunter Watts was at pains to differentiate the statist position of the SDF from the anti-statist strategies of the SLP:

> If we belonged to the 'let the pot boil over' school of revolutionaries, which we do not; if we thought it well to let the seething cauldron of discontent boil and bubble till it scalded capitalism to death, we should not be found advocating state maintenance of the children, for it will transform into consumers so many tiny human beings

cruelly condemned by the poverty of their parents to experience what it means to be 'non-effective consumers' that we cannot be sure that the adoption of the proposal will not give a fresh lease of life to capitalism . . . [22]

The clear assumption was that state maintenance was a demand which did not challenge the state and which could be granted by the state. The community of interests between the working class and the state is clearly expressed by the definition of children as consumers within capitalism rather than as part of an oppressed class.

In somewhat contradictory vein, J. Hunter Watts later argued in the same pamphlet that state maintenance for children would be a step towards a 'cooperative commonwealth'.[23] At one and the same time, then, state maintenance was viewed as a contribution to the maintenance of capitalism and as a step towards an alternative political system. In the educational strategies of the SDF one thus sees a position which differentiated itself from the classic Marxist position in respect of the role of the state in maintaining capitalism.[24]

The differences between the ILP and the SDF on the question of state maintenance did not focus on alternative analyses of the role of the state but on who was responsible for bearing the cost. The SDF believed that the state should bear the full cost for feeding all children whose parents wanted them fed. The ILP, however, believed that such proposals eroded parental responsibility and backed state maintenance with the proviso that parents contributed towards the costs.[25]

Because the SDF did not view its demand as a threat to the state it was able to organize initiatives on this question with bodies which took an explicitly reformist position on the state. In January 1905, for example, a conference was jointly organized with the London Trades Council — with TUC backing.[26] Later in the same year the TUC adopted the policy of state maintenance as raised by Will Thorne.[27] He was to play an important role in Parliament in 1906, as Labour MP for West Ham, promoting Labour's Education (Provision of Meals) Bill. For this effort the following acknowledgment was made in the SDF year book: 'The only socialist measure at all successfully promoted by the Labour Party during the session was the Education (Provision of Meals) Act . . . '[28]

Throughout its existence the SDF continued to prioritize welfare provision within the framework of the educational state apparatus. Its 1907 conference condemned the Provision of Meals Act as a sham in that the cost of food could not be covered by rate-borne expenditure.[29] The conference of the following year heard reports of the work of London members who had petitioned the LCC to implement existing legislation and had organized meetings to demand that the Act was made compulsory and that the Imperial Exchequer provide grants for food.[30] Subsequently the conference carried a motion stating that state maintenance for all children in state schools should be financed by the national exchequer and not by local authorities through the rates.[31] This had the effect of placing financial demands upon the central state without challenging the structures of the state implementing such a demand.

The SDF's understanding of the state as a benevolent institution capable of acceding to working-class demands underpinned its demands for a '. . . national system of education . . . free and secular and under complete popular control'.[32] This position was also accepted by the Labour Party as part of its 1906 election manifesto and no candidates were to be endorsed who did not accept this demand.[33] It is important to clarify what is meant by 'complete popular control' for at first it appears that the SDF was arguing for state resources to be brought under workers' control. What was intended, however, was that education should be brought under direct control of a directly elected body responsible for education. The power of the state as such was not challenged but the nature of the electoral process was. As indicated in Chapter 1, since the 1902 Education Act election of local education authorities had been subsumed within the structure of local government. The type of system advocated was one which recalled the earlier system of election to school boards and which ensured that those candidates specifically interested in education, and education alone, were elected.

Education was important to the SDF for it believed that education — any education — could sweep away ignorance and lay the basis for socialism.[34] Thus the SDF was involved in the Socialist Sunday School movement — which will be discussed in the next chapter — to assist in the education of children as a supplement to the curriculum of the elementary schools. The SDF's educational campaigns stressed access to state education and the removal of impediments, such as hunger and poor health, which prevented children learning. As far as the curriculum itself was concerned the SDF opposed religious education and argued that education should be fully secular. There was no great attempt to spell out the precise nature of the curriculum, for the main priority was access to the curriculum as it currently existed. As Brian Simon has put it, socialists in the SDF and ILP alike 'stood in the classic tradition of humanist education of the past'.[35]

The SDF campaigns relied on the activity of prominent individual members such as the Countess of Warwick, Mrs Bridges Adams, Will Thorne and George Lansbury who promoted educational questions because of their individual concerns and circumstances.[36] This is elaborated for example by the Countess of Warwick in a volume of her autobiography, *Afterthoughts*:

> The first vital experience that I had in the labour movement was when Mrs Bridges Adams, Will Thorne, J. R. Clynes, John Gorst and various others of us tramped the country to try to arouse sufficient feeling to enforce compulsory feeding of starving

children. It was an exciting period, for we all had the cause deeply at heart. I had visited hospitals in plenty, and seen the victims of malnutrition . . . Naturally I felt that I had to throw myself into the fight and joined up. Will Thorne was then the dominant personality of our group.[37]

Despite their activity there is little indication that the same enthusiasm was directed to developing their political positions on educational questions: throughout its existence the SDF/SDP maintained a strategy of reliance upon the state to provide and extend education. The same adaptation to a statist framework for education was to be found in the BSP, formed out of the SDP in 1911.

The Positions of the BSP

In 1911 on the initiative of the SDP a unity conference was held, attended by delegates from many ILP branches, Clarion Clubs, socialist societies and Labour Representation committees to establish the British Socialist Party (BSP).[38] The newly organized group aimed to achieve socialism, meanwhile supporting 'all measures that tend to protect the life and health of the workers and to strengthen their struggle against capitalist class'.[39] As before emphasis was placed upon the 'education of the people in the principles of socialism'.[40]

The new group — still dominated by Hyndman and the politics of the old SDF — was formed at a time of growing industrial unrest particularly in the docks, railways and mines. Increasingly, militant trades unionists were turning towards syndicalist politics to provide strategies for the working movement. As I have explained earlier, the SDF had seen the development of socialism solely through political parties. The BSP continued this line. At its founding congress, the BSP declared its intention of establishing 'a militant socialist party in Parliament and local bodies . . . ' and although it subsequently encouraged its members to become involved in trades unions it was within these parameters.[41]

Tom Mann, the former dockers' leader, was to join the SDP briefly on his return to England from Australia, but resigned shortly after the 1911 conference, stating in his resignation letter:

I find myself not in agreement with the important matter of Parliamentary action. My experiences have driven me more and more into the non-Parliamentary position and this I find is most unwelcome to most members of the Party. After the most careful reflection I am driven to the belief that the real reason why the trade union movement of this country is in such a deplorable state of inefficiency is to be found in the fictitious importance which the workers have been encouraged to attach to Parliamentary action . . . economic liberty will never be realised by such means.[42]

Future issues of the *Industrial Syndicalist*, founded by Tom Mann to agitate and organize on syndicalist lines, elaborated the differences with the BSP on the state:

> The political socialist sees in everything the need for the state or the municipality to do something, thereby forgetting the class nature of the state and his own teaching that anything to be done, must be done by the workers themselves, and that no laws will be enforced effectively in the workers' interests, until the workers can enforce it themselves.[43]

It was the BSP's antipathy towards trade union intervention in this period of industrial unrest, James Hinton has argued, which led to a decline in the organization's membership by two thirds by the outbreak of war from a figure of 35,000 at the founding conference.[44]

Policies on Educational Welfare and Intellectual Needs

Demands on the state to extend educational provision continued unassisted by trades union pressure organized by the BSP. By 1911 legislation on feeding and medical care had been extended and many authorities had taken advantage of the enabling legislation to introduce their own schemes, albeit still inadequately financed by the National Exchequer.[45]

The BSP then turned its attention to the extension of such provisions and the basis of their financing. The whole cost of education, including feeding, was to be borne by the state centrally.[46] The question of children's physical needs was linked to their 'mental' needs. Opening the 1914 BSP conference John Stokes, amidst applause, referred back to the origins of the BSP's current education policy: 'Thirty years ago the old SDF pointed to the stomach as the seat of learning . . . and demanded that complete maintenance by the community was the right of every child born in a civil state.'[47] Here again we see the elision between the community and the state, in the same way as we earlier saw in the SDF the elision between the nation, the state and the working class. It is against this same political concept of a benign state that arguments were put forward on the type of education to be received by children: 'Let the individual child be studied scientifically and sympathetically that body and mind may be properly fed and trained. We want a cultured and educated people to take full possession of the glorious future that awaits them.'[48]

The emphasis on 'proper' education is also seen in a contemporary article in *Justice*.[49] In both these examples the nature of feeding and training is not explored, 'proper' suffices as a means of elaboration. The state schools are to be given the task of educating working-class children defined as part of the 'people'. I have previously indicated how this denial of children as part of an oppressed class indicated a positive view of the possibility of achieving significant reforms within the state. It also helps to explain why so little attention was paid to the curriculum. Debates about the particular curriculum needs, for example, of the working-class would not arise given that these educational needs were seen to be the same as the needs of the people as a whole. When attention was occasionally directed towards the content of education this was directed in a negative way, citing what was *not* required in a curriculum: 'Education was the only groundwork upon which any successful revolution could possibly be based. Even among socialists there was a lack of clear conception of what education really meant. They had no right to subject the child to any form of education which had profit for this object or the dissemination of any particular kind of theological dogma.'[50]

Religious knowledge was opposed and education was not to be subordinated to the claims of industry.[51] The organization was rather more vague about its own alternatives: students were to have a grounding element of knowledge to fit them for citizenship;[52] the aim of education was to produce 'intellectually eager men and women with emancipated minds and broad sympathies'.[53] This latter aspect provided their alternative framework in that it suggested that the removal of ignorance and the desire for knowledge would automatically ensure that people would accept the 'socialist message'.

The BSP's Receptiveness to the Educational Positions of the Progressives

Such a view implicitly rejected a class-based analysis, for it assumed that through the eradication of ignorance alone society would be transformed. The emphasis is upon the changed perceptions and understanding of people rather than upon the nature of state institutions in capitalist society. This approach allowed for a receptiveness towards the ideas of the progressive education movement. State schools were criticized for their tendency to 'tradition, conservatism, officialism, and a love of the artificial'.[54] Such sentiments echoed those expressed by Edmond Holmes, the former chief educational inspector, in his extremely popular book *What is and What Might Be*,[55] in which he criticized the general practice in elementary schools and blamed the materialistic outlook on life prevalent in the West.[56] Another BSP contribution defined the position thus: 'It is not a matter of appointing working class managers and working class education committees as much as getting control over the curriculum, the books used, the "atmosphere" of the schools.'[57]

Certainly the BSP, like the progressives, welcomed a freer approach in the school's 'atmosphere', as this extract from the Earl of Lytton's address to the 1916 Conference for New Ideals in Education indicates:

> It is not a definite educational philosophy that we wish to propound from the platform, still less is it a particular educational curriculum. We do not advocate a curriculum, but rather a method, or perhaps not even a method, but a point of view, an attitude towards education... the means of ensuring as far as possible in all education the free, spontaneous individual experience of pupils.'[58]

Challenges to the Emphasis on Equality of Access to State Education

In addition to responding positively to the new thinking in education put forward by the progressives, some BSP members also started to reassess the hitherto accepted view that access to existing state education was a correct socialist line.[59] In a polemical article, Litchfield Wood, the editor of *The Link*, argued that the 'proletariat must cease to worship the educational shibboleths of the bourgeois before it can gain emancipation'.[60] His analysis was developed along Marxist reductionist lines. The present system of education had followed the development of bourgeois society, and thus the main emphasis had been on knowledge to run the industrial machine.

Counterposed to 'knowledge' was 'intelligence' which was seen as the discovery of relations, the object being to 'guide the child to the establishment of relations, ready made knowledge and facts being taught only where absolutely necessary, or as material for the exercise of intelligence'.[61] A similar sentiment is found in an article a few months later which defined education as 'deliberately and cleverly designed to supply a cheap supply of ready-made clerks, or to produce human machine minders'.[62] The alternatives were described as 'clear thought, brain formation and development, healthy minds, bodies and morals'.[63]

These approaches looked at education in the context of the economic function that it performed within capitalist society and argued that education in state schools was geared simply to the economic needs of capitalism. There was then in some way a break with earlier discussion in the SDF which had focused simply on the demands to be made upon the state. Here we also find discussion of the function of the existing education which was provided by the state. However, these analyses of the function were not accompanied by demands upon the state to acquiesce to suggested changes.

The BSP Response to the 1918 Education Act

It was not until the state itself was developing new structures for education — in this case the 1918 Education Bill — that the BSP turned its attention to analyzing the nature of education and then developed specific demands for change and campaigns to achieve them.[64] The Fisher Bill was welcomed. Previous policy for educational efficiency in the interests of the nation was reiterated: unless the physical needs were met the best education system in the world would be largely wasted and 'the efforts of the finest teachers will be nullified'.[65] The whole curriculum should have, the BSP argued, a 'much more democratic colouring'.[66] Another desirable feature was the teaching of 'liberty, equality, fraternity' (*sic*) as this would be better 'for the race'.[67] Thus again we see the conflation of the needs of the working-class with the needs of the nation. The 'new' aspect of policy was the endorsement of aspects of education which 'brought out' children's 'latent possibilities',[68] in other words an endorsement of the educational philosophy of the progressives.

It should be remembered that these positions were being advocated in 1917 at the end of the imperialist war, against a background of growing political and industrial unrest in the country. New working-class organizations such as the shop stewards' movement were starting to be built and the effect of the revolution in the Soviet Union was being felt throughout the labour movement. The BSP was playing a campaigning role in such activities. I highlight these features of the political climate to contrast them with the type of educational policies being advocated by the BSP. Leading activists were involved in solidarity work with the Russian Revolution, principally through the 'Hands Off Russia' campaign, and others were prominent in the new National Workers Committee.[69] In its general practice the BSP was attempting to place itself at the head of working-class forces challenging the state.

On the educational state apparatus it took a less clear cut oppositional line. The articles written in the BSP paper, *The Call*, by John Maclean are an exception to this approach. He analyzed that the function of education in a capitalist society was to produce 'better wages slaves or better producers of commodities'.[70] He then went on to argue that it would, however, be reactionary to oppose educational reforms, such as the Fisher Bill, 'over which we as voters have a slight control . . . it is our special business to see that all public education institutions be used for the creation of intelligent, class conscious workers.'[71] Part of the overall class struggle 'must be for absolute control of all educational agencies' which cannot be postponed until working-class control has been achieved.[72] These positions broke with the mainstream of the BSP educational argument in several ways. The type of education to be given in the country's schools was to be determined by the outcome of the class struggle. That is, the question of education could not be settled within the existing state educational apparatus, instead it would be determined by the broader class conflicts in society as a whole. Further, Maclean was not accepting that the needs of the working class could be identified with those of the nation: the working class had particular needs which required a particular education.

His contributions marked a move away from an approach which simply made propaganda about educational questions and which saw access to existing state provision as the main priority. Whether educational changes were to be finally realized depended upon the balance of class forces in society at large to effect those changes and not upon the generosity of the state. However, such a line was not integrated into the broader strategies of the organization. Writing six months later, Fairchild, the BSP secretary, re-iterated the argument for (individual) equality of opportunity for all, rather than developing Maclean's view about the different needs for different classes.[73] The framework for discussion was that put forward by bodies of the state. The BSP's response focused on the extension of state provision to the individual child, irrespective of class. In so doing it was unable politic-ally to challenge the state's strategy in that it accepted many of the implicit assumptions on which such educational strategy was based.

The Policies of the SLP

In contrast the much smaller Socialist Labour Party (SLP) challenged theoretically the educational framework of the state. The SLP was a small Marxist organization formed through a split from the SDF in 1903. It was very much influenced by the American Marxist Daniel DeLeon and whole-heartedly embraced his view of industrial unionism, as popularized by the American 'Wobblies'.[74] Although the SLP welcomed this type of trade union activity it was highly critical of the existing unions which were dismissed — leadership and rank and file alike — as reformist. Thus they distanced themselves from the syndicalist activities of Tom Mann and his supporters for these were based on existing trade unions. The SLP believed that in order to overthrow the state and establish an 'industrial republic' the working class needed to be educated in class conscious education. As DeLeon expressed it in his 1904 Scottish tour: 'The foundation of the socialist movement was the education of the working class.'[75] The organization believed that there was no possibility of change in the interests of the working class in existing capitalist society. The SLP's rejection of the structures of the working-class movement to facilitate such a change, coupled with their rigorous autodidactism, set them apart from the rest of the socialist movement.[76]

The organization's small base was in Scotland and the North: in 1911 there were three branches in London, by 1918 there were none.[77] After the founding of the Communist Party leading members Thomas Bell, Arthur McManus, and William Paul, the widely acclaimed author of *The State, its*

Origins and Function, led the majority of the organization into the Communist Party.[78] A small rump, however, continued to produce *The Socialist* well into the 1920s during which time the coverage of education issues was extended.[79]

The SLP's Keen Interest in Education and Learning

Several analyses have been offered by former SLP members to account for the organization's intense interest in learning. In his autobiography, T. A. Jackson, a former member who later became a Communist Party luminary, attributed it to higher educational standards in Scotland and a greater respect for learning.[80] This factor is also evident in the autobiography of James Clunie, who subsequently became the national organizer of the Central Labour College. His writing is peppered with references to an eclectic range of writers: William Morris, Leibknecht, Lewis H. Morgan, Dietzgen — an SLP favourite — Robert Burns, Engels, Marx, Smith (*Wealth of Nations*) and Whitman (*Leaves of Grass*).[81] He describes his attitude to learning thus: 'Books to me became symbols of social revolution: through reason, enlightenment, and unity'.[82] The esteem in which learning and those responsible for its dissemination, teachers, were held is indicated by the way in which John Maclean is mentioned: 'If I must select one who influenced my life more than any other it was John Maclean, the Glasgow *school teacher*' [my emphasis].[83] Later, Maclean is described as the 'political *school master* [my emphasis] [from whom] I was given a sense of historical values and was informed that the British working-class was the most astute in the world . . . '.[84]

It was not simply that John Maclean was revered as in incisive politician but that that reverence was couched in an educational discourse. The SLP's own education with its perspective of creating politically conscious workers covered broad areas. It specifically opposed the concept of neutral education, as espoused for example by the Workers' Educational Association, and described this approach as capitulation to capitalism:

> . . . all modern education is hopelessly biased in favour of the perpetuation of capitalism . . . revolutionary socialism dare not permit its educational work to be conducted by any workers' educational association which prides itself upon being 'neutral' regarding the interests of Capital and Labour. In the class struggle the 'neutrals' so called, are *always* subtle and sinister elements in opposition to the workers.[85]

In line with its criticism of the existing structures of capitalism, the SLP argued that revolutionary socialists needed their own education which they could organize and control themselves, independent of capitalist bodies.

The SLP's Attitude to State Education

This rejection of capitalist-financed education for adults was paralleled by their attitude towards state education for children. When I discussed the BSP I highlighted the organization's lack of theoretical perspectives on the state's educational role and the response of socialists. In sharp contrast the SLP considered the question of the state to be a very important one. It underpinned its attitude to the Labour Party and other groups it defined as reformist because of such groups' attempts to work in the state's framework.[86]

This concern was reflected in the election platform on which the SLP stood — for the purpose of educating the working class about the futility of Parliamentary strategies — in the 1918 election. Arthur McManus, chair of the National Shop Stewards' Movement, in Halifax,[87] J. T. Murphy in Gorton, and William Paul in Ince, put forward general and specific alternatives to the state in its various forms. Standing for Soviets and the Bolshevik revolution they argued against Parliamentary democracy. They specifically advocated sound general and technical education for all under community control; responsibility for the care of all widows and orphans also under community control; for nationalization of land, railways, mines, and transport, and for instruments of social service to be the 'communal property of the people'.[88] Throughout the programme the emphasis was on the abolition of the capitalist state and its replacement by institutions under forms of workers' control. The emphasis was not on reforms of existing state structures but on alternatives to the very structures themselves. Thus demands were not put forward about educational provision or state maintenance since these would have indicated an acceptance of the possibility of reform within the existing state. Rather, the SLP chose to focus on the types of control needed to ensure that the existing structures of capitalism could no longer exist.

The SLP's view can perhaps best be expressed by reference to the popular work of William Paul, written prior to the Russian Revolution in 1917, *The State, its Origin and Function*.[89] It came to be widely read in the socialist movement at a time when many classic Marxist texts on such questions were unavailable in English (or yet to be written).[90] Paul traced the historical development of the state from Athens, through feudalism to the rise of industrial capitalism, and ended with revolutionary socialist alternatives. Viewing the state as a product of a particular stage of historical development, he explained its contemporary role as a tool of capitalism: 'State control is the most oppressive form of capitalist administration.'[91] In much of the book he specifically took issue with views of the state put forward by the Labour Party and the Fabians. He criticized the Fabian equation of municipalism with socialism arguing that the reforms afforded by municipalism reinforced capitalism and perpetuated class rule.[92] The state was defined as the armed forces, police, spies, legal machinery, education, and Parliament. Democratic control of the existing state was, he argued, an impossibility because it was an attempt to make geographically elected institutions (i.e. Parliament) conduct an industrial process.[93] The alternative was a social revolution resulting in a socialist republic with government of industry administered on behalf of the whole community.[94] These alternatives would be opposed, he argued, by the capitalist class who would rely on an extension of the state's activities to counter them.[95] The continued existence of capitalism was attributable to property owners who equated the state with society in order to hide the class nature of their own activity and deceive the working-class.[96]

His explanation of Labour's positive attitude towards the state included a criticism of Labour leaders for their failure to acquaint themselves with practical experience of the international class struggle and with the works of scientific socialism, namely the writing of Marx, Engels, Liebknecht, Bebel, Kautsky, Lafargue, DeLeon, Labriola and Morris.[97] I have described Paul's book at some length for it offers the reader a clear account of the SLP's approach to the political strategy which informed their specific educational positions. Thus the 'conspiracy theory' offered by Paul to explain the way in which capitalism equated the state with society is also found in educational articles in the SLP's paper, *The Socialist*. An article of February 1920 explained that under capitalism workers were taught to read and write merely to understand the orders of their masters and were instructed in subjects designed to make them proficient wage slaves.[98]

The SLP's line on the impossibility of working within the state's, or labour movement's, existing structures to effect change did not prevent them from developing their own blueprints for a future school curriculum and inviting other socialists interested in education to contribute to their pages. Among the contributions were Mrs Bridges Adams,[99] a former member of the London School Board, whose articles included those criticizing religious teaching in schools and the education provided by the WEA.[100] The point of such articles was not to make demands upon the state as such but rather to educate the paper's readership on what constituted class conscious education.

The SLP's Work with Young People

Because the SLP both rejected direct intervention into state education and believed that the education of the working-class was the key to a successful revolution it directed its efforts towards the education of its members and young people. The SLP saw its work with young people as explicitly oppositional. Children were regarded as politically conscious and were taught about the state and the nature of state education.[101]

Prominent in this field was Tom Anderson — sufficiently respected at the time to be given the honour of giving John Maclean's funeral oration[102]

— who founded the Proletarian College in 1919 'to teach the young workers of the country the absolute necessity for the abolition of the present political state and the inauguration of an industrial republic, the teaching being based on the ten proletarian maxims'.[103] These maxims, drawn up some time before by Anderson and taught at the SLP's Sunday schools, included the following:

> No 5: Thou shalt teach Revolution, for revolution means the abolition of the present political state, and the end of capitalism, and the raising in their place of an industrial republic.
> No 9: Thou shalt perform a mission in society by achieving an ideal of a fuller and higher life for all, in the abolition of classes, and by the regulation of industry by the Industrial Republic, which shall end the political state.
> No 10: Thou shalt remember that the economic structure of society determines the legal and political superstructure . . . it is not men's consciousness which determines their life; on the contrary, it is the social life which determines their consciousness.[104]

This practical approach to the education of the young as much as its theoretical stance distanced the SLP from groups such as the BSP. Little love was lost between the two organizations: the BSP condemned their erstwhile colleagues as 'impossibilists'; the SLP countered that the BSP's concerns for state maintenance were reformist and assisted in the maintenance of the capitalist state.[105] Ironically, the SLP's position on the state, as expounded by William Paul, was widely respected within the socialist movement, while its positions on educational alternatives were largely ignored. It had the capacity to produce powerful propaganda but rejected the mechanisms by which that propaganda could be directed into action — the existing trade union and labour movement.

The Policies of the WSF

A contemporary organization which shared the SLP's contempt for Parliamentary action[106] was the small Workers' Socialist Federation (WSF), as it was known in 1918, formed from the East London Suffrage Federation by Sylvia Pankhurst.[107] It, too, defined itself as a propaganda organization intent on educating the working class, especially working-class women, in socialist ideas, so that they might understand the nature of the class society. It defined its attitude towards learning thus: 'The printing press is the machine gun for the slaves against slavery.'[108]

Like the SLP it called for the abolition of capitalism with the establishment of a common social order to be achieved by socialist revolution.[109] But unlike the SLP it paid little attention to a theoretical position on the state. Various pamphlets were printed by the WSF between 1918 and 1920 on the soviet experience, Ireland, Communist Hungary, a translation of Kollantai's *Communism and the Family*, pamphlets by Sylvia Pankhurst and Eden and Cedar Paul on the schooling for the future and independent working-class education respectively, but there was nothing theoretical published on the state.[110]

Educational Discussion within the Pages of the *Woman's Dreadnought* and the *Workers' Dreadnought*

The *Workers' Dreadnought* and the *Woman's Dreadnought*, its predecessor, had regular coverage of contemporary educational questions. It discussed ideas of the progressive movement, gave support to the victimized teachers Mr and Mrs Higdon and their strike school at Burston, and covered activities by the National Federation of Women Teachers (NFWT) and the Women Teachers' Franchise Union (WTFU).[111]

As will be elaborated in Chapter 5, many leading members of the NFWT were supporters of the Women's Freedom League which took a positive attitude to the labour and socialist movement before, during, and after the war. The Women's Freedom League worked with the East London Federation of Suffragettes on specific issues, most notably in this period for the repeal of section 40d of the Defence of the Realm Act.[112] NFWT members who contributed to the pages of the *Woman's Dreadnought* included Theodora Bonwick, the campaigner for sex hygiene.[113]

Like the BSP and the NFWT, the WSF's paper gave sympathetic coverage to the ideas of the progressive movement. Its press included articles on Homer Lane's Little Commonwealth,[114] the work of Maria Montessori,[115] and a progressive school in Burges run by Mr and Mrs Faria.[116] Space was given to Margaret MacMillan of the ILP and to the independent socialists Eden and Cedar Paul to write a series of articles on their definitions of socialist education.[117]

The Pauls described the maintenance of capitalism through state education and called upon workers to form their own educational institutions outside the state's framework.[118] However, whilst arguing for independence from the state they also suggested that state education in its initial phase was a progressive development. Echoing Dewey's early writings[119] they argued that public elementary schools were founded out of 'liberal and humanist impulses' which were subsequently expelled by the more pressing needs of capitalism. Thus, they argued that possibilities for improvement existed, but only in the years of schooling before puberty. After that the mind formed its own general theories and philosophies of life and hence was easily influenced.[120]

The positive attitude towards state education was mitigated, however, by their analysis towards state control of teachers: 'Revolutionists, no less, are many of our elementary school teachers, but they are shackled and gagged by the system under which they work.'[121] What was offered was a confused position which both argued that the state had control over what was taught in schools and that alternatives within the system were possible. When they went on to elaborate such alternatives, however, they looked to the Progressive Movement which sought to 'provide for the plastic mind of childhood an environment wherein can flower individual development which shall ensure for the young their rightful place in the fashioning of a new world'.[122]

The Pauls' solution to the oppressive nature of state education was to develop alternatives outside the educational state apparatus rather than to challenge the existing balance of class forces which gave rise to the existing state. Such strategies operated within an educational discourse. Children were to be educated in schools 'founded, run and staffed by ourselves',[123] within the workers' movement, outside the state framework. This venture would begin to 'liberate our children's minds from the octopus like tentacles of the class state'.[124] Thus while the oppressive role of the state was recognized, no strategies were elaborated to challenge effectively that general situation.

As I have said, the WSF seems to have had no independent initiatives towards the school curriculum, but it nevertheless opened the pages of its press to contributions from various writers on educational matters. These included articles by T. Islwyn Nicholas, protégé of Tom Anderson, and 'General Secretary of the International Proletarian School', who advocated revolutionary teaching 'that it might be the means of bringing about the day when the working class would take charge of the means of life'.[125]

In line with its feminist politics articles were included which were of special interest to women: in addition to the articles cited above submitted by the NFWT, there was coverage of educational development in Soviet Russia, which dealt with issues from a woman's perspective.[126] Practical measures were also taken which were aimed at the specific needs of working-class women. A nursery, The Mothers Arms, a cost price restaurant, and a toy-making factory were set up by Sylvia Pankhurst in the East End.[127] In addition, crèches were organized on Sunday afternoons to allow women to attend demonstrations, with the caveat: 'Mothers are asked to bring their own cushions for babies in arms'.[128]

Muriel Matters, of the Women's Freedom League, was appointed to run the nursery on Montessorian lines and lectured throughout the country on Montessori's work to large audiences. A meeting organized on this topic by the WSF in Manchester attracted eight hundred people.[129] She also wrote articles for the *Workers' Dreadnought* to explain Montessori's 'scientific systematic education of the senses'.[130]

The peculiar origins of the WSF from a militant feminist suffrage group campaigning amongst working-class women in East London, allowed the organization to attract interest (and contributions to its paper) from a broader political spectrum than its contemporary rival socialist groups. The women in the NFWT, for example, who supported suffrage agitation did not necessarily embrace Sylvia Pankhurst's revolutionary socialist views, but recognized that her organization offered an avenue for the dissemination of feminist educational ideas. The WSF, for its part, was happy to support the women teachers' demands for equal pay.[131]

In the WSF we see an unusual combination of revolutionary socialist propaganda on similarly anti-parliamentarian lines to that of the SLP and feminism derived from the militant suffrage movement. It was a small organization, whose influence owed its origins to the actions of its founder and main proponent Sylvia Pankhurst. The openness shown to individual socialists and feminists to express their opinions within the pages of its press encouraged debate on educational matters. However, it was able to do little to provide a coherent strategy in opposition to state educational policy. The influence of the WSF, small though it was, waned after the Communist Party was formed and recognized by the Comintern. During the 1920s the main organization, other than the Labour Party, to exert any influence in the socialist movement was the Communist Party, formed mainly from the BSP with the addition of some leading members of the SLP and some independent socialists.

The Nature of the Communist Party's Politics

The early years of the CP continued to be dominated by the perspectives of its predecessor, the BSP, to the extent that the 'Report on Organization' presented by the Party Commission in the 1922 annual conference criticized the organization's practice in bald terms: 'Our task is not to create some propagandist society or revolutionary club, but to create an efficient machine of the class struggle, of confronting the complicated and centralised apparatus of the state, and eventually taking in hand the organization of production itself'.[132]

In analyzing the extent to which the educational strategies of the BSP or SDF were anti-statist it was noted that these socialist organizations accepted a statist framework for educational policy, even in periods of intense class conflict as epitomized by the 1911 strike wave and the shop stewards' movement at the end of the war. A consideration of the CP's educational strategies needs to be made against a political situation *less* favourable to socialist organizations. The CP was formed in a period of political and economic downturn which was to deepen during the 1920s. In its early years the shop stewards' movement was defeated, the Geddes cuts in capital and revenue expenditure in the public sector were introduced, the triple alliance of major industrial unions collapsed. The subsequent failure of the General Strike consolidated these defeats for the socialist movement.[133] Even at its inception, the CP had only 12,000 members. Its early progress was described by its own leaders thus: 'The Party has made no real progress either numerically or in terms of influence'.[134]

The 1922 Party Conference, however, marked a turning point in the way the CP saw its role. Attention was given to organizing its influence in the working-class movement through a centralized approach.[135] Henceforth the CP saw itself not as a propaganda organization but as one committed to organizing and developing strategy for the working-class movement. The way in which such intervention in the labour movement was to be achieved was through organizing trade unionists at their place of work. The same approach was developed for the education sector. Members were instructed to join their trades unions, stand for positions, organize groups of sympathizers and campaign to transform unions into revolutionary organs on the basis of industrial unionism.[136]

Educational Strategies of the Communist Party

The policy for education, which the party as a whole endorsed, encompassed previous BSP policy in its demands for the free provision of existing state education 'up to the highest stages'.[137] In addition, attention was paid to the curriculum based on a Marxist analysis of the existing curriculum rather than the critique offered by the Progressives. The character of education was to be altered by removing from the curricula 'teaching of a servile character or instruction biased in favour of the capitalist class, and to substitute scientific teachings that interpret history, economics and social life from the working class point of view'.[138]

As I elaborated in the last chapter, the 1918 Education Act was introduced on the basis of uniting the nation by appealing to individuals across class allegiances, and this ideology was accepted by the Labour Party. By the early 1920s, however, the CP had rejected such a strategy for education in favour of one based on the needs of the working class as a class. The difficulties of developing this strategy amongst teachers were spelt out in an article by 'School Drudge'.[139] Castigating the education given in state schools because it 'arises in a primitive manner out of the false, misleading mists of religious dualism',[140] the writer also questioned the viability of relying on teachers to act as agents of change:

> There is no hope of putting an end to capitalist wars if we have to depend on the teachers and their influence in the class room. The handful of socialist left-wing teachers realise this... [teachers] stand as the most damning indictment of state education, and as proof of its wonderful efficiency. For teachers are the product *par excellence* of a brain numbing machine, capitalism's means of deadening the minds of its victims so that they may put up with its

evils with cow-like contentment and do its bidding with un-questioning servility.[141]

The article finished by endorsing the need for organization amongst teachers while recognizing that the CP would be able to do little amongst teachers other than 'to prepare the minds of a minority of present teachers and of an increasing number of coming teachers and lay plans in readiness for the future social revolution'.[142]

As I will expand in Chapter 6; the CP's strategy in respect of teachers foundered on the very nature of teachers' political and ideological allegiance to the state. This was discussed in a response to the article by 'School Drudge' from a 'socialist teacher':[143] teachers themselves did not recognize the nature of the school system and curriculum. The alternatives posed to it by Progressives such as O'Neill and McMunn also failed to recognize 'the political and social basis of education — how it is a product, not a cause of a social system'.[144] The author also recognized that 'of course, if a teacher did begin to tackle the fundamentals (history, say) in the proper way, he would soon find himself lying on the street on the back of his neck!'[145]

The constraints placed on the very few CP teachers in the 1920s caused difficulties for the CP's strategy which placed trade union activists in the educational sector at the centre of its educational strategies. By the mid 1920s, there was a shift to campaigning also amongst parents on educational questions, and amongst young people and school children themselves.[146] In some areas campaigns were waged against Empire Day or to demand that the local authorities provide sufficient clothing or boots for children.[147]

However, the increasing isolation of the CP within the working-class movement, particularly after its explusion from the Labour Party in the mid-twenties, meant that its policies, like those of its Marxist predecessors, became simply propagandist, 'exposing' the nature of capitalist education. This stance reached its culmination in the 'Class against Class' election programme adopted for the 1929 election, which described the CP's attitude to the Labour Party thus: 'Class is against class. The Labour Party has chosen the capitalist class. The Communist Party is the party of the working class.'[148] In frenzied tones the document stated: 'Children are taught various religions, dragooned into imperialist demonstrations, taught perverted history and all their mental processes brought under the strict supervision of capitalist teaching.'[149] There followed a list of 'demands' which covered the nature of the school curriculum, the funding of education, the pay and con-ditions of teachers.[150] In adopting an explicitly anti-statist position the CP also adopted a sectarian approach to the main party in the labour movement. This ensured that its ideas would remain isolated from the main debates within the movement.

In analyzing the educational strategies of the CP in this period I have drawn attention to the broader political, economic and ideological climate within which this socialist organization was operating. Nevertheless, it is questionable whether the specific strategies adopted, which centred initially on state employees, would have been any more effective in the context in which the Communist Party's predecessors worked.

By the end of the decade the CP's influence had waned considerably.[151] In part this is no doubt due to the circumstances of its operation; nevertheless its growing sectarianism towards the labour movement in a period of increasingly repressive state activity suggests that the reasons for its lack of resonance within the working-class movement cannot be attributed solely to the political period.

An Assessment of the Overall Educational Strategies of Socialist Organizations

Stuart Macintyre, in his thorough discussion of Marxist autodidactism in the post-war period,[152] has developed questions about the relationship between state education and Marxists' own education. In this study of the position of socialist organizations on the state and education his view is endorsed: that prior to 1917 there was an absence of political strategy amongst socialist organizations, and they were isolated from the working-class movement.[153] Further, I believe that his view is generally correct that the economic and political conditions did not exist in the 1920s for the Marxist political strategy put forward to succeed.[154] However, I question his suggestion that there was a decline in autodidactism because of the increased provision of secondary education. Secondary education, he has argued, disseminated a syllabus consonant with the dominant national culture and this contributed to the decline in Marxist self-education.[155] This suggests both that elementary education did not play this role — which was not the view held by contemporary socialists[156] — and that state schooling did have a direct impact upon the positions held on education.

Clive Griggs, working in a non-Marxist framework, has suggested, on the contrary, that schooling had little effect on the interests of trades unionists in education.[157] In his study on the educational positions of the TUC, he has analyzed the educational background of prominent TUC members based upon their memoirs and concluded:

> ... one searches in vain for any substantial writing about their schooldays... This general lack of schoolboy memories suggests that for most working-class men such time as they did spend at school was too brief and infrequent for it to have been of major consequence. For those who therefore recorded their lives later the sentence or two afforded to their time spent at school was in proportion to its significance in their lives.[158]

Griggs acknowledges the role played by Will Thorne of the SDF and Pete Curran of the ILP, both from the Gasworkers' Union, in the early years of the century at the TUC. He attributes most of the resolutions discussed at the TUC congress between 1895 and 1911 to these two men but attributes this to their political allegiance, rather than to their educational backgrounds.[159]

My study of the memoirs of members (and former members) of the socialist groups under consideration has revealed little correlation between individuals' schooling and their interest in educational questions. In addition, descriptions of self-education are frequently related to the individual's wider political perspectives rather than being seen as a substitute for a non-existing secondary education. Will Thorne explained that he had little time for self-education, but was concerned about state provision of education on behalf of the unskilled workers he represented in the Gasworkers' Union.[160] On the other hand, Ben Tillet and Thomas Bell who did little to campaign in any guise for educational reform described at some length their interest in self-education. Thomas Bell described his joining of the SDF as attributable to a desire to gain knowledge about socialism. He subsequently expanded about the reading he undertook: 'I carried the first nine chapters of *Capital* to work and read on the trams to and from work and during the meal hours.'[161] Ben Tillet, however, explained that he started to study Latin and Greek whilst working on the docks with the intention of improving his own circumstances by becoming a barrister.[162]

Stuart Macintyre's point is valid if socialists saw their wide interest in reading and knowledge simply as a substitute for lost opportunities which should have been provided by the state. Yet there is little indication in the writings I have read to suggest that self-education was seen in this light. Rather, as Macintyre acknowledges in the bulk of his text, socialists in the Labour Party saw knowledge itself — without concerning themselves too much about what that knowledge was — as power, creating enlightenment and socialism. Marxist socialists, particularly in the post-war period, situated learning and education within the broader context of the needs of the class struggle. It was not a question of learning for learning's sake but how knowledge could assist in building the class struggle. The extent to which Marxist socialists, who held the latter view of knowledge and education, bothered to discuss with any seriousness the role of the state in education depended on their overall analysis of the changes needed in society and the ways in which they would be achieved. The correlation between individuals' own schooling and education within the socialist movement was not the issue, but rather the analysis of the general political situation, including education, and the orientation of the socialist movement towards the wider labour movement.

Thus although the SLP paid particular attention to a theoretical exposition on the role of the state — to the extent that Ramsay MacDonald[163] felt obliged to refute the arguments of William Paul — its attitude to the working-class movement as it presently existed ensured that little progress was made in implementing its own demands.

In the period between 1900 and 1930 there were seen to be favourable circumstances in which the socialist movement could develop anti-statist positions. Yet, as has been indicated, little was achieved in this respect in the pre-war period, a period which cannot be described as one witnessing a defeated socialist movement. In assessing the relative weakness of the CP strategy in the 1920s, attention is drawn to the theoretical tradition on which it was founded and its own mixture of propagandism and sectarian intervention into an essentially conservative workforce.[164] Such a position indicates that political weakness on the part of socialists, as well as a successful hegemonic strategy on the part of the state, was attributable to the broad consent achieved for a statist perspective. At the start of this chapter I made reference to the scant attention paid by historians to the educational positions of socialist organizations. Perhaps this is partly explained by the importance that socialists themselves attached to developing a theory and practice of education to challenge state strategies. Even the Plebs League, set up to promote workers' self-education along Marxist lines, paid scant attention to the role of elementary education under capitalism.[165]

To suggest for reasons of contemporary political expediency that the failure of socialist educational alternatives to the state in this period was reducible to the strength of the state alone is to mis-estimate the nature of socialist educational strategies in this period. The state's ability to gain consent for its positions also owed much to the weakness of those strategies drawn up by its opponents.

Notes and References

1 Arthur Henderson (Secretary of the Labour Party), *The Aims of Labour, op. cit.* See in particular Appendix 2, 'Labour and the new social order'. David Coates, *The Labour Party and the Struggle for Socialism, op. cit.*; Ross McKibbin, *The Evolution of the Labour Party 1910-24*, London, Oxford University Press, 1974.
2 That there is scant reference to the child education policies of socialist organizations in the following texts, for example, is perhaps understandable, given the writers' concerns: Tom Bell, *The British Communist Party: A Short History*, London, Lawrence and Wishart, 1937; Guy Aldred, *Communism — A Story of the Communist Party*, Glasgow, Strickland Press, 1943; D. M. Chewter, *The History of the SLP of Great Britain from 1902 until 1921 with Specific Reference to the Development of its Ideas*, B. Litt. thesis, Oxon., 1965; Henry Collins, 'The Marxism of the SDF', in Asa Briggs and John Saville (Eds), *Essays in Labour History 1880-1923*, London, MacMillan, 1971, pp. 47-69; Chishichi Tsuzuki, *H. M. Hyndman and British Socialism*, ed. Henry Pelling, London, Oxford University Press, 1961. However, equally scant attention is given in works specifically dealing with adult education in the socialist movement such as Stuart Macintyre, *A Proletarian Science, Marxism in Britain 1917-33*, Cambridge University Press, 1980; Ian Hamilton *Education for Revolution: The Plebs League and the Labour College Movement 1918-21*, MA thesis, Warwick, June 1972; Walter Kendall, *The Revolutionary Movement in Britain 1900-21: The Origins of British Communism*, London, Weidenfeld and Nicolson, 1969.

3 On the other hand studies of labour movement education policies have generally
   ignored the positions of organizations to the left of the Labour Party. For example,
   Clive Griggs, *The TUC and the Struggle for Education 1868–1925*, Lewes, Falmer
   Press, 1983. Even in Brian Simon's two volumes covering this period, *Education and
   the Labour Movement 1870–1920*, *op. cit.*, and *Politics of Educational Reform
   1920–1940*, *op. cit.*, there is little reference to the policies and activities of socialist
   organizations to the left of the Labour Party. Indeed, in the second volume, there is
   no discussion at all of the Communist Party, although there are a few references to
   the Teachers' Labour League in which the CP was prominent.

4 See Kendall, *op. cit.*, Collins, *op. cit.*, Tsuzuki, *op. cit.* See also A. L. Morton and
   George Tate, *The British Labour Movement*, 1st edn, London, Lawrence and
   Wishart, 1956, reprinted 1973, pp. 163ff.; James Hinton, *Labour and Socialism: A
   History of the British Labour Movement 1867–1974*, Brighton, Wheatsheaf, 1983,
   pp. 40ff.

5 Simon (1974) (1), *op. cit.*, p. 174.

6 J. T. Murphy, *Preparing for Power*, first published 1934, reprinted Pluto 1972, p.
   74.

7 *Ibid.*

8 Engels, 'May 4th in London', 1890, in Marx and Engels, *Articles on Britain*, Progress
   Publishers, Moscow, 1975, pp. 402–3. See also Engels writing to F. A. Sorge, 10
   November 1894: 'The SDF . . . has managed to transform our theory into the rigid
   dogma of an orthodox sect . . .', as quoted in Collins, *op. cit.*, p. 48. Similar views
   were expressed of the role of Hyndman by other socialists of the period, for example,
   'The practical application which he gave this doctrine [Marxism] was violently
   sectarian and his manner of stating it was often arrogantly disputatious' (Edouard
   Bernstein, *My Years of Exile — Reminiscences of a Socialist*, London, Leonard
   Parsons, 1921, p. 205); 'Hyndman . . . impressed me as a mystic whose presence
   belonged to a world far from my humble environment and not at all like the disciple
   of Marx that his writings seemed to bear out. He gave us a few words of advice, how
   to behave and work for the social revolution and the party and we left quite
   unmoved . . .' (James Clunie, *Labour is my Faith: The Autobiography of a House
   Painter*, Dunfermline, 1954, p. 92).

9 *Annual Conference Report*, SDF, 1906. *Annual Conference Report*, SDF, 1909.
   (On this occasion the vote was 125–2 against affiliation.) Members such as Cllr. Dan
   Irving in Burnley and Quelch in London favoured affiliation. See also Morton and
   Tate, *op. cit.*, pp. 228–30.

10 See Collins, *op. cit.*, p. 55 for an account of its position that strikes — short of an
   international general strike — were harmful to the working class, as expounded in
   its manifesto to the trades unions issued in 1894. This is also discussed in Murphy, *op.
   cit.*, p. 75.

11 Hence their emphasis on education. See Tsuzuki, *op. cit.*, Murphy, *op. cit.*, Morton
   and Tate, *op. cit.*

12 In 1885 four SDF candidates ran in London; in Newcastle in 1891 three SDF
   members were elected. See Hilda Kean, *Towards a Curriculum in the Interests of
   the Working Class*, unpublished MA thesis, Institute of Education, University of
   London, 1981, pp. 39–40; Simon, *op. cit.*, pp. 149–55; Paul Thompson, *Socialists
   Liberals and Labour: The Struggle for London 1885–1914*, *op. cit.*, pp. 1011f.
   However, Helen Taylor, a successful SDF candidate on the London School Board,
   was criticized by Hyndman for being too devoted to the board which he called 'that
   feeble middle class body' (as quoted in Tsuzuki, *op. cit.*, p. 62). Candidates were
   also stood in borough council elections. For example, two stood in Hackney in 1903,
   and in a subsequent by-election in 1904 E. C. Fairchild stood and was elected
   (Andrew Rothstein, 'An SDF Branch 1903–6', *Our History*, CP no. 19, Autumn
   1960).

13 Simon (1), *op. cit.*, pp. 133–6; M. E. Bulkley, *The Feeding of Schoolchildren*, Ratan Tara Foundation, London, G. Bell, 1914, pp. 24–6.

14 Simon, *ibid.*

15 Will Thorne, *My Life's Battles*, London, George Newnes, 1926, p. 60.

16 Countess of Warwick, 1906, *op. cit.*, p. 32.

17 *Morning Post*, 29 October 1900, as quoted in Tsuzuki, *op. cit.*, p. 148.

18 Rose Jarvis, 'State Maintenance', in *Socialist Annual*, SDF, London, Twentieth Century Press, 1906.

19 *Annual Report*, SDF, 1905.

20 Zelda Kahan, 'State Maintenance', in *Social Democrat*, February 1911.

21 J. Hunter Watts, *State Maintenance for Children*, London, Twentieth Century Press, 1904.

22 *Ibid.*

23 *Ibid.*

24 For example, in his refutation of the German Workers' Party programme Marx regarded elementary education by the state as 'Altogether objection-able . . . government and church should rather be excluded from any influence on the school' (Marx, *Critique of the Gotha Programme*, *op. cit.*, p. 333).

25 See the debate on this at LRC conference, 26 January 1905, in *Annual Report*, LRC, 1905. Thorne moved an amendment 'in favour of state maintenance of children as a necessary corollary of universal compulsory education and as a means of arresting that physical deterioration of the industrial population of this country'. Ramsay MacDonald (of the ILP) argued against this, stating that if working-class children were fed and clothed 'working class rents would go up by a corresponding amount' (*Annual Report*, LRC, 1905). In a report of the debate, *Labour Leader*, (ILP), 3 February 1905, argued that Thorne had gone too far on that occasion. Kier Hardie (ILP) also advocated this position on payment, saying that loans should be made to fathers to pay for the state provision of meals: 'Feed my Lambs' in *Labour Leader*, 9 June 1905). For an account of the ILP position see David Howell, *British Workers and the ILP 1888–1906*, Manchester, Manchester University Press, 1983. See also Edmund and Ruth Frow, *A Study of the Half Time System in Education*, Manchester, B. J. Morton, 1970; and Fenner Brockway, *Socialism over Sixty Years*, London, George Allen and Unwin, 1946, pp. 54ff. The Frows deal with SDF/ILP differences; Brockway describes the practical activities of ILP members, especially Jowett, on Bradford Council.

26 Later in the same month the LRC organized a special conference in Liverpool on provision of meals for school children at public expense. Simon (1), p. 281. *Annual Report*, TUC, 1905.

27 Thorne, of the Gasworkers' Union, represented the TUC at the organizing committee for the TUC/SDF conference on state maintenance (*Annual Report*, TUC, 1905). He was part of the TUC sectional committee on education which also included T. Whitehead, Ben Tillett, Alfred Evans, W. A. Appleton, J. Cuthbertson, J. C. Gordon, W. Davison, and J. O'Grady. The Gasworkers moved a detailed reso-lution to the TUC in 1905 on free medical advice and inspection. Griggs, *op. cit.*, p. 151.

28 Fred Knee, 'Socialism in Great Britain in 1906', *Socialist Annual*, SDF, Twentieth Century Press, 1907. This was moved by Thorne for the Gasworkers at the LRC in 1905 (see n. 27) and subsequently included in the SDF election programme of 1906. See Simon (1), p. 282.

29 Moved by Dan Irving of Burnley. *Annual report*, SDF, 1907.

30 *Annual Report*, SDF, 1908. The SDF organized a public meeting to demand that the LCC put into force the Provision of Meals Act. Speakers included Lady Warwick, Will Thorne and Victor Grayson (*The Times*, 8 January 1908, p. 14).

31 Moved by Dan Irving, SDF, *ibid.*

32 *Ibid.*
33 It was moved at Labour Party conference by Pete Curran of the ILP and stated that state schools should be under the control of and administered 'by directly elected representatives of the people' (*Conference Report*, Labour Party, 1906). Thorne subsequently introduced a bill on the broad lines of TUC policy to Parliament on 2 March 1906, omitting references to control. This indicates the similarities between the SDF and ILP on educational policy: access, provision, equal oportunity, despite the supposed differences between a reformist and revolutionary organization.
34 Herbert Burrows, Kentish Town SDF: 'The party which got hold of the children got hold of the future nation.' *Annual Report*, SDF, 1904; Macintyre, *op. cit.*, p. 157.
35 Simon (1), *op. cit.*, p. 147. *Annual Report*, SDF, 1906: Policy discussion on secular education. *Annual Report*, SDF, 1908.
36 For example see n. 30; *The Times*, 28 September 1908, Mrs Bridges Adam speaking at a Moral Education conference on secular education. Will Thorne described both his own lack of education and his being taught to read and write by Eleanor Marx as a spur to his own political activities on the question (Thorne, *op. cit.*, p. 214, etc.). George Lansbury, *My Life*, London, Constable, 1928. See especially p. 276 for an account of his own educational concerns. Margaret Blunden, *Countess of Warwick*, London, Cassell, 1967, especially pp. 168–89. See Guy Aldred, *No Traitor's Gait*, 3 vols, Glasgow, Strickland Press, 1956–63, pp. 88–9 for an interesting account of the Countess's 'conversion': 'It would be difficult to decide how far the countess really sympathized with socialism, but certainly she was one of the most remarkable women of her time.' Mrs Bridges Adams, the Countess of Warwick's secretary, had stood for the London School Board and had been elected as an ILP member for Greenwich in 1897 and 1900. She initiated and became the pro-tem secretary of the National Labour Education League (*Labour Leader*, 23 November 1901). Throughout her life she wrote articles for various publications including *Clarion*, *Socialist*, *Woman's Dreadnought*, and *The Link*.
37 Frances, Countess of Warwick, *Afterthoughts*, London, Cassell, 1931, p. 233.
38 Morton and Tate, *op. cit.*, p. 240.
39 *Ibid.*
40 *Ibid.*
41 As quoted in Morton and Tate, *op. cit.*, p. 240.
42 Letter quoted to H. W. Lee, SDP secretary (*Justice*, 11 May 1911) as reprinted in *Industrial Syndicalism* (Introduction by Geoff Brown), Documents in Social History no. 3, Nottingham, Spokesman, 1974, Introduction p. 11.
43 'Osborne Judgement Outcome' by G. Tufton in *Industrial Syndicalism*, March 1911, p. 21, as reprinted in Brown, *op. cit.*, p. 323.
44 Hinton, *op. cit.*, p. 90. See Morton and Tate, *op. cit.*, p. 240 for estimated figure of 35,000. It should be remembered that Hyndman and the old guard's support for the 1914 war led to a major split. Subsequently the BSP joined the Labour Party in 1916 (Morton and Tate, pp. 240–47).
45 See Brockway, *op. cit.*, for an account of the Bradford feeding schemes; Bentley B. Gilbert, 1970, *op. cit.*, especially pp. 113ff., for an account of the legislation; Sir George Newman, *op. cit.*, especially p. 207, for developments in London; M. E. Bulkley, *op. cit.*; and H. E. Haward, *op. cit.*
46 Samuel Williamsburgh, 'The Educational Mix-up', in *British Socialist*, August 1913 (continued in September 1913).
47 Chair's address in *Annual Report*, BSP, 1914.
48 *Ibid.*
49 *Justice*, 1 March 1913.
50 Introduction by Dan Irving, *Annual Conference Report*, BSP, 1912.
51 *Annual Conference Report*, BSP, 1912; Williamsburgh, *op. cit.*; Ray Olden, 'An Open Letter to a Critic of Education', *The Link*, October 1912.

52 Williamsburgh, September 1913, *op. cit.*
53 Ralph Morley, 'Socialism and Working Class Education', *Socialist Record*, (internal journal of the BSP), October, 1912.
54 Norman Young, 'The Why Attitude in Education', *The Link*, May 1912.
55 E. Holmes, *What Is and What Might Be*, London, Constable, 1912.
56 *Ibid.*, Preface.
57 A. G. Angus, 'Technical Education', *The Link*, November 1912.
58 *CNI Report*, 1916. For details of the Progressives' work with working-class children, see Gerard Holmes, *The Idiot Teacher*, London, Faber and Faber, 1952; H. Middleton, 'Developments in Self Activity in the Elementary School', in Ernest Young (Ed.), *The New Era in Education*, London, George Phillips and Son, p. 20; Norman Macmunn, *The Child's Path to Freedom*, London, Curwen, 1926, 1st edn, 1914, rewritten 1920; W. David Wills, *Homer Lane*, London, George Allen and Unwin, 1974; Hilda Kean (1981), *op. cit.*, pp. 25–38.
59 Ralph Morley, *op. cit.*
60 Litchfield Woods, 'Knowledge or intelligence?', *The Link*, April 1912.
61 *Ibid.*
62 Ray Olden, *op. cit.*
63 *Ibid.*
64 Editorials on the Bill in *The Call*, 19 April 1917 and 26 April 1917.
65 *The Call*, 26 April 1917.
66 *Ibid.*
67 *Ibid.*
68 *Ibid.*
69 Kendall, *op. cit.*, Hinton, *op. cit.*, Morton and Tate, *op. cit.*, Murphy, *op. cit.*
70 John Maclean, 'Independence in Working Class Education', *The Call*, 20 September, 1917.
71 *Ibid.*
72 *Ibid.*
73 E. C. Fairchild, editorial on 'Rights of Youth', *The Call*, 21 March 1918: 'Let the working class demand education for its sons as though they were the children of princes wisely instructed.'
74 Murphy, *op. cit.*, pp. 87–93.
75 Quoted in Macintyre, *op. cit.*, p. 19.
76 Kean (1988) *op. cit.*, p. 101.
77 As listed by the SLP itself, there were three branches in London: London Central, London North, and London East (*Socialist*, January 1911). In the branch directory in *Socialist*, 18 September 1919, none are given for London. However, there are estimates that the paper received a wide circulation. Challinor gave a figure of 3,000 for 1914 rising to 20,000 by the end of the war. Influence was particularly strong in Clydeside (Ray Challinor, *John S. Clarke: Parliamentarian, Poet, Lion Tamer*, London, Pluto, 1977, p. 37).
78 *Socialist*, 6 May 1920; Bell, *Pioneering Days*, *op. cit.*; Morton and Tate, *op. cit.*, p. 295.
79 Many of the articles were about the lessons of the Proletarian Schools which I will discuss in the next chapter. It also contained articles by Mrs Bridges Adams on religion in schools (*Socialist*, 17 June 1920), unemployment and starving children (21 October 1920) and clerical schools (4 November 1920). J. R. Sullivan contributed a series of articles on education in England which covered in detail the nature of the school curriculum (*Socialist*, 26 February, 1920, 11 March 1920, 18 March 1920, 1 April 1920, 8 April 1920).
80 T. A. Jackson, *Solo Trumpet — Some Memories of Socialist Agitation and Propaganda*, London, Lawrence and Wishart, 1953, p. 64.
81 Clunie, *op. cit.*

82 *Ibid.*, p. 82.
83 *Ibid.*, Foreword.
84 *Ibid.*, p. 62.
85 William Paul, *Scientific Socialism*, Glasgow, SLP, pp. 29–30.
86 Macintyre, *op. cit.*, pp. 19f.; D. M. Chewter, *op. cit.*; Murphy sums up their stance as follows: 'The SLP did more than any other party in this country to explain the Capitalist state as the executive committee of the capitalist class' (*op. cit.*, p. 89).
87 Halifax was chosen because the sitting member was Whitley, responsible for the report on workshop committees (Bell, *op. cit.*, p. 156).
88 *Ibid.*
89 William Paul, *The State, its Origin and Function*, Glasgow, SLP, 1917. See Bob Davies, *op. cit.*, for an account of the St Helen's Socialist Society reading of chapters of Paul's work, and Macintyre, *op. cit.*, p. 95.
90 Paul's work predates English translations of many important Marxist texts. *The Critique of the Gotha Programme* was not available until 1919, *The German Ideology* was not available until 1933 and then only in extract form. Lenin's *State and Revolution* was first published in 1919, and his *Left Wing Communism: An Infantile Disorder* in 1920. The works of Luxemburg and Gramsci were not available. The emphasis on economistic Marxism and the lack of development of ideological questions is not surprising in this context (Macintyre, *op. cit.*, pp. 68–9, p. 195, p. 214).
91 Paul (1917), *op. cit.*, p. 177.
92 *Ibid.*, p. 179.
93 *Ibid.*, p. 194.
94 *Ibid.*, pp. 194–9.
95 *Ibid.*, p. 199.
96 *Ibid.*, p. 181.
97 *Ibid.*, p. 200.
98 J. R. Sullivan, 'Education in England', *Socialist*, 26 February 1920.
99 See n. 36.
100 'Independent working class education in Britain and the Communist Young International', *Socialist*, 19 August 1920; 'Unemployment and C3 clerical schools', *Socialist*, 4 November 1920; 'Theological camps in the People's Schools', *Socialist*, 17 June 1920.
101 A full account of their youth work and the role of Tom Anderson will be given in the next chapter. The object of the Proletarian College for 15 to 25-year-olds, founded in 1919, was 'to teach the young workers of the country the absolute necessity for the abolition of the present political state and the inauguration of an industrial republic, the teaching being based on the ten Proletarian Maxims' (as printed in 'Fat Bourgeois', a lesson given to Bridgeton Socialist School in 1919, Glasgow, 1919).
102 PRO: CAB 24/160 CP 476, 6 December 1923.
103 See n. 101.
104 'Fat Bourgeois', *op. cit.*, p. 21.
105 Editorial on the founding conference of the BSP. J. Hunter Watts argued that demands such as state maintenance were revolutionary. The SLP countered that they were reformist (*Socialist*, November 1911). See *Annual Report*, SDF Conference 1904, for details of SLP expulsions. For other comments on the same proceedings see Bell, *op. cit.*, pp. 38f.; Guy Aldred, *No Traitor's Gait*, *op. cit.*, p. 156; T. A. Jackson, *op. cit.*, for his own involvement in these events.
106 See Lenin, 'Left wing communism: An infantile disorder', in *Selected Works*, London, Lawrence and Wishart, 1969, pp. 560–70. The positions of the SLP and Sylvia Pankhurst alike are criticized.
107 The WSF was formed in May 1918; prior to this it had been called, for a period, the

Workers' Suffrage Federation. Initially the ELSF had published *The Woman's Dreadnought* which changed its name to *Workers' Dreadnought* (Silvia Franchini, *Sylvia Pankhurst 1912-24: Dal Suffragismo Alla Rivoluzione Sociale*, Pisa, ETS Universita, 1980, p. 164).

108 As reprinted on all WSF pamphlets.

109 *Ibid.*

110 L. A. Motler, *Soviets for the British: A Plain Talk to Plain People: The Russian System Explained*; Bukharin, *Soviets or Parliament*; Sylvia Pankhurst, *Rebel Ireland: Thoughts on Easter Week*; Patricia Lynch, *Scenes from the Rebellion*; Mary O'Callaghan, *The First Sinn Fein Member of Parliament*; Charles Henry Schmidt, *The Hungarian Revolution — An Eyewitness Account*, translated M. P. Shiel; Kollantai, *Communism and the Family*; Eden and Cedar Paul, *Independent Working Class Education* (WSF 1918–1930).

111 Report of WTFU activity at NUT conference in *Woman's Dreadnought*, 18 April 1914; T. G. Higdon, The Burston Rebellion', *Woman's Dreadnought*, 8 August 1914; 'A Village in Revolt', *Woman's Dreadnought*, 19 May 1917; article on Homer Lane's Little Commonwealth, 24 October 1914; on Burston, 27 October 1917; picture of the opening of the Burston Strike School, 26 May 1917; series by Muriel Matters on Dr Montessori starting Christmas 1917; account of the LCC attitude towards the NFWT on women's pay, 19 March 1918.

112 Les Garner, *Stepping Stones to Women's Liberty*, London, Heinemann, 1984, p. 41; Frank Mort, *Dangerous Sexualities: Medico-Moral Politics in England since 1830*, London, Routledge and Kegan Paul, 1987, pp. 199, 207–8.

113 Theodora Bonwick, 'What the child should know', *Woman's Dreadnought*, 18 July 1914. See also *Woman's Dreadnought*, 8 March 1914, for an account of a meeting addressed on this topic by Theodora Bonwick, and *Workers' Dreadnought*, 2 December 1916, for an interview with Mrs Drake on the same topic. See Hilda Kean, *Deeds not Words: The Lives of Suffragette Teachers*, Pluto Press, 1990, for details of Theodora Bonwick's life and politics.

114 *Woman's Dreadnought*, 24 October 1914.

115 Series of articles by Muriel Matters: *Workers' Dreadnought*, Christmas 1917, 19 January 1918, 13 April 1918.

116 *Workers' Dreadnought*, Christmas 1917.

117 Margaret MacMillan (on child nurses), 'What to do — the trained woman', *Women's Dreadnought*, 7 August 1915; Eden and Cedar Paul on socialist education (and progressive education), *Workers' Dreadnought*, 20 July 1918, 27 July 1918, 3 August 1917, 10 August 1917, 17 August 1917, 24 August 1917, 7 September 1918, 14 September 1918.

118 *Workers' Dreadnought*, 20 July 1918.

119 John and Evelyn Dewey, *Schools of Tomorrow*, New York, E. P. Dutton and Co. 1915; John Dewey, *The School and Society*, 2nd edn, University of Chicago Press, 1915; Kean (1981) *op. cit.*, pp. 16–20.

120 *Workers' Dreadnought*, 10 August 1918.

121 *Ibid.*

122 *Workers' Dreadnought*, 3 August 1918.

123 *Workers' Dreadnought*, 14 September 1918.

124 *Ibid.*

125 T. Islywn Nicholas, 'The Missing Tactic', *Workers' Dreadnought*, 8 January 1921.

126 For example, Lunatcharsky, 'Revolutionary Education', *Workers' Dreadnought*, 8 January 1921.

127 *Woman's Dreadnought*, 12 September 1914, 19 September 1914, 10 October 1914. Sylvia Pankhurst, *The Home Front*, 1932, republished Cresset Library, London, Hutchinson, 1987, pp. 173–4, 425–9; Franchini, *op. cit.*, p. 147.

128 *Woman's Dreadnought*, 11 July, 1914.
129 *Workers' Dreadnought*, 16 March 1918. Pankhurst, *op. cit.*, p. 425.
130 *Workers' Dreadnought*, 19 January 1918.
131 *Workers' Dreadnought*, 9 March 1918; coverage of the election of Miss Conway to the presidency of the NUT and her position on equal pay (6 April 1918); for coverage of the Rhondda teachers' strike, 22 March 1919 and 12 April 1919.
132 'Report on Organisation' by Inkpin, Pollitt and Palme Dutt, presented by party commission to annual conference, CPGB, 7 October 1922. This was described by Pollitt, *op. cit.*, p. 155, as 'the turning point . . . it represented for us all . . . a new conception of what a communist party is, how it works, the functions of its press, the correct methods of work in the factories and workshops, and localities, and the decisive place that agitation and propaganda occupy in the work of a communist party.' See also Raphael Samuel, 'Staying power: The lost world of British communism, Part Two' in *New Left Review*, 156, March/April 1986, pp. 65–6.
133 Noreen Branson, *History of the Communist Party of Great Britain 1917–1941*, London, Lawrence and Wishart, 1985; pp. 1–15; James Hinton, *op. cit.*, pp. 131–47.
134 'Report on Organisation', *op. cit.*, p. 10.
135 *Ibid.*, p. 13.
136 *Ibid.*, pp. 36ff. 'Communist Industrial Policy: New Tasks for New Times', *Congress Report*, Communist Party, 1923, pp. 7–8.
137 'Communist Parliamentary Policy and Election Programme', *Congress Report*, Communist Party, 1923, p. 14.
138 *Ibid.*
139 School Drudge, 'The No More Warriors', *The Communist*, 19 August 1922, p. 7.
140 *Ibid.*
141 *Ibid.*
142 *Ibid.*
143 *The Communist*, 9 September 1922.
144 *Ibid.*
145 *Ibid.*
146 *Workers' Weekly*, 19 February 1926, covers organizing parents' councils in Blaydon for feeding and clothing. *Workers' Weekly*, 26 February 1926, the formation of the Young Comrades League 'to counteract false and anti-working-class teaching in the schools; to fight for better conditions, both inside and outside school . . .'
147 *Education Worker*, April 1928, describes action in Leyton; *Education Worker*, May 1928, has an article on Empire Day by Mark Starr; *Education Worker*, June 1928, on action in Leyton on Empire Day; *Workers' Weekly*, 4 January 1924, for boot campaign by Port Glasgow workers.
148 'Class Against Class', *General Election Programme*, Communist Party, 1929, p. 10.
149 Branson, *op. cit.*, pp. 31–51; 'Class Against Class', *op. cit.*, p. 26.
150 *Ibid.*
151 Branson, *op. cit.*, p. 48, p. 52.
152 Macintyre, *op. cit.*
153 *Ibid.*, pp. 236ff.
154 *Ibid.*
155 *Ibid.*, p. 238.
156 See nn. 100, 139, 143, 148, for references covering the period of Macintyre's study. For an interesting — though slightly later — comment see a letter to which T. A. Jackson replied on what Communist Party members should do with their children on Empire Day in Raphael Samuel, 'The lost world of British communism: Two Texts', in *New Left Review*, 155, January/February 1986.
157 Griggs, *op. cit.*, pp. 213–23. Griggs bases much of his argument on the auto-

biographies written by individual trades unionists. I would suggest that an exploration of autobiography as a genre and the restrictions this places upon the way in which working-class writers assume they should write is also an aspect worth exploring. See Hilda Kean, *English Teaching and Class*, ILEA, 1988, pp. 26–41.

158 Griggs, *op. cit.*, pp. 214–15.
159 *Ibid.*, pp. 86–7.
160 Thorne, *op. cit.*, p. 217.
161 Bell, *op. cit.*, p. 65.
162 Tillett, *Memories and Reflections*, London, John Long, 1931, p. 43 and p. 94. He later comments (p. 271): 'If I have one grouch against the world rather than another, the lack of opportunity for acquiring education in my earlier days is that one big grouch.'
163 Macintyre, *op. cit.*, p. 178.
164 See Chapter 6, nn. 85–100.
165 See Kean, *State Education 1988, op. cit.*, pp. 106–7. For background to the ideas of the Plebs League and independent working-class education see Hamilton, *op. cit.*, and J. H. Roberts, *The National Council of Labour Colleges: An Experiment in Workers' Education*, M.Sc. thesis, Edinburgh, 1970.

Chapter 3

Activities of Socialist Organizations with Children of Socialists

In the last chapter I analyzed the extent to which the educational strategies of socialists were statist in character. Here consideration is given to the educational practice of socialist organizations in relation to the children and young people of the socialist movement itself. As can be seen from Figure 3.1 some of these organizations were short lived and all took their political impetus from the type of socialism advocated by particular adult socialist groups.

My analysis of children's and youth organizations, in particular the Socialist Sunday Schools (SSS), The Young Comrades League (also referred to as the Communist Children's Group), Young Socialist League (YSL), Young Communist League (YCL) and the Proletarian Schools Movement (PSM)[1] will focus on two related areas. The first is the extent to which such organizations were perceived by their adult sponsors to be in opposition to state elementary education. The second focus will be the nature of the cultural function of these organizations. They did not exist simply as an alternative to the elementary schools nor as a training ground for young socialists. They performed an additional important role in the building of a socialist *cultural* alternative to the dominant ideology. The children of socialists, often portrayed as the future hope of socialism, were gradually introduced to the values and ethos of socialism in a broader context than that offered by the family.

The State's Attitude and Actions towards Socialist Children's and Youth Groups

Irrespective of the actual positions taken by these youth organizations, all were the victims in some form or another of state repressive strategies. These strategies focused on the explicit — or implicit — views of socialists that children were political. However, the extent to which the SSS or the other, more militant, groups can be called oppositional owes more to the interpretation of Parliament, the Home Office and Special Branch and local

Figure 3.1   The Relationship between Adult Socialist Organizations and Youth Organizations Discussed in Chapter 3

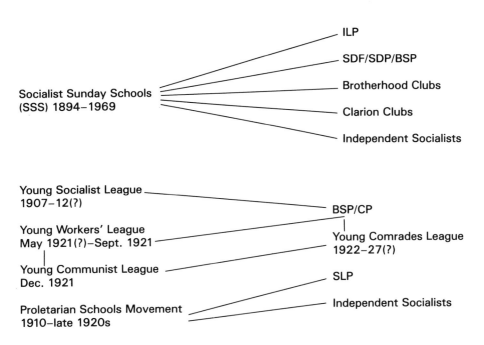

education authorities that it does to the actual activities of such organizations. Although all the groups under discussion did, in various ways, define themselves as socialists, there were absences which existed in respect of their orientation towards state elementary education.

In 1897, according to the ILP paper, *Labour Leader*,[2] there were only fifteen SSS in the whole of England and Scotland. At the height of the organization's peak in 1923 the SSS's own publication gave a national (weekly) attendance figure of 5,268 children.[3] Yet despite the very small size of the SSS movement — the first socialist organization for children in this period, organized in a non-sectarian way[4] — it faced staunch opposition from right wing forces and state apparatuses.

As will be expanded later, the movement defined itself in opposition primarily to the work of the religious Sunday Schools and the militarist scout movement rather than to the work of the elementary schools.[5]. Yet some of the earliest attacks on the movement came from the local state. In the early years of the century several London SSS met in premises of the London County Council (LCC). Against a background of well publicized criticism of the SSS movement as indoctrinators of children, the LCC decided to ban schools from meeting in its premises.[6] In response there were demonstrations in which children participated fully, waving small red flags to indicate their opposition.[7]

The exclusion of the SSS from the premises of local authorities seems to have done little to restrict its growth. Perhaps it is a measure of the success of the socialist movement that a children's Non-Socialist League was set up in specific opposition to the SSS, and to socialism and agnosticism in general.[8] Such hostile activities focused on the political and 'religious' nature of the SSS rather than any orientation the SSS may have had towards state education itself. That *children* were participating in explicitly political activity was cause enough for opposition.[9]

A different form of opposition faced the youth organizations in the post-war period. Like their adult counterparts, the SSS and Proletarian Schools Movement (PSM) were subjected to surveillance and their activities were commented upon in the weekly Cabinet reports on subversive activities.[10] This repressive stance was increased during the 1920s, accompanied by attempts to ban such schools for the teaching of 'sedition'. The Cabinet and Home Office papers reveal a similar response to that found in the coverage of Communist Party activities. A Private Members' Bill was introduced by Sir John Butcher in 1922, with the backing of the British Empire Union and the support of the Home Office.[11] Ostensibly the legislation was designed to protect children from seditious teaching. In reality it became part of the wider campaign to discredit even mildly progressive organizations with the taint of Communism. As discussed in Chapter 1, this was part of the strategy of sections of the ruling class to ensure that the Labour Party never became a party of government.[12] Thus the work of the SSS, which by the 1920s were increasingly dominated by the politics of the ILP and Labour Party, was caricatured as inextricably linked with that of the PSM, which owed its origins to the Socialist Labour Party (SLP), and of the Communist children's groups, linked to the Communist Party.[13]

The introduction of the Seditious Teaching Bill encouraged increased surveillance of youth groups and the seizing of their publications.[14] The first attempts to introduce such legislation were thwarted and the second attempt failed at the Lords' stage on the dissolution of Parliament in 1923.[15] No such legislation ever reached the statute books. However, these attempts had fulfilled an important function in creating a wider concern about the activities of socialist youth organizations. The Cabinet discussion on this legislation, which was subsequently reintroduced on several occasions, led to consideration of similar restraints on adult communist organizations, but this was rejected in this form.[16]

Although it was made clear to some over-enthusiastic MPs that the SSS and PSM were entirely unrelated to the schools under the remit of the Board of Education[17], nevertheless some of them availed themselves of the opportunity subsequently to launch attacks on the Teachers' Labour League attempting to make (unfounded[18]) direct links between communist teachers, state schools, and the 'subversive' activities of socialist youth organizations. It was not until 1927 that Joyson-Hicks, then Home Secretary, intervened to differentiate between the communist and socialist youth organizations.[19] This attempt to isolate communist organizations from the socialist and labour movement in general complemented the positions of the TUC and Labour Party. By 1927 both conferences had disassociated themselves from the Communist Party, proscribed the organization and estranged its members from the ranks of the trade union movement.[20]

Subsequently, the work of the CP youth organizations, alongside their adult counterparts, although *not* the SSS, continued to receive the attention of the state authorities. On one occasion, a march by the Young Pioneers in Greenock was banned;[21] on another, publications coming into the YCL offices from abroad were confiscated by Customs and the GPO,[22] as an alternative to prosecuting the YCL for publication of seditious material. Similarly, no legal action was taken against the bulletin of the Communist Children's Groups, described as a 'melancholy periodical', on the grounds that this would lead to questions in Parliament and additional publicity.[23] Because of its data on communist organizations, adult and youth alike, the Home Office knew how small such organizations were. It tended to adopt a more sober assessment of their strength and influence than those Conservative MPs and Special Branch officers whose hysterical urgings were still being heard at the end of the 1920s.[24]

The Response of Socialist Youth and Children's Organizations

The way in which the socialist youth movements resisted these post-war attacks helps reveal the differences in their general outlook. The SSS, not unnaturally, felt aggrieved that the proposed legislation against seditious teaching was being directed against them rather than the communist groups, whose own propaganda was being cited as the rationale for legislation. An editorial of the *Young Socialist* maintained that far from being seditious, the SSS movement was religious: '. . . in spirit and idealism it is "religious" in the best sense of the meaning of that word. It confines itself to the broad essentials of the socialist humanitarian faith, its main purpose being to extend the sympathy and understanding of the young with regard to the society in which they live.'[25]

All SSS were asked to organize demonstrations and send letters to the Leader of the Opposition.[26] Subsequently successful libel action was brought by adult teachers in the Hammersmith SSS against local Conservatives who had accused them of instructing children in blasphemous and seditious teaching.[27]

The Communist Party adopted a different line. Dave Springhall, the YCL leader,[28] argued that the legislation was an attack on the work of the

YCL and not upon a 'school'. In an exchange of views between himself and Alfred Russell, of the Glasgow SSS, in *Workers' Life*, Springhall maintained that 'the Tories have no objection whatsoever to the present abstract teaching of "love and justice" of the SSS' because such schools ignored the existence of the class struggle.[29] He also rejected the concept of teaching socialism 'by blackboard lectures given by greybeards . . . '[30] He went on to explain that the YCL school groups were the only sound bodies for socialist youth because they 'understand that the schools are part and parcel of the capitalist state machine'.[31]

The Position of Socialist Youth and Children's Organizations on State Education

As has been seen, the state chose to adopt a repressive stance towards these youth organizations because of their political involvement with children and young people, rather than because of any activities directed towards the state educational apparatus. Yet, to varying degrees, the socialist groups did direct their attention to state education.

On first appearance it would seem that the SSS modelled its practice upon activities for children conducted outside the state school by the churches in religious Sunday Schools. One of the early accounts of a typical SSS session describes physical drill for boys and scarf and flower drill for girls. Hymns from the Labour Church Hymn Book were sung, an address was given and there was a recitation or a solo.[32] Such a programme bears a stronger resemblance to the church Sunday Schools or Boys' Brigade than to those of the elementary schools.

However, a closer study of some of the later debates inside the SSS movement reveals different aspects of the movement' work. In an article in the *Young Socialist* in 1911,[33] Fred Coates, the national secretary, set out the argument for teaching socialism to children. He realized that some parents objected to this on the grounds that children should be unbiased and decide their views later for themselves, but refuted this on the grounds that children were receptive to ideas from many quarters including those from their parents and friends. He also argued in favour of teaching socialism to counter the religious lessons given in the state elementary schools. These lessons were opposed to socialism; the history given in schools was also distorted: 'In the whole school curriculum there is a bias — intentionally or unintentionally — in favour of existing institutions.'[34]

Here then one is presented with the beginnings of a critique of state education; it is also indicated that the SSS had a role to play in providing an alternative to state education. It is important to note that Coates confined his remarks to the work of the SSS in their *own* schools: there is no suggestion that these ideas should be taken up by local education authorities or individual state schools. His sentiments are echoed in contributions in a contemporary debate in the *Clarion*.[35] While the bulk of the contributions focused on the desirability, or not, of teaching socialism to children, the relationship between the SSS and state schools was also covered. The secretary of the Ilford SSS, for example,[36] believed that children did not hear much good about socialism at elementary school and therefore 'it is to protect children and parents against these insidious reactionary influences that the SSS is necessary.'[37] Other contributors believed that teaching children in a 'scientific manner'[38] or placing 'the facts of life before children in true perspective'[39] would ensure that children would become socialists in the long term. However, there is no suggestion that the teaching of 'true facts' ought to be carried out in elementary schools as well. An example of the different emphasis given by the SSS to the subject matter of the elementary schools is the following: 'In the story of Columbus our day schools tell of the gold he discovered, whilst we show how, by his discovery of America, he helped to find a new home for a number of his and other country men.'[40] This example is also revealing for what the SSS did *not* say about the colonizing role of Columbus!

The articles I have referred to here were not written by Marxists or by socialists seeking to challenge the state educational system. Indeed many of the contributors stress the reasonableness of their approaches: 'I have never heard of a SSS where children were taught politics . . . the whole thing [the socialist ten commandments] might be a blend of Thomas à Kempis and the Moral Instruction League,'[41] or 'We merely want to give children an education which will be helpful to them in after life.'[42] Nevertheless there is no suggestion that the SSS should — or could — become the good practice of the state elementary schools. In some ways, then, the activities of the SSS — at least in the pre-war period — *were interpreted* by such socialists as oppositional to the state's activities, although the type of oppositional stance put forward was rather different to that of the PSM or YCL.

A different attitude towards state education was found in the YCL and Young Comrades' League. They held the view that state education needed to be given a Marxist analysis and that activities needed to be organized against the type of educational provision and curriculum content offered by state schools. This position was taken from the line of the Young Communist International: 'The object of the children's sections is to enlist the children of the proleteriat in the class struggle and to give them a communist outlook so that they may become active fighters in the communist movement.'[43] They were counterposed to the SSS: 'In contradistinction to the state school and the SSS the communist sections are based upon "education by doing".'[44]

Schools were seen as fulfilling economic and ideological roles under capitalism which would be challenged by children and young people attending them: 'Today, more than ever before does the ruling class endeavour to estrange the proletarian children from the proletarian class; to teach them to oppose their own struggling parents, their brothers and sisters . . . [the school is] an institution for the training of servile and submissive wages slaves, a nursery for the future scabs and white guards.'[45] Children were to organize themselves. They were encouraged to apply the schooling they received in reading, writing and arithmetic to working-class ends, and to give alternative interpretations to the history and civics taught in state schools.[46] This position of the Young Communist International was echoed in the policy for education adopted by the Communist Party in 1923.[47] It called for the removal of teaching in favour of capitalism and the substitution of 'scientific teaching from a working-class point of view'.[48]

During the *early* twenties the communist youth organizations were not simply making demands upon a hostile state but campaigning inside state institutions. The emphasis was not on changing the structure of the schools but upon the possibilities for change opened up *inside* institutions through children's own organized activity.[49] The function of the education offered to children and young people in the YCL and Young Comrades' League was to assist their political intervention in the state schools. The education was not seen as an end in itself or as a means to an abstract socialist awareness, but as a mechanism by which political change could be effected against the capitalist state. In this period the YCL advocated the supervision of the curriculum by representatives of workers' organizations and pupil councils.[50] The interest in the state curriculum was also seen in the tableaux presented by the Young Comrades' League during May Day celebrations. One of the tableaux was of a class at work supervised by a teacher holding a cane and accompanied by the slogan: 'Down with Capitalist Teaching in Schools' and 'We want Workers' History'.[51]

The position which advocated direct activity in favour of alternatives to state education was altered by the late 1920s. The emphasis was no longer on possible change inside state institutions. The education of the state was counterposed to the class struggle outside the schools. Thus the YCL opposed the raising of the school leaving age to sixteen on the grounds that workers were withdrawn from industry, would not receive wages and thus lower standards of living would arise.[52] Vocational education — outside the school — was needed so that young people 'will become trained, capable and self reliant workers, playing their part in the class struggle today and building socialism in soviet Britain in the future'.[53]

The previous view that children should combat the teaching they were offered in schools changed into one which advocated that they left schools as soon as possible: the sole object of capitalist education was to convince people that capitalism was good. The solution was to build an alternative education machine, through struggle.[54] In a similar vein the Labour Party proposals for the extension of secondary education were opposed on the grounds that 'secondary education is entirely divorced from production and productive labour and therefore manifestly incapable of training the working youth for its ultimate destination — the industries'.[55] The solution offered was 'a full blown socialist factory-school system'.[56]

By the mid 1920s an analysis of capitalist education was being developed which reasserted the ideological and economic function of state education while denying the possibility of change within those institutions. The focus for propaganda on the curriculum, Empire Day, became an attempt to 'expose' capitalist education. Leaflets on one day of the year substituted for ongoing activity.[57]

In effect the youth organizations of the CP, despite their protestations to the contrary, had developed their political *analysis* of the state school at the expense of *campaigning* for changes in that education. In this respect their *de facto* position had become similar to that of the PSM, the youth group organized by the SLP. In these schools the children were taught that they had 'a mission to perform, that mission is the abolition of wage slavery'.[58] Given the expected imminence of a socialist revolution heralding an industrial republic,[59] children were to be equipped to enter a communist state.

Although SLP members developed propaganda about the need for workers' control of the curriculum there is no indication that children were to play any part in the process. The weekly activities of the Proletarian Schools went on alongside that of the state schools rather than as a preparation for intervention in them. It is ironic that, in some respects, the militant Marxist analysis of the SLP on state education[60] had something in common with the general position of the SSS: both existed alongside the state schools rather than as training grounds for intervention into the state's schools.

It was stated earlier that a central feature of the state's opposition to socialist youth movements was the opposition to young people and children being treated as political beings. Children were viewed in various ways by socialist groups including as recipients, because of their age, of one form or another of 'education'. Whether or not this education had an orientation towards the state's schools it was clearly seen, like children themselves, as being part of the socialist movement. Children were seen as being a visible part of the socialist movement's practice and culture, and specific attention was directed by all socialist groups to the nature and special problems of children.

Concepts of Childhood in Socialist Youth and Children's Organizations

The attitude of the SSS towards the children who attended its schools was broadly of two kinds. On the one hand they were regarded as individual children who would be exposed to an atmosphere of 'love and justice',[61] which would have a beneficial effect on their own growth: 'To build up the city of love in our own hearts, and so bye and bye help to build it up in the world.'[62] On the other hand, they were regarded as a definite and specific part of the general socialist movement. Their involvement in the socialist movement would both enhance their own development and, more significantly, influence for the better the type of movement the adult socialists were building: 'Children have hitherto little attention paid to them, they have been made little of . . . They now ask to be regarded as a definite part of the movement and to receive a definite standing in it . . . [the socialist movement will represent] a manifestation of the new socialism [which] . . . will be one with all that is noblest and fairest in human life . . . '.[63] Children were seen, particularly by adults who aligned themselves with the ILP,[64] as the very future of the movement: 'The children's education matters far more than the conversion of a whole packed meeting of middle aged persons.'[65]

The fact that, at least in the early years of the SSS, adult members of the SDF, the ILP, and, in Scotland, the SLP, who often entered in bitter disputes with each other, could form a working relationship within the SSS movement was attributed to the positive role played by the children. One reads, for example, that Archie McManus, the editor of the *Young Socialist*, and ILP member, had been invited to take up a seat on the Young Socialist Industrial Exhibition Committee being organized by the SDF. To this offer he responded with enthusiasm: 'Surely the day cometh quickly when love shall reign and the earth be glad!'[66]

In addition to being educated in socialist 'cultural' activities, children were also initiated in other socialist practices. They regularly participated in May Day rallies, having their own brakes and platforms,[67] and engaged in philanthropic activities.[68] It was also thought suitable that they should be involved in campaigns against vivisection.[69]

However, as discussed earlier, even these types of political activity caused concern among some adult members of the SSS. There was a view that the SSS should have a role preparing children for future engagement with political ideas while protecting them from the excesses of existing capitalist ideology.

This protective view was rejected by the Marxist youth organizations, although the communist groups were at pains to stress the recognition of the special needs of childhood. They insisted that children had a present role in the class struggle. Children's groups were to be built up with the full individual activity of children 'according to the special features of childhood'.[70] These special features included campaigns of particular *immediate* relevance to children: provision of free meals, nature of the curriculum and discipline of elementary schools.[71]

The social needs of children were also catered for by the YCL. A children's march in support of the miners ended with oranges, sweets and organized games.[72] There was a special Young Comrades Badge of a hammer and sickle set against a camp fire on a red flag and a uniform of red and grey.[73] The adoption of a political position which advocated children's political activity was counterposed to that of the SSS which sought to maintain a paternalistic attitude. This position inside the CP was not, apparently, accepted without dissent. According to the recollections of David Ainley, district secretary of Manchester YCL in 1923 at the age of 16, there was 'bitter opposition'.[74] The CP disassociated itself from its previous stance applicable when it had participated in the SSS: 'We wanted to do away with the paternalistic attitudes towards children and draw them into the revolutionary movement.'[75]

This position gave rise to various political problems: the support and consent of parents was required if children were to be politically militant; yet, children were not to be treated paternalistically. Children were encouraged to take political initiatives; yet, the Young Comrades' League and YCL were inextricably linked with the CP which formed overall policy for the British Communist Party's groups.

The Young Comrades' League existed in areas where the CP had a significant industrial base, such as South Wales, or parts of Scotland. In such areas parents' groups were encouraged to campaign alongside children.[76] While children in the SSS were denied autonomy from adults in that political self-organization and activity were not encouraged, children and young people in the YCL and Young Comrades' League faced a different sort of lack of autonomy. Although it is true that the YCL was answerable to the district committees of the CP and not to local organizations, nevertheless it did not have political autonomy from the CP.[77] The YCL became the frequent recipient of criticism from the CP and the Young Comintern,[78] often for having simply carried out the line agreed by the CP itself. Thus in a 1923 issue of the *Workers' Weekly* we read an article praising the social aspect of the YCL activities: 'The Marxian theory of surplus value will not appeal to a young boy as much as the opportunity for a football match, a Sunday ramble, an evening cycle run or a swimming competition.'[79] Two years later the same publication is criticizing the YCL for being a 'glorified social club', rather than a recruiting ground for party members.[80]

Further, despite the enthusiasm expressed towards socialist children in the publications of various youth organizations, all of the organizations faced the problem of lack of adult support. Successive conferences of the SDF and ILP alike passed motions calling upon their members to take more active interest in the work of the SSS.[81] Even youth organizations such as the Young Socialist League, and the Young Communist League, set up by the BSP and CP respectively and having strong organizational links with adult bodies, had similar problems.[82]

The Role of Socialist Youth Organizations in Providing Alternative Cultural Activities

Children's and young people's socialist organizations were regarded by socialists and the state alike as part of the culture of the socialist movement.[83] This is true irrespective of whether they existed to counter elementary education, to educate children for a future socialism or to assist in campaigns for improvements in state schools. These organizations also fulfilled the (unstated) function of providing socialist education for socialists' *own* children. Adult socialists might not be in the position, because of the general political climate, to offer working-class children in general the kind of education they believed in. Nevertheless, they were able to exert direct influence over the alternative educational and social activities in which their own children participated. Annie Davison[84] interpreted her father's enthusiasm for her participation in the SSS in two ways: 'He was very keen on his children learning as much as possible, even though he hadn't the money really to educate them very well.' And: 'They [her parents] wanted their children to learn that socialism was a good way of life.'[85] Such an approach, which might be called by subsequent generations 'lifestyle politics', is reflected both in accounts of socialists' memories and of their involvement in the SSS and in the way in which they explained their allegiance in contemporary accounts.[86] Socialists have brought with them fond memories of times spent many years previously in the children's groups.[87]

The SSS movement was seen by contemporary socialists, in many cases, to be an epitome of the socialist movement in general and a body to which people 'converted'. This attitude is particularly prevalent in the portrait gallery series in the early editions of the *Young Socialist*. Here socialists, usually adults, active in the SSS, would give an account of their political involvement and activities. Although it is true that the SSS did attract a range of socialists, including those in the ILP and Labour Church, who maintained their religious beliefs, the language of 'conversion' to a *new* faith is frequently seen in these portrait gallery contributions. Involvement in the SSS was discussed alongside socialists' general lifestyles. Frequent references were made, by members themselves, to their vegetarianism or abstention from alcohol, and of their conversion from non-conformist religions to socialism — as an alternative religion.[88] This was in addition to their party political and trade union allegiances.

It was not, then, that children were simply *taught* about socialism in lessons at the SSS, although this did happen, but that it was hoped that they would be imbued with the socialist lifestyle, which covered many aspects: 'Socialist children are expected to be an example in cleanliness and tidiness at all times — just as they are also expected to be very exemplary in fair conduct and good manners... To be dainty and clean in person, dress and habits, is not only, I might say, the first mark of good manners, but it is a safety, as we all know, to health... but it is also a virtue.'[89] Children were to act as 'examples', to be 'missionaries'[90] for socialism by their very conduct and morals. Through their own behaviour the socialism discussed by adults was to be exemplified.

Lessons were given in the SSS on morality: how children could learn from the habits of social animals; how a child's life was like a garden in which weeds like deceit and carelessness and disobedience spread up; how brotherliness was to be acquired as a daily habit.[91] The lessons of the Moral Instruction League were used.[92] The 'brotherliness' mentioned above was encouraged in specific practical ways. For example, children were asked to send money in support of the miners locked out in Yorkshire.[93] Other currents inside the SSS, more concerned with socialist aspects of education, drew up socialist catechisms, songs and questions and answers on socialism and specific lessons on socialism.[94] A socialist ten commandments was put into verse by Thomas Campbell of Govan:

> All good things gathered from the earth,
> By toil of hand and brain,
> Instead of going to the few,
> The workers should retain.[95]

The SSS provided an opportunity for working-class socialist adults to engage in a direct way with different educational pedagogic theories. The current tending to favour an ethical moralistic approach also was inclined to endorse similar educational views to those of the progressives. There are frequent references in discussions on pedagogy to the 'drawing out' of children's capacities.[96] Those socialists who favoured an explicitly socialist content were more concerned with the content of lessons than with any educational pedagogy.[97]

Not unnaturally, the socialists who believed that the 'teaching in the SSS is an attempt, however imperfect, to unite ethics and religion'[98] were opposed to the didactic teaching of socialism and made this opposition clear: 'It is not the object of our school to turn out previously class conscious individuals who have lost much of the joy of childhood in an attempt to grapple with Marxian economics.'[99] The main target for such a view was the Proletarian Schools Movement, in which Tom Anderson was the leading light.[100] In these schools, children were taught definitions of socialism, the ten proletarian commandments, based on dialectical materialism, and various parables. The story of Humpty Dumpty was used as an analogy for the fall of the capitalist class in Russia.[101] Other parables were new: 'Once upon a time there lived in a city, called Capital, a lady and gentleman who had so much money they did not know what to do with it; there was Lord and Lady Ne'er work . . . It was the first of May and a very strange thing happened, for that very morning Mr. and Mrs. Labour had a baby'.[102] There was a special socialist alphabet for children[103] and socialist songs, which were printed in *Revolution*, the chorus of a typical one being:

> Class conscious we are singing,
> Class conscious all are we;
> For labour now is digging,
> The grave of the Boorzh-waw-ze.[104]

Irrespective of the particular content offered in the different socialist and communist youth groups, an opportunity was also afforded to working-class socialists to assist directly in the education of their own children. Socialists active in the youth movements would have been prevented from teaching children in the state schools because of their lack of formal qualifications. In the SSS and other groups workers from all walks of life, particularly manual workers, were active in teaching the young people of the socialist movement. Indeed there are very few examples of elementary school teachers participating in this aspect of socialist life.[105]

Occupations of those active in the SSS movement (as described in *Young Socialist* portrait galleries) included: engineer,[106] mason,[107] stonemason,[108] blacksmith,[109] compositor,[110] textile worker,[111] and pattern maker.[112] Many of the socialists active in the SSS were active trades unionists. A prominent example was Alex Gossip, who played a full part in the Sunday Schools in Glasgow and Fulham while being general secretary of the Furniture Trades Union and being active in left-wing movements such as the Hands Off Russia campaign and the National Unemployed Workers Movement.[113]

Training sessions for SSS teachers were organized to raise pedagogical questions and to give advice on approaches to lessons.[114] That trade union and socialist activists were involved in the SSS indicates, as we have said, that the movement was seen as an integral part of the culture of the socialist movement.

Interpretation of Practice

In consideration of the extent to which these socialist organizations were oppositional in the sense of being anti-statist, a distinction has been made between the actual practice of such youth groups and the adult perceptions of that practice. It is clear that the actions of the PSM and groups of the Communist Party were intended to prepare, in different ways, children for their part in the broader class struggle, rather than necessarily focusing on the educational state apparatus as such. The perspectives of the SSS were not directed to challenging the state in any fundamental way. Nevertheless, the types of activities offered to children were unlikely at that period to have been available in elementary schools.

Writing of the differences between the content of his SSS lessons and those he gave in elementary school, Walter Scott mused: 'I wonder how the boys and girls in our Sunday School would like to have lessons in their day schools like those they get on Sundays. I have learned in Canning Town [SSS] that these are the very lessons that should be taught'.[115] Clearly Walter Scott regarded himself as offering a different perspective to that presented in the state schools. That the SSS provided a different perspective is not in doubt. Whether that perspective is anti-statist is much more doubtful. The adult organizers of the SSS, like their counterparts in the state schools, were unwilling to adopt anti-statist strategies.

In the next chapter consideration will be given to the nature of teachers as state employees in this period and the extent to which discussion of their radicalization can take place without reference to their ideological commitment to the state.

Notes and References

1 I do not intend to deal with the Young Socialist League or Young Workers' League, which were shortlived. I also will not focus on the work of the Young Socialist Citizen Crusaders on the grounds that it was set up with a particular anti-militarist, pro-peace position, rather than as a socialist organization *per se*. See Kean, *State Education 1988, op. cit.*, p. 127. For further details of activities of socialist groups opposed to the war see Sylvia Pankhurst, *op. cit.*; Sheila Rowbotham, *Friends of Alice Wheeldon*, Pluto, London, 1986; Ken Weller, *'Don't be a Soldier! The Radical Anti-War Movement in North London 1914–1918*, London, Journeyman, 1985.

2 *Labour Leader*, 20 November 1897 (articles on the founding of Canning Town SSS). There were London branches in Walthamstow, Dalston, Battersea, Bermondsey, Fulham and Tottenham and eight others in the rest of England and Scotland.

3 Regular membership figures were not issued by the SSS nor, when they did appear, were they in a consistent form. The early figures simply recorded children and adult attenders. The later ones also include adolescents as a separate category. It is also unclear whether all the attenders were members. However, the following figures do at least give some indication of the size of the organization. The dates refer to the month the figures appear in the *Young Socialist*:

National Attendance

	Children	*Adults*	*Total*
Jan. 1905	1,643	582	2,225
Mar. 1911	4,558	1,266	5,854
May 1923	5,268	1,313	7,401*
May 1926	1,097	226	1,503*

* including adolescents.

Some indication of SSS strength is also given by their own figures of the print run or number of copies sold of *Young Socialist*. The print order for March 1911 was 3,000. *Young Socialist* (January 1914) reported 6,000 copies sold of one issue. The average monthly sale as given in May 1920 was 5,043. These were small attendance figures compared to those of the religious Sunday Schools. For example in *Young Socialist* (February 1905) an attendance for Shoreditch SSS is given of eighty children and three adults. In the adjacent area of Old Street, the Leysian Mission, a Methodist mission, had huge attendances at its groups. In 1902 there were nearly seven hundred children on its Sunday School books, with an average attendance of four hundred and eighty (E. Margaret Pook, *The Leysian Mission 1886-1986, A Century of Caring*, Epworth Press, 1978, p.11). Lantern services were so popular that children queued to get in (p. 18). The bank holiday outing was attended by 1,600 children and adults in 1905 and three trains were booked for them (p.21) From the late 1890s the following clubs were run: Girls' Parlour, Boys' Club, Cricket Club, Gym, Women's Total Abstinence Group, Coal Club, Boot Club, and Sports Club. In addition there was a relief committee and a doctor in attendance to offer milk and nourishment. It was not that the SSS were offering a cultural and recreational facility where none existed but were setting up their groups in competition with religious organizations.

4 Although different groups tended to dominate different SSS according to the groups' strength in the locality, nevertheless nationally the SSS contained various socialist groups' members. *Young Socialist* (May 1902) reports both the SDF and ILP conferences welcoming the work of the SSS.

5 *Young Socialist*, March 1901 and April 1902. See brief typewritten history of the SSS by Jean Simmons in the Marx Memorial Library.

6 Reports of LCC in *The Times*, 10 June 1907, and 12 June 1907. A motion was carried by sixty-six votes to forty preventing the council schools being used by the SSS and terminating the tenancies of the SSS in Fulham, Hammersmith, and North and South Islington.

7 The SSS organized support from the LRC, ILP, SDF, and Trades Councils (*Young Socialist*, June 1907). Demonstrations took place in Victoria Park and Trafalgar Square (*Young Socialist*, July 1907; *The Times*, 29 July 1907). Support was received from Will Crooks MP and from Councillor Sanders (*Young Socialist*, March 1907). At the Trafalgar Square demonstrations letters were read from sympathetic MPs. Speaking against the eviction by the LCC and Willesden Council, Mrs Bridges Adams argued that schools should belong to the people; councils knew that an education in theology was the best way of deadening the intellects of children. Alfred Pung Hazell, superintendant of North Islington SSS, and SDF member, believed that the *Red Catechism*, which he wrote, was used by the LCC as a reason for evicting the SSS (*Young Socialist*, March 1911.

8 *The Times*, 30 November 1911, reports a meeting of the Children's Non-Socialist League under the presidency of Lord Ancaster set up to campaign in every area where the SSS existed. In the same year the Anti-Socialist League organized a meeting at NUT conference chaired by Mr Reg Wilson of Upper Hornsey Road school (*The London Teacher*, 1 May 1911, p.191).

9 .There was even controversy amongst socialists on the question (see nn. 33-42).

10 For example PRO: CAB 24/96 CP 491: 'The SSS are doing much harm...At Aberdare a Proletarian School has been opened by Tom Anderson.' James Stewart, an SLP member from Wallsend, was imprisoned under the DORA for one month for publishing an article likely to cause disaffection in *Young Rebel*, a duplicated paper aimed at children and young people. Mrs Julia Kavlovsky of Newcastle SLP was imprisoned alongside him for distribution of the publication (*The Times*, 13 July 1918, p. 3; *Socialist*, August 1918). After the war James Stewart was also imprisoned for a speech he gave to unemployed workers in Wolverhampton (*Workers' Dreadnought*, 21 July 1921).

11 The Bill was introduced on 10 February 1922 by Sir John Butcher, Conservative MP for York 1910-23, but fell in May 1922 crowded out by the Labour Party Right to Work Bill. It was reintroduced by Butcher in March 1923 when it received a second reading (102 votes to 20) and was in the House of Lords when Parliament disbanded on the calling of a general election. On reaching the Commons on 27 March 1923 (*Hansard*, Fifth series, vol.162, cols. 273-74, 1924) Butcher described it as 'a bill to prevent teaching of seditious doctrines or methods to the young'. He referred to the work of the YCL whom he accused of establishing schools. He developed his argument by implying that the SSS and Communist Sunday Schools (presumably the PSM or Communist children's groups) were the same thing: 'The object of the Bill is the protection of children... Can it be maintained that the state which has

recognized its obligations to protect the bodies of children is not bound to protect their souls and their minds from contamination in their early and impressionable years?' The British Empire Union's backing is mentioned in *The Times*, 22 April 1922 and 9 February 1922. The British Empire Union issued a pamphlet 'Danger Ahead' on the socialist and proletarian Sunday Schools, naming teachers and castigating the National Labour Colleges reading list: 'Not one book recommended is by an English writer' (copy in PRO:HO 45/1189/3 no. 323141). See Beatrix Campbell, *The Iron Ladies*, London, Virago, 1987, p. 57, for the support the Bill attracted from Conservative women.PRO: HO 45/11895 includes a note 323141/18 dated 10 February 1922: 'The object of this bill is admirable and it seems to me well drafted for effecting its purpose. Prosecutions under it would be few in number and might sometimes fail, but it will certainly be of some use in protecting children from the poisonous effusions of international communists. The true communist having no belief in parental rights would take more delight in corrupting other people's children than his own . . . It might of course be argued that a good deal of history taught in schools tends to bring the King and constitution into contempt and even promote dissatisfaction with the administration of justice, but such an argument would be too disingenuous to convince any sane person . . .'

12 A Conservative election leaflet warned against the SSS, saying: 'Children are being baptised into the Communistic faith . . . the elder children are even taught the principles of street fighting and how to blow up bridges, render roads useless, and a dozen other useful forms of warfare' (quoted in Richard Lyman, *The First Labour Government*, Chapman, 1957, p. 256). The Conservatives deliberately created red scares. The monthly 'Gleanings and Memoranda' linked the Labour Party to Communism. A popular party poster read: 'MacDonald for Moscow; Lloyd George for Limehouse; Baldwin for Britain. Keep the Home Fires Burning' (as quoted in Lyman, *ibid.*, p. 38). See also Robert Rhodes James *Memoirs of a Conservative*: *J.C.C. Davidson's Memoirs and Papers 1910-1937*, London, Weidenfeld and Nicolson, 1969, for the fears of revolutionary activists, although small in number, obtaining influence in the trade union movement (p. 227). See H.A. Taylor, *Jix*: *Viscount Brentford*, Stanley, Paul & Co., 1933 on the creation of 'red scares' and 'Bolshevist spies' in this period (pp. 181, 195 and 236-8). The surveillance reports of this period frequently refer to the communist 'threat', for example, PRO: CAB 24/96 CP 500, Industrial Disturbances. Memorandum by the Minister of Agriculture and Fisheries 26 January 1920: ' . . . we appear to be drifting with our eyes open into a possible disaster, in a few weeks' time, without making any serious effort to organise against it . . . the vital importance and urgency of counter revolutionary propaganda on the largest and most vigorous scale that can be organised by the government. So far we appear to be ignoring the poison which is being distilled in our midst and leaving the masses at its mercy without providing any antidote.' See also PRO: CAB 24/97 CP 544, 'Revolutionaries and the Need for Legislation' circulated by the Home Secretary 2 February 20; PRO CAB 24/180 CP 236, memo by the Home Secretary 11 June 1926 on Russian 'gold' and CAB 24/180 CP 244; CAB 24/80 CP 237, Legislation Committee report recommending statutory secret strike ballots; CAB 24/179 CP 136, 25 March 1926, Report of the Public Order Committee on the need to strengthen the law on sedition (rejected in the short term); CAB 24/175 CP 420, 9 October 1925, Report by Attorney General on the desire for making strikes against the state illegal, although recognizing the inability to frame satisfactory words.

13 This line was promoted by Conservative MPs. At a meeting held to discuss the Seditious Teaching Bill (*The Times*, 27 February 1923) it was stated that three types of schools existed: socialist, proletarian and communist which were similar to each other. It was said that the SSS was increasing its numbers all over London. According to the speakers at the meeting the SSS had a doctrine of overthrowing the

social system and replacing it with a workers' republic. For its part the SSS strongly disassociated itself from the PSM and communist groups. Writing in *The Times* of 8 February 1923 Stanley Mayne, then secretary of the National Council of the British SSS, said: 'We do not teach or encourage blasphemy. Our attitude in the matter of deity is clearly stated in our constitution, namely, 'the teaching to be non-theological in character, paying exclusive attention to the present life and its duties'. It was 'ethical in outlook and religious in spirit and idealism [covering] the broad essentials of the socialist humanitarian faith'. An editorial of *Young Socialist* (May 1922) conveys a similar line. Nevertheless hostility against the SSS continued. Replying to his letter in *The Times*, Lady Asquith (6 February 1923) continued to make links between SSS and communism and made specific accusations against Mayne as a state employee (he worked for the Ministry of Health). See a reply by Mayne in *The Times*, 27 February 1923. For its part Tom Anderson, of the PSM, responded in cavalier fashion: 'We are not concerned with the state, we know what it is. We teach science first, foremost and at all times. We tell the children of the working class why they are poor . . . we tell them that the next stage of development is a spurious state socialism after the pattern of the ILP sprinkled with a spurious Christianity . . .' (Tom Anderson, *A Few Pearls*, July 1923).

14 Winston Churchill, incensed by copies of the *Young Communist* sent to him by Sir John Butcher, wrote to the Home Secretary (HO 45/11895 no. 323141/31, 16 May 1922): 'Have we to accept the position that 10,000 copies of this seditious publication are being circulated every month among the children attending the SSS, or is any action contemplated to protect children against this poisonous propaganda? (In response the Home Secretary informed him that the YCL had a small membership and that the circulation of *Young Communist* was small. The membership of the YCL was estimated at 700, that of the PSM considerably less.) Copies of the Bulletin of the Communist Children's Groups were sent by Lord Syndenham to the Home Office, together with copies of the *Young Communist*. The headline of the copy of *Young Communist* stating 'British Section of the YCL' was indicated by Sydenham: 'Degradation of Britain in this'. He called for raids on the Communist Party head-quarters (HO 45/11895 no. 323141/31, 15 May 1923). The police wanted to prosecute. However, rather than initiate legislation against the youth communist press directly Scotland Yard seized publications coming into the Communist Party headquarters from abroad. The Home Secretary's initial opinion was to 'prevent the post office from affording facilities for the distribution of any printed matter issued under their auspices . . .' (HO 45/11895, no. 323141/72, 31 August 1923), but this was subsequently reconsidered. During 1923 there were regular reports to the Cabinet (in the reports of revolutionary and subversive organizations) of the YCL's activities: CAB 24/160: CP 202, 19 April; CP 219, 26 April; CP 232, 3 May; CP 239, 10 May; CP 249, 17 May; CP 256, 31 May; CP 265, 7 June; CP 277, 14 June, etc.

15 The Bill received a second reading and in due course went to the Lords where it was carried by 102 votes to 20 in July 1924 (HO 45/11895: 32314/80) but fell due to the disbanding of Parliament. It received the support of British fascists (pamphlet on Communist Sunday Schools in HO 45/11895: 32314/99). A similar bill was intro-duced by Sir Philip Richardson, 20 February 1925, which received a second reading, 24 April 1925. Subsequently a seditious and blasphemous teaching bill was intro-duced by Capt. Holt in February 1927. This time the bill was moved in terms of defending the future of the empire: 'The future of the empire depends entirely on whether our children grow up into useful and loyal citizens' (HO 45/13756: Capt. Holt on the second reading, 11 March 1927). It was passed in the Commons by 213 votes to 85, with the backing of Joyson-Hicks, Home Secretary, who sought to use it to concentrate on the role of the CL rather than on the dwindling activities of the Proletarian Schools Movement. Several problems appeared at the committee stage and it was not passed due to several wrecking amendments; it fell on 15 December

1927. It was reintroduced 4 May 1928 by Sir George Hume, Tory MP for Greenwich, but the House was 'counted out'. When a further bill was introduced on 1 November 1929 by Commander Southby it was agreed to oppose it as serving no useful purpose, and a similar stance was adopted in response to attempts by Wardlaw Milne on 31 October 1930 in respect of YCL literature.

16 On the reintroduction of a seditious and blasphemous teaching bill by Capt. Holt, 11 February 1927, (which received its second reading 11 March 1927 by 213 votes to 85) the Home Office note reads: 'I think this bill will get a second reading. It gives in regard to children what I really want in regard to adults' (HO45/13756 no. 481582, 26 February 1927).

17 In a letter to the Home Secretary on 23 March 1922 (HO 45/11895 no. 323141/27) Austin Chamberlain wrote that he had received lots of letters concerning the Proletarian Schools: 'Fisher tells me these proletarian and communist schools are not held in grant aided schools nor taught by grant aided teachers and that he therefore has no control over the matter.'

18 Moving the second reading (see footnote 15), Capt. Holt attempted to draw links between the Young Communists and the Teachers' Labour League. While obviously the TLL and the YCL were both — at that time — bodies containing Communist Party members and their supporters, there is no evidence that communist school teachers were involved in the running of the YCL or Young Comrades' League (YC des L). Indeed, it is also true that very few teachers were involved in the SSS.

19 He argued that the SSS were perfectly legal and that members should differentiate between those and the proletarian and communist schools. The Proletarian Schools had died down and now the threat lay with the YCL, with its 300 members. Alongside this is a typewritten note from HRS, 22 February 1927, stating that the SSS 'do not appear to be either seditious or blasphemous' (HO 45/13756 no. 481582, 11 March 1927).

20 *Annual Report*, TUC 1926; *Annual Report*, Labour Party 1926. Branson, *op. cit.*, pp. 1–15. See Ruth and Edmund Frow, *The Communist Party in Manchester 1920–26*, 1978, Appendix 2: in an interview David Ainley describes the moves locally to prevent the Communist Party using the Labour Hall for its youth communist group.

21 On one occasion a march by the Young Pioneers (a young Communist Party group) in Greenock was banned. (HO 45/11895 no. 88, 11 December 1924, and 102/3, 29 June 1925, includes notes from New Scotland Yard on the numbers of children in Greenock YCL and complaints about the way in which the march was dispersed.)

22 See n. 14.

23 PRO: HO 45/11895 no. 323141/73. Action was also demanded by the British Empire Union against *Proletcult*, issued by the PSM in Scotland. The Procurator Fiscal had declined to prosecute on the grounds that the issues contained 'merely the usual Young Communist (sic) stuff encouraging class hatred, scoffing at Christianity as a religion established for the benefit of the bourgeoisie, and preaching no war and marxian economics'. The Home Office had never heard of it (HO 45/11895/75 no. 323141/75, 17 September 1923).

24 The Cabinet took the decision to oppose the private member's bill introduced by Commander Southby, Conservative MP for Epsom, in November 1929 on the grounds that it 'serve[d] no useful practical purpose'. Similar legislation was again introduced by Sir John Wardlaw Milne, Conservative MP for Kidderminster, on 31 October 1930. This received a similar response: 'While the YCL is so misguided as to circulate rubbish of this kind, there is no need for Parliament to waste time on a measure to protect children against seditious and blasphemous teaching' (HO 45/13756 no. 481582). It should be noted that the work of the communist youth organizations is not being ignored but rather that the particular repressive measures suggested are rejected as bad tactics.

25 *Young Socialist*, May 1922.
26 *Young Socialist*, May 1923.
27 *Young Socialist*, January 1926.
28 He was a leader of the YCL and acting secretary of the Young Comrades' League. In 1926 he was arrested under the Emergency Powers Act and sent to Wormwood Scrubs for two months hard labour for sedition (*Young Comrade*, June 1926).
29 *Workers' Life*, (continuation of *Workers' Weekly*), 1 April 1927.
30 Probably a sideswipe at Tom Anderson and the PSM.
31 *Workers' Life*, 1 April 1927. Alfred Russell, writing in the *Workers' Life* issue of 25 March, had made the point that the seditious teaching legislation was 'a tribute to the wisdom of beginning with the young'. Russell also argued (*Workers' Life*, 15 April 1927) that individual SSS had control over their own affairs and therefore could be socialist, while he accepted that many did ignore the class struggle. Springhall, in the same issue, conceded that Russell was one of the few in the SSS movement with a working-class conception of what a children's movement might be.
32 In addition 'at homes' were held on Saturdays in Winter, when there were songs, games and dancing. In Summer months there were picnics and rambles (*Young Socialist*, 7 July 1901, and 8 August 1901).
33 *Young Socialist*, December 1911.
34 *Ibid.*
35 Edited by Robert Blatchford.
36 T. A. W. Connell, letter in *Clarion*, 30 June 1911.
37 *Ibid.*
38 Letter from SSS teacher of three years standing in *Clarion*, 7 July 1911.
39 Letter from E. H., Islington North, in *Clarion*, 7 July 1911.
40 John Hirst, secretary of Yorkshire SSS union, letter to *Clarion*, 11 August 1911.
41 For details of the lessons of the Moral Instruction League see n. 92; T. A. W. Connell, letter in *Clarion*, 30 June 1911.
42 Letter from teacher of three years' standing, *Clarion*, 7 July 1911.
43 *Bulletin for Leaders of Communist Children's Groups*, EC of YCI, English edn, 2, 1, 1924.
44 *Ibid.*
45 *The Child of the Worker*, EC of YCI, Berlin 1923, p. 12 and p. 16.
46 *Bulletin for Leaders of Communist Children's Groups, op. cit.*
47 *Communist Parliamentary Policy and Electoral Programme*, Communist Party, 1923, p. 14.
48 *Ibid.*
49 In due course the view which denied the possibility of change inside institutions became dominant (Branson, *op. cit.*, pp. 31–51).
50 Report on YCL, *Workers Weekly*, 23 June 1923. An example of joint children's/adult action is given in *Workers' Weekly*, 4 January 1924. Unemployed parents organized to keep their children at home from school in Port Glasgow until the council agreed to supply them with boots.
51 *Young Comrade*, June 1926.
52 William Rust, *The Case for the YCL*, YCL n. d. (1927?).
53 *Ibid.*
54 *Ibid.*
55 *Young Worker*, 10 July 1926. Kean (1981) *op. cit.*, pp. 56–7.
56 *Young Worker*, 10 July 1926.
57 The *Rhondda Fach Gazette*, 16 June 1928, reports protests of Liberal and Labour members of the Rhondda Education Committee against seditious leaflets distributed to children by the Communist Party on Empire Day. The leaflets included the

slogans: 'Join the Young Comrades League and vote for free meals in schools and free boots', 'No more caning in schools. No patriotic teaching in schools. Smaller classes and better schools', 'Refuse to sing patriotic songs. Refuse to salute the Union Jack. Don't stay away but protest in school.' Tom Thomas, Communist member for Ynyshir, retorted that politics were already in the schools.

58 Tom Anderson, 'How to open and conduct a school', *The Revolution*, official organ of the socialist school, Glasgow, April 1918.

59 J. R. Sullivan, 'The revolutionary nature of school studies', *Socialist*, 18 March 1920.

60 See Chapter 2, nn. 89–97.

61 The first editorial of *Young Socialist*, 1, 1, January 1901, reads: 'Love for your mother, your sister and your brother, for your schoolmates and your playmates, for the dog and cat, for the primrose sweet and the daisy with its peeping eye, for "everybody and everything" . . . *that*, love, is to be the spirit, the note of our magazine.'

62 Editorial, *Young Socialist*, 1, 3, January 1901.

63 Editorial, *Young Socialist*, 2, 4, April, 1902.

64 The ILP conference of 1904 (*Annual Report*, ILP, 1904) passed a motion recommending ILP members to withdraw their children from school until the time for religious education had passed every day. This didn't stop many of them adopting a religious stance *towards* their socialism. This view is well expressed by Lizzie Glasier: 'The teaching of the SSS is an attempt, however imperfect, to unite ethics and religion . . . it is the religion of love' (*Young Socialist*, August 1906). As I mentioned in Chapter 2, the ILP held the view that the spread of education — of any kind — would assist in the success of socialism: 'The socialist movement owes its position today to the spread of education more than any other factor' (H. C. Shears, *Socialist Policy: Reform or Revolution*, ILP, new series 17. 1919).

65 Isabella O. Ford addressing an anniversary meeting of the Huddersfield SSS (*Young Socialist*, July 1904). Isabella Ford had joined the ILP in 1893 and was one of its executive members. She was particularly active in the late 1880s with women textile workers, becoming president of the Tailoresses Union. Subsequently she became an active campaigner for womens' suffrage and a member of the executive of the NUWSS.

66 *Young Socialist*, November 1902.

67 There were twelve brakes for children and a special platform for the SSS at the 1905 May Day rally (*Young Socialist*, June 1905). At the 1912 demonstration in Hyde Park there were forty brakes and the following speakers: Alex Gossip, Margaret MacMillan, J. Hunter Watts, and Val McEntee. Singing was conducted by Miss Smart of Hackney (*Young Socialist*, June 1912).

68 For example, a concert was given to the local workhouse by the West Ham school, who sung the cantata 'Washing Day' (*Young Socialist*, July 1901); entertainment was provided by the Glasgow school for the local poorhouse (*Young Socialist*, November 1901); the same school gave entertainments to the Woodlee Lunatic Asylum (sic) (*Young Socialist*, December 1901).

69 This was supported by the London SSS (*Young Socialist*, March 1910).

70 *League Training Syllabus*, YCL, 1925(?).

71 *Young Worker*, 26 June 1926, for example, reports a deputation to a headmaster in Fifeshire complaining about a teacher who had used the cane thirty-seven times in one day. This deputation was supported by the Trades Council. The deputation had proved successful so the group was now campaigning for free boots and clothing, backed by the Cowdenbeath Trades Council and the Fife Council of Action. They were suggesting a stay-in strike, refusing to do lessons and 'to generally make a nuisance of themselves' until their demands were granted. Parents' as well as children's meetings had been organized. See Ainley in Frow, *op. cit.* Appendix 2, p. 75, for reference to Manchester campaigns against the cane.

72 *Young Worker*, 5 June 1926.
73 *Young Comrade*, July 1926 and May 1927, *Young Worker*, 18 June 1927. The wearing of the Young Comrades' League badge caused consternation in Hendrefadog at a school attended by Cliff Roberts, whose headmaster asked the local education committee to ban it (*Young Worker*, 19 Novermber 1927). There were also Young Comrades' League banners. See photograph in Hywel Francis and David Smith, *The Fed, A History of the South Wales Miners in the Twentieth Century*, London, Lawrence and Wishart, 1980, opposite p. 109.
74 Ainley in Frow, *op. cit.* The records of the CPGB tell a different story. The resolution of the sixth conference of the CPGB, 17 May 1924, reads: 'The steps taken by the EC of the league to build up a strong communist childrens' movement receives our keen approval.' (*Speeches and Documents of the Sixth Conference of the CPGB*, Communist Party, 1924, p. 43.)
75 Ainley in Frow, *op. cit.*, Appendix 2.
76 For example, see n. 71. A strong parents' council was formed in Greenock where children were active in the schools (*Young Worker*, 11 September 1926). The 1924 Communist Party conference (*Speeches and Documents, op. cit.*) stated that women should be active in Communist Children's Groups, which were to be under the aegis of the YCL. Parental support was also needed for the YC des L delegation to the USSR (*Young Worker*, 4 June 1927). Nevertheless, we also read reports of the YC des L wanting to run their own activities. *Workers' Weekly*, 7 March 1924, reported that at the first conference of Communist Children's Groups the children were insistent that the *Young Comrade* was really their own paper while recognizing the need for backing from parents. At the Young Comrades' League conference in 1926 (*Workers' Weekly*, 26 February 1926) 13-year-old A. Campbell, son of 'Johnnie', was elected chair. School group papers were produced such as *Red Cracker*, (*Young Worker*, 5 June 1926) or *School Torch* (*Young Worker*, 29 May 1926). Unfortunately, these are not extant. The Annual Report of the Young Comrades' League for 1925 refers to the paper written 'largely by the children themselves' and the existence of eighteen groups (Report of YCL, *Annual Party Conference Report*, Communist Party, 1925). The Young Comrades' League choir sang at the London demonstration of 3,000 on 'Youth Day' (*Young Worker*, 10 September 1927).
77 However, according to Margaret McCarthy, writing of her days in Manchester YCL, there was greater autonomy for the YCL than that enjoyed by the ILP Guild of Youth: 'Of especial interest to me in the YCL was the autonomy it enjoyed and its enormous liberty to conduct and organise its own affairs. This was in the greatest contrast to the state of dependence in which the remaining socialist youth bodies were maintained by the adult organisations which, sternly patriarchal, were far from encouraging the youth sections, and appeared to be in some fear and mistrust of them, controlled, hampered, and restricted all signs of youthful individuality and independence.' (Margaret McCarthy, *Generation in Revolt*, London, Heinemann, 1953, p. 77).
78 The 1924 report of the Central Executive Committee of the Communist Party to the National Party Congress of 1924 stated that the YCL was in a 'semi-disorganised condition ... circulation of the *Young Communist* was very low' (*Report of the Central Executive Committee*, Communist Party, 1924, p. 11). The Cabinet papers also reveal this criticism. PRO: CAB 24/160 no. 239, 10 May 1923, includes a reprimand for the YCL by Moscow for its lack of success: '... nor can we perceive any earnest endeavours to penetrate the masses of working class youth and into the shops, to raise the question of the economic representation of the former and to establish trade union factions and shop nuclei.' PRO: CAB 24/160 CP 249, 17 May 1923, reports a memorandum of Charles Redfern, YCL secretary, saying that the organization was '... in a terrible state ... absolutely bankrupt'. Subsequently the

YCL was reprimanded by the YCI for not having subscriptions (CAB 24/160 CP 265, 7 June 1923). A motion of censure was passed, shortly after, upon Charles Redfern for not having carried out instructions (CAB 24/160 CP 285, 21 June 1923).

79 *Workers' Weekly*, 9 June 1923.

80 *Workers' Weekly*, 23 January 1925.

81 The SDF conference in 1907 passed a motion from Anfield saying that if local SSS did not exist then branches should set one up (*Annual Report*, SDF, 1907). Two years later, a similar motion was carried, which indicates a lack of progress (*Annual Report*, SDF, 1909: Central Islington branch urged every branch to set up a SSS). *Young Socialist*, October 1907, reports the ILP conference passing a motion saying that members should take more interest in the work of the SSS.

82 See n. 78. The Young Socialist League (YSL) defined itself primarily as an organiz-ation set up to 'convert' young people to socialism (article by J. Zimmerman in *Link*, January 1912) and expressed this in proselytizing tones: 'Socialism alone stands virgin pure, offering to man the bounteous gifts of nature . . . Revolt against misery, poverty and degradation, the true children of capitalism which spread darkness, and evil over the earth and obscure the rays of justice, which bring life and health to all men' (appeal by John Scurr, president of YCL, in *Link*, November 1911). *Link* of May 1912 talks of a crisis in the organization and asks for adult support. The BSP conference of the same year passed a motion from Stepney, where the YSL was strong, calling for closer links between the two organizations (*Conference Report*, BSP, 1912). The YSL reformed itself after the war into the Young Workers' League, holding its first conference on 27 March 1921, and agreed to affiliate to the Young Communist International (*Young Worker*, May 1921). In a few months time it became the Young Communist League. The first issue of the *Young Communist* (December 1921) says it was formed from a fusion of the YWL and the International Communist School Movement: 'Hitherto, the education of children and youth of our class, was left to a few, unnoticed, hardworking, painstaking and enthusiastic colleagues who realised the importance of their task and had to be content to meet in small schools, and joining with each other in singing our rebel songs. But that was only the beginning . . .'

83 An exception to this is the position taken by the Communist Party on the SSS in 1924. A report of the first conference of the Communist Children's Groups (*Workers' Weekly*, 29 February 1924) states that they regarded the SSS as outside the workers' movement and apart from the class struggle. They rejected intervention in the SSS as a waste of time. Less than a year before the YCL had approached the SSS calling for 'fraternal delegates' to the SSS conference in Edinburgh and had appealed for a united front on specific issues including the enrolling of the 'proletarian child in the struggle of its class' (*Workers' Weekly*, 14 April 1923). Their appeal was rejected.

84 Interviewed by Jean McCrindle and Sheila Rowbotham in *Dutiful Daughters*, Harmondsworth, Penguin, 1979, pp. 62–6.

85 *Ibid.*, p. 65.

86 Margaret McCarthy, *op. cit.*, p. 38, described being taken to the Accrington SSS where her mother was a BSP member. Thomas Bell, leading Communist Party member, wrote a most interesting account of the relationship between his politics and personal life in *Pioneering Days*, London, Lawrence and Wishart, 1941. He included his attitudes to marriage 'On economic grounds I had convinced myself that it was criminal for a worker to attempt to keep a wife, home, and possibly children on the beggarly wages they paid . . . to me marriage and the family was a bourgeois trap . . .' p. 85), his wife's refusal to wear a wedding ring, his commit-ment to vegetarianism and sending his son, Oliver, regularly to SSS.

87 Annie Davison (McCrindle and Rowbotham, *op. cit.*) recalled going to give readings to the SSS of the BSP, anarchists, and other groups, for which she received

elocution lessons. Interviewed some sixty years later she could still recite the precepts and declarations she learnt and remembered the stories she was told. In a recent letter to me from Sadie Fulton (15 May 1987) she described her memories of the SSS in Glasgow in the 1920s: 'My years with the SSS were always full of friendship and harmony.'

88 Alfred Russell refers to himself as a vegetarian (*Young Socialist*, August 1903), James Love as an 'apprentice vegetarian' and as a teetotaller (*Young Socialist*, October 1903); John Sarson used to be a church elder (*Young Socialist*, November 1905); and John Munroe used to be a Calvinist, but was now a Unitarian (*Young Socialist*, September 1904). Several members were in the Labour Church: Samuel Horsfal, Thomas Hardy, and Henry Emmins.

89 Article by Lizzie Glasier, *Young Socialist*, February 1905.

90 Editorial on the war, *Young Socialist*, September 1916.

91 *Young Socialist*, January 1905 and January 1906.

92 A plan of the Moral Instruction League's lessons was described as follows in *Young Socialist*, June 1903. It included: Patriotism; the vote, the nation and its government, society as an organism, universal brotherhood, peace and war; international relations, the value of arbitration, tidiness, fairness, courage; when alone, darkness, shadows and strange noise; manners, cleanliness; cooperation; the will; self respect; ideals. Many of the Moral Instruction League publications (Letter from George Berry, *Clarion*, 28 November 1911) were written by F. J. Gould who gave up teaching to work full time for the ethical movement. He was a former member of the Leicestershire School Board (*Young Socialist*, March 1912). He also wrote a child's version of Plutarch. He was a popular speaker on education: he gave a lecture in the USA in the Spring of 1914 (*Young Socialist*, June 1914) and spoke to meetings of the NUWT (*The Woman Teacher*, 17 December 1926) and SSS (*Young Socialist*, September 1903). In 1916 he aligned himself with the jingoists from the former SDF and formed the National Socialist Party, under whose aegis he wrote a socialist plan for education issued in 1918. See also F. J. Gould, *The Life Story of a Humanist*, Watts & Co., 1923.

93 Editorial, *Young Socialist*, Novermber 1905.

94 Kentish Town SSS, for example, described lessons given on people's natural right to land (*Young Socialist*, April 1904); Alfred Pung Hazel, SDF member and superintendent of the North Islington School, drew up a red catechism which included questions and answers on subjects such as socialism and the working class, hungry children, hospitals and machines (*Young Socialist*, July 1906).

95 *Young Socialist*, March 1908.

96 A letter from Isabel Wright stated the lessons were 'purely educational in the sense of drawing out the latent thinking capacities in scholars' (*Clarion*, 7 July 1911). John Hirst referred to their work with young children 'drawing out their ideas' through finger plays, picture books and plasticine (*Clarion*, 11 August 1911). An article in *Young Socialist*, April 1909, discusses the syllabuses of the Lancashire and Cheshire Union drawn up by Miss Dora Walford on Pestalozzi's line that character should be the supreme aim of education, and instruction should be imparted by 'drawing out'.

97 George Whitehead in an article on 'What to teach' argues that instruction should impart hatred of social evil and show capitalism as bad and socialism as good, rather than concerning itself with abstract virtues (*Young Socialist*, February 1913). An article by Margaret McDougall on a model lesson on private ownership is included in *Young Socialist*, July 1906.

98 Lizzie Glasier, *Young Socialist*, August 1906.

99 Fred Coates, national secretary of SSS and ILP member, writing in *Clarion*, 28 July 1911.

100 See Kean, *State Education*, 1988, pp. 328–9 for a description of Tom Anderson.

101 J. T. Murphy writing in *Red Dawn*, March 1919.

102 'The Land of Joy' by Margaret Johnson in *Red Dawn*, March 1919.
103 For example: 'C is for Connolly whom the government shot, D is for DeLeon who could not be bought, T is for Trotsky the man that you know . . .' (*Red Dawn*, April 1919).
104 *Revolution*, February 1918.
105 One of the very few examples I could find is Walter Scott, a Shoreditch teacher and member of the Canning Town SSS (*Young Socialist*, April 1905).
106 George Seagers, *Young Socialist*, May 1905; Maitland James Neil, secretary of Clydebank Trades Council, LRC and ASE member, *Young Socialist*, June 1905.
107 Charles Taylor, *Young Socialist*, November 1905.
108 William Fisher, assistant general secretary of his union in Gateshead, *Young Socialist*, September 1906.
109 John Storrie, delegate to Paisley Trades Council, *Young Socialist*, November 1906.
110 A. P. Hazell, *Young Socialist*, March 1911.
111 James Searson, *Young Socialist*, November 1903; George Boothroyd, *Young Socialist*, March 1903.
112 James Love, delegate to Paisley Trades Council, *Young Socialist*, October 1903.
113 He was superintendent of Glasgow SSS until he resigned in 1901 to take up the post of general secretary of his union in London (*Young Socialist*, December 1901). See Stanley Harrison, *op. cit.* He was close to the Communist Party in the postwar period but never actually joined. John Brotherton, Labour MP for Gateshead in 1923, was also active in the SSS (*Herald Book of Labour Members*, S. V. Bracher, Daily Herald, 1923).
114 Classes were run in Accrington on the art of securing attention, the art of questioning, problems of individuality and the theory of education (*Young Socialist*, July 1912). The teachers' class in Lancashire studied Hebart and Margaret MacMillan (*Young Socialist*, April 1909). The SSS nationally set up an education bureau in 1914 to improve teaching methods. 'Professional' assistance was used here: four of the eight members of the committee possessed MAs (*Young Socialist*, August 1914).
115 *Young Socialist*, April 1905.

Chapter 4

The Statist Perspective of Teacher Trade Unionists

In my discussion of the strategies of socialist organizations towards state education I suggested that much of the political and ideological dimension of such responses failed to provide an oppositional stance. In discussing the role of teacher unions in the period I will also argue that despite their trade union militancy, as documented by, for example, Roger Seifert,[1] teacher unions held political and ideological allegiance to the state. I will explore both the positions of teachers and the function they were required to perform by the state *outside* the confines of the educational state apparatus. Too often the focus upon teachers' role entirely within the accepted parameters of educational discourse had led those writers keen to see themselves outside the norm of the discourse into untenable positions.

A Critique of Lawn's Methodology

A particularly good example of a proponent of this weak methodology is Martin Lawn. A consistency of approach is apparent in his various writings.[2] He has made, and continues to make, much of what he considers to be his novel approach towards teacher unionism in this period. Few studies, he correctly argues, have looked in detail at the formations of teachers' organizations, struggles and cor.flicts, occupational ideologies and relations with the state and other agencies.[3] He also emphasizes that a comparative approach is needed to understand the political, economic and social relations of teachers in society.[4] However, Lawn's present and past readings of teacher politics in the period 1900–1930 have done little to provide credibility to the approach he advocates. His tendency to analyze the trade union actions of teachers without placing these in a political context has led him to overestimate the political and ideological autonomy of teachers and in turn, as Seifert has noted, to overestimate the radicalization of teachers in this period.[5]

Lawn's first book (with Ozga) started to develop an analysis of teachers' role which moved away from the professionalist lines advocated by Tropp.[6] It argued that professionalism constructed as an ideology by the state was employed by organized teachers in oppositional anti-statist ways. Further, Ozga and Lawn invested the trade union militancy of the period of their study (1910–20) with a radical, socialist, political consciousness. Little attempt was made to explore the concept of 'politicization'. In their survey of Marxist theoreticians they concentrated on the writing of Poulantzas, with whom they have several differences: 'While we place the state at the centre of events we do not see it as incorporating the teachers within it, as state personnel, or as members of the ideological state apparatus, or members of the new middle class oppressing the working class from whom they are supposedly separated ideologically.'[7]

In refuting Poulantzas's view of state employees they conflated the ideological and political relationship between employees and the state with the employees' subjective perception of that relationship. It seems that Poulantzas's analysis was interpreted as a slur on militants' political integrity: 'How for example does Poulantzas establish that a social worker, engaged in sympathetic industrial action with other workers, does not question his [sic] function within the ideology of the state apparatus?'[8] It is clear, even from *their* choice of quotation, that this was certainly not Poulantzas's position: 'Agents of the state personnel who go over to the side of the popular masses often live their revolt in terms of the dominant ideology . . . even sections of the state personnel which go over to the popular masses . . . [do not] normally challenge the political position between rulers and ruled that is embodied in the state.'[9] Indeed their historical study of the period 1910–20 showed neither that teachers were not incorporated nor that they challenged politically the position between 'rulers' and 'ruled'. Although Ozga and Lawn rejected the view that class location is simply economically determined they nevertheless failed to deal adequately with the ideological or political determinants of this location, as raised by Poulantzas. While it is commonly accepted[10] that Poulantzas's positions on the question of class determination changed, there seems to be a misunderstanding of his position. Indeed, his actual position is of greater relevance to the understanding of the relationship between state and teachers in this period than Ozga and Lawn would have us believe.

It is true that Poulantzas, in his desire to avoid economism, rejected a concept of class determined purely by economic relations. Writing from an unsympathetic stance, Ellen Meiksins Wood has characterized Poulantzas's differentiation between working class and *petit bourgeoisie* as a 'political-ideological division': 'He is suggesting that political and ideological relationships may actually take precedence over the relations of exploitation in the "objective" constitution of classes, and that political and ideological divisions may represent essentially class barriers.'[11] On the other hand, Bob Jessop has interpreted Poulantzas's position less sharply, reminding us that

Poulantzas saw the class location of the *petit bourgeoisie* 'in terms of its capitalistically unproductive economic role, its political work of supervision and control, and its ideological role of mental labour — all considered as movements within the social relations of production.'[12]

However, it was not just timeless economic relations which determined this class position but 'class strategies crystallized within class alliances that determine class position in the class struggle . . . '[13] To turn to Ozga and Lawn's original point: by simply looking at teachers' economic circumstances without looking at their class location in political ideological terms it *is* possible to read teachers' moves towards the labour movement as a radical political move. But if the *political* consciousness of teachers is analyzed — as I will do later in this chapter — it suggests rather, as Poulantzas does, that teachers did not 'challenge the political position between rulers and ruled'.[14] The politicization of teachers did not lead to an opposition to the state, but to a willing participation within its structures.

Lawn has attempted to modify this stance in his latest book, *Servants of the State*.[15] Reference is made to the political allegiance of teachers as a fact in their relationship to the state, without clearly defining that politicization. Lawn continues his view that trade union action was of a radical socialist nature. In addition he has suggested that teachers' support for the Labour Party was an anti-statist stand. He suggests, without justification, for example, that the campaign to affiliate the NUT to the Labour Party in 1917 was conducted on 'a straightforward Marxist ticket'[16] under the leadership of G. D. Bell, a moderate Freemason member of the Labour Party![17] He notes the Labour Party programme, *Labour and the New Social Order*, which I discussed in Chapter 1,[18] and suggest that it was developing an anti-statist stand.[19] He fails to perceive, for example, that the emphasis within the document on community involvement in education carried with it not a radical 1980s stance of community-based political action, but a direct counterposition to policies based on class, as advocated by Willie Paul.[20] By the end of this work he does accept that teachers wanted state intervention in education and that they perceived it to be an impartial referee.[21] What he fails to recognize is that this benign attitude to the state was always present in the policies of the Labour Party, which, he has suggested, had such a radical effect on teachers!

In their initial study of teachers, Ozga and Lawn did not give information on the activities of teachers in this period of a sort to persuade the reader that teachers challenged the fundamental nature of the state or its right to control the educational system. Thus, on the basis of Poulantzas's criteria, it is not possible to construe teachers' class position as a political one. The NUT did not suggest that teachers or the 'ruled', the working class, control education in opposition to the status quo. The Teachers' Registration Council, for example, was essentially a move to control the entrance of teachers into the profession, not to control what was taught, nor what was provided by the state in the way of instruction.[22]

Indeed, the NUT suggested that teachers — and working-class representatives — take on a greater part *within* the state through the creation of
alliances and partnerships between teachers and the local or central state.
Part of this strategy included the support for teachers who stood for councils
or Parliament. Ozga and Lawn, for their part, described such teachers who
became Labour councillors or MPs as 'militant members', irrespective of the
nature of their socialist policies.[23] Ozga and Lawn both overestimated the
trade union militancy of the NUT while simultaneously investing it with
anti-statist policies. Trade union militancy is seen as following on from the
state's refusal to relinquish power to a TRC: '*Then* the teachers considered
other means of resisting the state's right to manage education' (my
emphasis).[24]

First, Ozga and Lawn have stated that trade union activity took place
after the failure of another strategy whereas, as will be elaborated, both
strategies were carried out concurrently. Secondly, trade union activity is
perceived as action in opposition to the state's right to manage education,
rather than as action to preserve working conditions or to improve salaries.
Thus the Hereford action of 1914 is seen as signalling new forms of action.[25]
Yet the actions prior to this in West Ham in 1907, and after it, in Lowestoft
in 1923, for example, were of a similar character and method of organization. The Rhondda strike action of 1919 is seen to be important because of
its militancy. The political (and geographical) location of this action in the
militant mining communities of the Rhondda is seen to be of less significance
than the fact that action was organized locally.[26] Ozga and Lawn deduce
that the reliance upon the local NUT association was a 'positive advantage
as a national strike would have broken a union so divided in working conditions, areas and organizations'.[27]

It was, however, the institution of a national salary scale, Burnham,
which the NUT willingly accepted that was to prevent localized action of
the same character as Ozga and Lawn described in the Rhondda, Burnham
was also important in effecting a change in the relationship between the
central and local state. Henceforth the local state would have less autonomy
in determining teachers' salaries, while it would continue to bear the brunt
of any teacher action deflected from the national state on to the local
administrators of education. In his latest work Lawn has suggested that the
state refrained from direct control of teachers partly due to the 'relative
strength and unity of the teachers and a lively local management, intent on
maintaining independence, financing control and keeping teachers in their
station'.[28] It is also clear that given such action by the local state and the
structure of Burnham tying teachers to the central and local state, *direct*
control was unnecessary.

The role of the local state and its relation to the central state is also one
which has been questioned by Ozga and Lawn. They characterized local
education authorities as 'local buffers, or indirect agents'.[29] This definition is
altered for the 1920s. Then the local state's existence is characterized as

'following the practice of colonial administration'.[30] This colonial definition has been expanded in their more recent article in the *British Journal of Sociology of Education*.[31] Here they appear to be saying that local government was based upon Lugard's system of colonial administration and thus the local state became a colony:

> Its essence was the appearance of decentralisation and devolution with a quasi-autonomous role of the 'native' which ensured their co-option, while the major powers of government remained firmly in British hands. In the control of education this was translated into the fostering by the Board . . . of teacher autonomy. As a strategy it involved the rejection of direct, prescriptive controls such as the direct employment of teachers by the central state. Its success depended on the widespread acceptance of the concept of partnership based on a broad consensus about education . . . In order to successfully promulgate the idea of partnership with the teachers, the central state needed to invoke the closely related concept of professionalism.[32]

The relationship, however, between the central and the local state as analyzed in Chapter 1 was not a new phenomenon of the 1920s, but one embodied in the 1902 Act.[33] In fact, from 1902 the relationship between the central and local state was the subject of much attention by the NUT. There were frequent calls for alternatives to the financial relationship between the two as characterized by the relatively small proportion of finance from the Imperial Exchequer and the relatively large proportion borne by the local rates.[34] Above all, teachers were anxious to see a well resourced local state with whom they could be in partnership. Ozga and Lawn interpreted this demand not as a 'real desire' of teachers, but rather as part of the 'state's [conspiratorial?] aim to create an ideology to licence a group of workers and to cut them off from their natural allies, the working class'.[35]

Although they rejected Poulantzas's emphasis on the political and ideological, here Ozga and Lawn subsumed the state's economic role within the ideological. They attributed change in the state's role to the strength of teachers' trade union activity and to strong class consciousness.[36] But simply to look at this militancy without looking at the role education was to play in *preserving* the state in a period of political turmoil — as expressed *outside* teachers' activity — is to misestimate both the state's and the teachers' strategies.

Ozga and Lawn's Historical Data

So far I have dealt with the broad relationship between teachers and the state Ozga and Lawn have presented. I now wish to consider some of the historical features and examples which Ozga and Lawn have used to back up their argument. They start their study in 1910, concentrating on 'agitation' for economic demands, for they see this to be the indicator for militancy. In doing so they ignore the broader expressions of empathy with the working class expressed by the NUT. At least from the turn of the century, there was an impetus towards the labour movement which was driven by teachers' concerns for the welfare of the working-class children they taught and their belief that Labour's welfare education programme would lead to improvements in children's lives.[37] Class size, for example, was an issue on which teachers felt strongly and on which they formulated progressive policy based on an alliance with the TUC, Labour Represent-ation Committee (LRC) and the Co-op, in order to improve education for children (and their own working conditions).[38] This was not a new pheno-menon produced in the ferment of wage militancy.

To back up their argument about the increasing militancy of teachers, Ozga and Lawn assert — without reference — that teachers joined the SDF (and ILP and Plebs League) and cite John Maclean as an example of a radical school teacher in this period.[39] I question the veracity of the former statement and the value of the latter. Although I have found much evidence of teachers' political involvement and activities in this period I have only come across one example of a BSP member[40] and no examples of SDF members.[41] In the *Plebs* from 1909 to 1920 there are three contributions only on elementary education, including one letter from one teacher.[42] I am unable to pursue Ozga and Lawn's sources, for none are cited.[43] This line of argument has been developed in Lawn's latest book, where again no refer-ences are given for the view that teachers worked with the SDF.[44]

As stated earlier, there was an increased politicization in the NUT during this period, but it is questionable whether that was attributable to the activities of socialist teachers like John Maclean. On the contrary, although the meetings at NUT conference of the Teachers's Socialist Associ-ation were well attended, the TSA's attempts to raise an alliance with the TUC and the Labour Party in the period before the First World War foundered.[45] It was not until the feminist teachers organized in the National Federation of Women Teachers (NFWT) and Women Teachers' Franchise Union (WFTU) that politics as such featured prominently in NUT dis-cussions at all levels . The feminists' contribution to teacher politics was skimmed over in one sentence in Ozga and Lawn's book.[46] In *Servants of the State* a chapter is allocated to the feminists but given Lawn's characteriz-ation of teachers' politicization little attention is paid either to the nature of the feminists' politicization or to its impact within the NUT.[47] The dis-cussions on the parliamentary franchise which NFWT and the WTFU[48] introduced into the NUT from 1910, in addition to their other campaigns for equal rights, highlighted the role of women teachers in the state. The argument of the feminists was that the state governed their whole life as women teachers, yet they were excluded from any decision-making role in that same state by their denial of the parliamentary franchise. It was this discussion which divided the union bitterly and helped prepare the way, at the end of the war, for an almost equally contentious debate on TUC/Labour Party affiliation. The politics which the feminists introduced into the NUT were not formed by the ILP (though many were Labour supporters) but by the militant suffrage organizations: the Women's Social and Political Union (WSPU) and Women's Freedom League (WFL).[49] The role of feminist teachers is of broader significance in this period. The introduction of Burnham, as said earlier, created a shift in the relationship between the central and local state. It was also important in preventing any realization of the demand for equal pay, even in particular areas where the feminists were strong, due to the national character of the new scales.

To look at politicization within the NUT by reference alone to the Rhondda teachers[50] is to ignore other political influences and to suggest that radicalization and politicization are one and the same thing. Ozga and Lawn have expressed enthusiasm for the actions of W. G. Cove and the South Wales teachers: 'The strength of the industrial union idea and its influence in the union came from the victory of the Rhondda teachers'[51]. However, they fail to explain adequately — in the light of *this* statement — why the South Wales teachers did not *organize* teachers nationally inside the NUT on their position.[52] In the same year that Cove took up office as president of the NUT — 1922 — the union elected Alderman Sainsbury, a well known Conservative councillor from London, to the vice presidency. Futhermore the founding of the Teachers' Labour League (TLL) in 1923[53] took place independently of the South Wales teachers. At the 1924 TLL conference in fact it was W. G. Cove who opposed affiliation to the Educational Workers' International (EWI) on the grounds that this would cause dissension in the union.[54] Locally in the Rhondda, militant action was less forthcoming in support of the married women teachers sacked by the council in the 1920s.[55]

These matters cannot be tackled just by referring to the internal dynamics of teacher union politics but by reference to the wider role for education within the state. Ozga and Lawn state that the 1920s witnessed 'attacks by the government [in the Geddes committee proposals] and the local authorities which severely damaged the gains of the post-war period and isolated teachers from the Labour movement'.[56] But teachers were not the only organized groups of workers to face defeat in this period. There was a general offensive by the state against the trade union movement.[56]

The NUT had been deeply affected by the broader political balance of forces in society. For example, it had been forced to take up the parliamentary franchise question precisely because of the political struggle *outside* teaching. The NUT had discussed TUC/Labour Party affiliation not just because of inadequate salary levels but because of the growing industrial unrest in society as a whole and the questions that that unrest raised about the future direction of British society.[58] Similarly, although there are specific features of state policy in education which affected teachers in this period, the general defeats in the union movement also affected teachers' ability to organize.

An understanding of this broader context for the state's strategy and teacher response is necessary as well in order to assess the state's repressive activities towards communist teachers in the 1920s. In their recent article Ozga and Lawn treat superficially the well known view of Lloyd George that 'in a revolutionary period . . . teachers seemed to be individuals in leadership roles' and state that the Conservative Party, in due course, 'became increasingly alarmed by the desertions of teachers from its ranks and towards a radical socialist party'.[59] Leaving aside Ozga and Lawn's characterization of the Labour Party in this period,[60] this phrase suggests that action was initiated against teachers because *teachers* were a threat and that it was for this reason that the Seditious Teaching Bill and Oath of Allegiance were discussed. I disagree. Education was important in the post-war period as a bulwark against class dissension. State education was an area comparatively *free* of political conflict, and therefore ideal, as Fisher saw, to promote social harmony and 'public good'.[61] For their part teachers supported legislation such as the 1918 Act, welcomed the Burnham proposals, agreed, at a specially convened conference with one vote against, to a wage cut of 5 per cent and endorsed much of Labour's programme for the extension of equality of opportunity by the state as presently structured.[62]

The activities of the TLL came to the attention of the Board of Education via the Home Office and Special Branch because of the state's concern to smash *Marxism* either by isolating it from the labour movement or by aligning it with the Labour Party in order to discredit the Labour Party.[63] The state, through its surveillance, was well aware of the small numbers of communist teachers. At the height of the 'red scares' the Home Office could only find seven English communist teachers.[64] Although a couple of Communist Party teachers were sacked for political activities it would be misleading to suggest that there were large numbers of left socialist teachers who somehow escaped such victimization.[65] Lawn fails to draw the readers' attention to the fact that 'victimized teachers' Dan Griffiths and Miss Spurrell, Labour and not Communist Party members, were *reinstated* in their teaching posts.[66] Even in an article attempting to argue that teachers were increasingly becoming radicalized David Capper, the TLL leader, could only cite two examples of victimization.[67] Lord Percy and Lord Fisher alike were fulsome in their praise of teachers' neutrality, commonsense, and professionalism.[68]

The actions against communists were part of the state's broader role in combatting Marxism in society generally, rather than because any specific threat was posed *inside* the education service. The mere presence of communists was enough to create a climate of opposition to even the mildest forms of socialism — outside the schools — for example, in the Socialist Sunday Schools. The effect of these general political strategies will now be explored in addition to particular conflicts within the NUT.

The State's Attitude Towards Teachers

This section starts by discussing the extent to which the state and teachers held common perceptions about the nature of state education and the role of teachers within that system. Ozga and Lawn have categorically stated that there is an 'unwarranted assumption that . . . [teachers] collaborate with the state at the ideological and political levels'.[69] Reference has already been made to my objection to an account of teachers' political roles which relies upon their subjective interpretation of such a role, rather than an objective assessment of their practice. Nevertheless, even on the subjective level, it is clear that the ideology which dominated organized teachers was one which perceived a commonality of interests between teachers and the state. It is inadequate to define this common perception as professionalism. Such a definition is too narrow to encompass an ideology which relates essentially to the nature of state education and accepts the state's right to organize such education.[70]

As stated in Chapter 1, education was a state apparatus which assumed an important role in the political and ideological fields in the post-war period. Even those educational initiatives which reacted most directly to economic need had a broader, ideological significance. For example, speaking to a meeting of the Association of Education for Industry in 1919, Fisher summed up his position thus:

> I have always felt the great problem for the next years is to bring the world of business and the world of education into clear connection. We have the same interests, and I believe that the solution of all the difficulties between capital and labour will ultimately lie not in the sphere of wages at all, not in any material sphere, but in the kind of improvement in the general condition which is due to the spread of knowledge amongst the people and the employers.[71]

A similar attitude was held by Lord Percy. As President of the Board of Education, later in the 1920s, he held that vocational education was a method of democratizing the school and in turn preventing discontent in industry.[72]

This political role for education was expressed more forcibly by Fisher in the Cabinet in debates on finance for the 1918 Act where he stated his belief that 'social peace' lay in the 'education of the democracy'.[73] The Labour Party also endorsed such sentiments, through the writings of its leadership, but also more specifically in the deliberations of the Advisory Committee on Education (ACE).[74] In a paper written in 1927 the ACE condemned 'any attempt . . . to impose on immature young minds any particular political doctrine'. Rather, the school would play its part in creating 'a new order of society' — a sentiment not dissimilar to that of Fisher's — if it made its single aim 'the strengthening of the character and development of the intelligence'.[75]

Such strategies relied on teachers for their implementation. Fisher saw teachers as central to maintaining a harmonizing role for education. Speaking at the Imperial Education Conference in 1923, he stated: 'The main business of the educational statesman is to provide the schools and colleges with an adequate staff of good teachers. If the teachers are efficient, the education will be good; if they are stupid and low-minded, the most elaborate system in the world will not prevent the education system of the country from being a hollow sham.'[76] Percy argued that his predecessor failed to allow for increased salaries and pensions with the result that Fisher's last two years in office were a 'discouraging period of disappointed hopes'.[77] Percy echoed Fisher's sentiments on education: 'A danger lay in the existence of such a thing as a purely elementary education, not concerned as a preparation for any further stage of initiation into responsible thinking and tending therefore to discharge youth into working life with no more than a child's thought and a child's knowledge.'[78] He also expressed similar views to Fisher on the role of the teaching force. Teachers, especially at the end of the war, had to counteract 'a revolutionary frame of mind'. And, according to Percy, they succeeded.[79] He quotes a London docker saying at the end of the General Strike: 'We have lost this strike because the public school spirit has got into the elementary school'.[80] The conclusion he reached about teachers was: 'The main impression that I carried away with me from those years was of the essential soundness of English school teachers'.[81] Nor was his perception of his attitudes coloured by the benefit of some thirty years of hindsight. Percy did not respond to the hysterial calls within his party for the political 'vetting' of teachers, through an oath of allegiance. He did not think 'loyalty' was a problem: 'I know that there is a good deal of unrest among teachers but I continue to think that there is no proper basis for it and this will be proved before very long'.[82]

To suggest that the Board of Education — as opposed to sections of the Conservative Party — held the view that teachers were undermining the fabric of society is to misunderstand the way in which education and teachers were viewed within the broader political context. Rather, as seen in a speech to the London Conservative Teachers' Association in 1927, Percy was seeking to draw the vast majority of the teaching profession towards a commonality of opinion on the nation's need.[83] This did not prove difficult. When Percy stated that the teaching profession condemned revolutionary and communist indoctrination in schools this was true.[84] It was also true that by the very quoting of such, unspecified, instances it served to *strengthen the status quo*. It isolated a very small number of protagonists while simultaneously suggesting their power: 'Ours is no longer a country to be enjoyed and exploited and loved for its advantages; it is a country to be saved.'[85] Percy even stated publicly that he was aware of the insignificance of the TLL and relied upon the strong opinion of the teaching profession to counteract such propaganda.[86] He stated his idea of the teachers' role in an address to the North of England Conference:

For besides the common duty of allegiance to the state, the teacher is bound to it by a special duty, which he has voluntarily undertaken. He applies to the state through its delegate, the local education authority, for a position as trustee for the education of its future citizens, and he accepts this trust from the state. His rights as a citizen, or rather, his exercise of these rights, is limited by his position, as are the civil rights of the judges of the high court.[87]

As stated above, he rejected the demand for teachers to take an oath of allegiance: it created a precendent regarding the relationship of teachers to the central state; and it was unnecessary.[88]

As discussed in Chapter 1, when Trevelyan was President of the Board of Education in 1924 he also recognized that the state had to have a specific strategy aimed at the incorporation of teachers within its framework. He advocated a triple partnership between the central and the local state and teachers. Teachers were to work alongside a largely unchanged educational state apparatus.[89] This view was subsequently developed by the ACE which stated that it was 'desirable that representatives of the teaching profession should be definitely associated with the administration of education'. The influence of teachers was to be institutionalized through advisory committees to local education authorities and a statutory advisory committee of the Board of Education, 'provided that the control of education through the elected representatives of the nation is maintained and the minister's responsibility to parliament remains intact'.[90]

It is against this background that the question of civil service status for teachers is considered. The state's concept of its own 'impartiality' would be threatened, even though greater financial control from the centre would be possible.[91] The state had no wish to be brought into day to day questions related to the teacher's job. The tendency would be for teachers to appeal to the Board on personal questions and for the Board to act as a court of appeal. The Board of Education would appear in the eyes of the educational world as an obstacle to educational progress: 'All the traditions of English education and of the civil service are against such a development and the system of party government has helped and would continue to help in securing freedom for education in this important sense.'[92] It would also suggest that the state was afraid to leave the exercise of teachers' influence to independent authorities.[93] The civil service concept conflicted with the 'neutrality' which was a central feature of the education system. The day to day management control of teachers would also have been weakened by a direct line of responsibility to a more remote body. Local control would have been diminished. Civil service status could provide stability and efficiency; it could not adequately maintain the ideological nature of state education.[94] In addition to the incorporation of teachers by consent, attention is also drawn to other — repressive — strategies. The surveillance of communist teachers was not a new phenomenon. As early as 1910 teachers' political activity was monitored.[95] There is an amusing account of Board of Education 'spies' being sent to report on an unemployed teachers' mass meeting: 'The teachers' meeting was the greatest fun. The place was packed . . .'[96] Enthused by their experiences, the 'spies' were subsequently sent to a demonstration on the same topic in Trafalgar Square. This time there was less to interest them: 'It was rather a damp raw day, not very suitable for warm displays of eloquence and both Phipps and I who attended on behalf of the Board got our feet rather cold and so didn't stay out the whole time.'[97] Records were also kept of teacher 'immorality' and decisions were taken on whether 'fallen women' were to be allowed further contact with small children.[98]

As a matter of routine newspaper cuttings, though not Home Office notes, were kept on teachers standing for election to councils, or Parliament, who had obtained press attention. These were teachers active in the NUT, or who had, in the case of Snelgrove in Sheffield, caused a stir by switching allegiance from Conservative to Labour. Press cuttings were also filed on those members of the public with past connections with the Board of Education, such as Michael Sadler.[99] The surveillance of communist teachers, however, was carried out primarily by the Special Branch and Home Office, rather than by the Education Board collecting newspaper cuttings. The emphasis in these reports is upon the links with the Communist Party and the Educational Workers' International, the international communist teachers' body. As with the reports on the YCL referred to in Chapter 3, close attention was paid to the TLL's financial difficulties. There were no reports of communist agitation *inside* schools.[100] It was precisely because such surveillance had been undertaken for a number of years that Percy recognised that while there was no real need to take action against communist teachers, nevertheless their small presence could be utilized in drawing the teaching profession — and public opinion — against Marxist ideas.[101]

In this respect the state's action mirrored that taken over the Seditious Teaching Bill (STB) which was discussed in Chapter 3. It had been clear that state schools were not the site for such 'seditious' teaching. However, by inserting an educational 'dimension' into such discussions over legislation it was possible to reassert the need for state schools to be a bulwark against such activity *outside* the schools. Both Simon, and Lawn and Ozga, have seen the STB as an attack on *teachers*.[102] But it was more complicated than that. Education, as I have explained, was seen as a vehicle for post-war harmony. There was a growing interest in matters educational and a widespread acceptance of the benefits of a neutral state education system. This consensual atmosphere ensured that education was 'appropriated' by different state apparatuses for different ends. The surveillance of the TLL, and the STB, were not needed to ensure the stability of the educational state apparatus. It was rather that they aided broader strategies: the defeat of revolutionary politics and the dramatizing of the communist threat.[103]

Lawn's situating of the surveillance of the TLL within the parameters of the educational state apparatus has led him to overestimate the threat actually caused by the TLL. The founding of the Conservative Teachers' Association (CTA) is seen as a response to the very real threat posed by the TLL in the early 1920s.[104] However, although there was a deputation of the CTA, composed of prominent teachers led by Crook, former NUT president and East Ham MP, to Baldwin in 1923, the CTA was not formed until 1924 on the instigation of the central Conservative Party office.[105] Its formation was welcomed by the Party chair, Davidson, who subsequently addressed local meetings in support.[106] Yet much of the *activity* of the CTA seems to have been undertaken in the later 1920s: a leaflet to recruit teachers did not appear until 1928.[107]

Crook had explained to Baldwin in the 1923 deputation that he had spent 1917 touring the country against Labour Party affiliation. He attributed the move to the Labour Party in the 1920s to cuts in superannuation and salaries.[108] But it was not until well *after* these debates on TUC/LP affiliation and *after* the Geddes cuts that it was felt necessary to form the CTA. The period was not one in which the left in the union was on the 'rise', but rather, in retreat. The CTA was not formed to counter militancy but to consolidate and rebuild its forces after the 'battle for socialism' had already been lost inside the NUT.

The Teachers' Response to the State's Educational Positions

My starting point here is teachers' analysis of the state's position on the nature and provision of education. Teachers accepted the state's right to determine the parameters of education. The majority of teachers identified with the state, seeing it as responsible for the nation's good.[109] The framework for educational debates was provided by the state's own initiatives. The NUT's position was responsive: calling on the Board of Education to implement the 1918 Act or to extend the legislation on school meals or to raise the school leaving age.[110] Stances were not determined by sharp *ideological differences*, but by specific tasks teachers were to undertake.

The annual Empire Day celebrations in which children were obliged to salute the achievements of the British Empire were enthusiastically supported by most teachers.[111] Criticism was raised by the NUT because such celebrations were compulsory only in elementary schools: this suggested that elementary school teachers (and their pupils) were less patriotic than their secondary school counterparts.[112] This slur was repudiated. The political correspondence in the NUT press from a few anti-imperialist teachers[113] was distinctly a minority view. The NUT participated in the Imperial Union of Teachers and in the Imperial Education Conferences and welcomed the British Empire exhibition.[114] The same approach is found in teachers' attitude towards 'excessive militarism' in schools. The objection to the officer training corps in schools was based primarily on the extra-curricular work involved for teachers rather than upon ideological objections.[115]

Although teachers endorsed the state's authority in determining education matters, this did not prevent teachers making demands upon the state. These demands were of a progressive character and were similar to the positions of the TUC and Labour Representation Committee (LRC).[116] It was not the case that the trade union activity in West Ham provided some kind of impetus for the NUT to discuss education from the perspective of working-class children and organizations.[117] By 1907 the national NUT conference had already adopted a progressive position on class size which included local work with the LRC and ILP.[118] Similar motions on education were prioritized to the top of the agenda even in years when pay, or the parliamentary franchise, or cuts, were of immediate interest. The 1911 conference which debated, amidst much excitement, the parliamentary franchise and condemned the Holmes-Morant circular, also discussed compulsory medical inspection of children, increased grants to Local Education Authorities from the central exchequer, and opposition to the raising of the school leaving age exemptions.[119] Top of the agenda for the 1912 conference was the extension of medical inspection — franchise was prioritized sixth and salaries ninth.[120] In 1921 the NFCT conference, which was often more progressive than the NUT, spent much time debating motions that called for the extension of secondary education, and democracy in schools.[121] Industrial action, TUC/LP affiliation and equal pay were not even on the agenda.

Like the TUC, the NUT opposed vocational training in that it acted both against the status quo in schools and against the concept of equality of opportunity.[122] But there were differences between the NUT and TUC on educational policy. Despite the attempts of socialists both in the NFCT and NUT to get the union to endorse policy on secular education this was not successful. The NUT opposed denominational religious teaching in state schools as this could penalize individual teachers' views, but fully supported the state's emphasis on religious education.[123]

The NUT supported TUC policy on the extension of the provision of meals for needy children. Indeed it was teachers themselves in some areas who had formed centres for feeding. In Southwark teachers formed the London Schools Dinner Association in the 1880s. Teachers also took the view that the serving of dinners was not their job and that school premises were inappropriate places for the eating of meals. Their desire to improve children's welfare conflicted with their desire to maintain their status.[124] Support for labour movement positions on educational provision was readily expressed in the election addresses of executive hopefuls and in the presidential addresses of the successful candidates.[125]

It was educational policy which became the rationale for positions on pay, conditions and status. For instance, the lowering of class sizes would lead to a healthier atmosphere for children and less pressure on teachers; the redistribution of imperial aid to finance stricken local education authorities would improve educational provision for children — as well as improve salaries.[126] Even in a period of cuts a similar stance was adopted. The 'platform on education' drawn up by the NUT in November 1922 as part of the general election 'campaign' made no reference to pay, the implementation of Burnham, or status. The teachers' financial circumstances were omitted in favour of an appeal for education 'in the needs of the nation'.[127]

The relationship between education policy and status and working conditions can be well exemplified by the debates on combined departments brought to the attention of the NUT first by the Equal Pay League and then by the NFWT. The amalgamation of boys' and girls' departments in elementary schools raised questions about the possible education provided for girls.[128] It also meant that women teachers were deprived of status and promotion prospects. The NFWT's opposition to amalgamated departments was supported by the NUT.[129]

To restrict a consideration of teachers' attitudes towards the state to an analysis of their concerns on pay, status and working conditions is to ignore the fact that the framework for their educational policies was, in fact, a statist one.

Teachers' Conflicts with the State on Pedagogy

Teachers endorsed the state's legitimacy in the area of educational provision. They took very different attitudes on pedagogical questions. It is upon such issues that teachers came into conflict with the state's representatives, in the form of His Majesty's Inspectors (HMIs), and also locally through local education authorities' inspectors. There was a double resentment against such men. First, HMIs held a position from which elementary school teachers had been effectively barred on the grounds of their own education and class background. Secondly, criticism of teachers' work was seen as an encroachment on the classroom expertise — and limited status — which elementary teachers *did* possess and which HMIs did not.[130]

Teachers might perceive their educational concerns and those of the state to be identical, but made a distinction when it came to the implementation of these concerns in the classroom. The anger which was expressed against the Holmes-Morant circular and vigour with which the expression was pursued epitomized long held resentment.[131] But it was not just against the inspectors' 'outside' interference that teachers railed. The NUT executive and London Teachers' Association (LTA) officers were also opposed to the work of the progressives, such as Montessori. *The Schoolmaster* denounced her for her audacity in suggesting *how* children should be taught. She was castigated because she was not a teacher, not English, and not aware of the difficulties elementary teachers faced:

From time to time American educationists have combined the pleasure of a trip to England with the duty of instructing us how to teach, and the Montessori evangel, based on the study of 'defective' children, is supposed to have brought the truth from Italy, as Augustine did to Kent; and what is indigenous is natural, evolutional, functional, and therefore more likely to be real and successful than any imported culture is a truth, which never crosses the minds of the critics who find fault with whatever is, and whatever is being done.'[132]

The book *What Is and What Might Be,* written by a former HMI, Edmond Holmes, also received short shrift.[133] These dismissive approaches were not shared by all sections of the NUT. Members of the NFWT often expressed the view that it was difficult summoning up any interest in issues of professional classroom practice amongst (male) members in NUT meetings. They rectified this with their own exhibitions and meetings. They welcomed Montessori's approaches, seeing parallels between the spirit of freedom she wished to encourage in small children with the spirit of freedom which they wanted in their own lives as disenfranchized citizens.[134]

The Dalton Plan was received with less hostility by *The Schoolmaster* because teachers' control and supervision were essential parts of the scheme.[135] However, the shying away from questions of educational philosophy and new ideas was evident in *The Schoolmaster*'s rejection of psychological theories to understand children's behaviour. Freud was criticized for being foreign and unnatural. Like Montessori, he was not an elementary school teacher: 'It is gratuitous, unnecessary and contaminating; taught to the young it may defile the thoughts of a life-time . . . [there is] found to be something particularly nasty at the bottom and part of those morbid erotical studies in which German psychologists have for a generation, now, taken such an unhealthy delight . . . '[136]

This fear, that their 'power' would be undermined, also characterized the approach of the NUT and LTA to the cinema. Educational films in schools, provided that they were suitable, were acceptable as long as the teacher could direct children's attention.[137] Films inside the cinema were a different matter. Here was recognized an area of influence on children's lives which excluded — and by implication undermined — the authority of teachers:

> Apart from the fact that much time would be wasted in going to and from places of entertainment, the cinema is not adapted for teaching purposes. The pictures are too rapid and cannot be assimilated . . . further by the withdrawal even for a short time from the teacher's influence there is something lost, for it is still true that moral power is affected by personality.[138]

From their feminist perspective on morality, the NFWT and NUWT were particularly interested in the cinema. This was seen as an area of professional life where they could legitimately pursue their political concerns.[139] This difference of gender perspective on educational matters is also found in discussions on sex hygiene. The NFWT favoured teaching sex hygiene to girls in elementary schools where parental consent was given; but for the mainstream of the NUT and LTA such ideas were anathema. It might be acceptable — to the NUT — for men and women in training colleges to be given such instruction themselves, but the needs of the professionals and the children in their care were seen as being distinct.[140]

There is little to suggest that in the sphere of educational practice the NUT (or LTA) adopted positions of a radical, or even progressive, nature. Any account of teachers' politicization during this period needs to recognize the conservative attitude to their work in the classroom.

The Attitude of Teachers towards the Central and Local State

Teachers accepted the state's authority to determine education, whilst maintaining their own rights to decide how to implement such policy inside the classroom. There was also an identification with the interests of the state on a broader level, which in turn reinforced teachers' attitudes within the specifically educational arena. Because of their broader allegiance to the state, for example during the First World War, teachers were politically incapacitated from defending their position in the educational sphere. Teachers saw themselves as exemplary citizens prepared to make sacrifices in the nation's cause. More than 20,000 teachers signed up during the war. Many were killed or suffered permanent disability.[141] This support for the state's cause was welcomed by the Board of Education[142] and the King and Queen alike: 'Their majesties are aware of the magnificent response which the education service throughout the country has made to the demand of the present time, not only in its contribution to the fighting forces, but also in the assistance which it has rendered in many kinds of important war work.'[143]

The majority of teachers was in sympathy with the state's war in the hope that this loyalty, this ideological and political commitment, would be rewarded after the war in the form of increased pay and status. This is not to say that NUT salary demands were abandoned but rather that they were shelved 'for the duration'. Even when a more militant motion was substituted at the 1916 conference for that of the executive it was still couched in terms of increased provision after the war.[144] And although there were protests, for example, against the use of unqualified and poorly paid 'supplementary' teachers during the war, the teachers' overriding political commitment weakened their economic demands.[145] The NUT conference in 1916, presided over by the Conservative president, listened to his speech attacking concientious objectors, even though education was regarded as an acceptable alternative for conscientious objectors by the state.[146] Letters in the NUT press reminding teachers that fellow colleagues were imprisoned (as conscientious objectors) received little sympathy.[147]

A similar loyalty was evident during the General Strike, when, as *The Schoolmaster* proudly asserted,[148] only a handful of teachers in the whole of London was unable to attend school. The education that teachers had provided the 'strikers' also ensured that the situation, as the state saw it, was restored to calm very quickly. For this, teachers were rewarded with additional holidays. Teachers' identification with the interests of the state operated on other levels too. There was a general acceptance of the need for economies and cuts in the public sector. In an editorial headed 'The Triumph of Reaction', the LTA bewailed the fact that teachers were always the first to be hit, while accepting that cuts were needed in order to pay for the war: 'The war must be paid for . . . we must forgo luxuries; we must exercise economies; we must live plainly; we must do without the frills and adornments of more prosperous days; all these things willingly conceded . . . [but] . . . why should the schools, the children, and the teachers be the first to be placed on the reduced rations?'[149] This view that sacrifice would be rewarded was even seen in respect of the Geddes cuts. A special NUT conference in January 1924 agreed to continue accepting a 5 per cent salaries cut to demonstrate their goodwill; an amendment to refuse wage cuts in localities which were still paying teachers below standard levels, was largely rejected.[150] By April 1925 *The Schoolmaster* could declare that there was cause for satisfaction that things were not worse.[151]

Alliances with the Local State

Teachers sought to intervene in the financial relationship between the central and local state to create a balance in favour of the local education authorities — and teacher incorporation. For a period of many years NUT and NFCT conferences alike backed policies calling on the government to increase imperial aid to local authorities. Local education authorities were increasingly facing financial difficulties paying for a national service from locally based contributions — the rates. Amongst other things friction was created on a *local* level between teachers and education authorities, bringing teachers increasingly into conflict with the local state. As NUT conference made clear, teachers wished to have a close relationship with the local state — but felt impeded by the conflicting pressures on local authorities to raise rates or keep salaries and educational provision at a low level.[152]

The NUT never argued for high rates, since this would adversely affect its strategy of local cooperation and deter sympathy from the public. Nor did it argue that all education should be financed centrally since this would have meant that teachers were 'state employees' and therefore not able to exercise the freedom they thought they possessed. Rather, they argued that since education was a national service, and a national investment, the state had a responsibility to finance education adequately.[153]

The West Ham dispute had been caused by the financial problems of West Ham Council. As an extra-metropolitan borough it was a highly rated area and contained a large school-age population. Forced to accept lower wage levels, teachers threatened resignation and reacted militantly to the Council's attempt to introduce strike breakers. Their actions were partially successful in this one area. But such local action was incapable of resolving the problems caused by the nature of central/local state financing.[154] What was adopted as a national strategy for the defence of educational provision and teachers' salaries was a partnership with the local education authorities. Close links with the local state were seen as a bulwark against the economies of the central state. This was a strategy favoured by the NUT throughout this period, from before the West Ham dispute to after the Geddes cuts.[155]

The debates which took place in 1919–20 on Whitley committees were a development of these earlier expressions of intent. The Whitley committees were promoted in a 'disinterested' way by the state:

> The government is not, of course, uninterested in the formation of these councils. Industry is becoming every day a more urgent problem, and it is more and more necessary for the government of the day to know the view of those immediately concerned in the several trades of the country. An industrial council is, therefore, useful to the government in providing *one voice* for the industry concerned [original emphasis].[156]

It was this one voice which was so attractive to the NUT. The conference of 1919 adopted policy on the Whitley councils unanimously as the only way in which salaries and avenues of promotion and status would be achieved.[157] This strategy was reaffirmed the following years in counterposition to one that envisaged a self-governing profession taking control of education. This latter position, advocated by the Rhondda men, attempted to invest the concept of status with the notion of workers' control. It failed to win support. Advisory committees on the lines of Whitley were seen as the avenue to 'joint control and full partnership' with the local education authorities.[158] This strategy proved to be non-controversial during the 1920s, even though it had proved to be of little benefit in defending teachers against the centrally imposed Geddes cuts.[159]

In addition to this general strategy the NUT — and NUWT — sought to stand teachers for local councils. The NUT thought that, irrespective of party allegiance, the fact that a councillor was a teacher would ensure the representation of educational interests. Teachers, as exemplary citizens, were encouraged to take an active part in public life. Publicity in NUT journals was given to the candidature of teachers — without reference to party politics — on the assumption that such information was an adequate incentive for securing the vote of NUT members.[160] The NUWT did not take such a simplistic view.[161]

During the West Ham and Lowestoft disputes by-elections were called and teacher candidates stood on a platform of support for the teachers. It is within *this* context of teachers' acceptance of state legitimacy and the desire to be incorporated into the administration of the local state that I will be discussing their particular attitude to trades unionism.[162]

The Nature of Teacher Trades Unionism

I believe Lawn is right to reject Tropp's analysis of the steady advance of teachers, because of the downturn in the 1920s;[163] nevertheless, there is a great deal of continuity in the *dominant* positions adopted by the NUT and NFCT in this period with respect to their relationship with the broader trade union movement. The intense debate in 1917 on TUC/LP affiliation, however, cannot be seen simply as a new phenomenon caused by a rise in the cost of living and a fall in wage levels. This debate took place against increased politicization in the country at large and amidst sharpening class conflict. It also occurred after the ground had already been prepared for the introduction of explicitly political questions into the NUT by feminist teachers a few years before. Again political issues were brought into the union, from the wider campaigns being undertaken in society, by teachers.

From before the turn of the century NUT members were sympathetic to a relationship with the wider trade union movement. Although it was the action of the 1897 conference in supporting the children of the Penrhyn quarrymen that was later summoned as a precedent in the 1913 debate on the support of the children of the Dublin transport workers,[164] other, less memorable, discussions on trade unionism also took place. Sections of the National Federation of Class Teachers, in particular, favoured working with other unions, and did so in certain areas. Class Teachers Associations in Rhondda, Merthyr, Darwen, Carlisle, Keighley, Todmorden, Southampton and Hackney were affiliated to local trades councils. In some areas teacher delegates held important offices.[165] ILP members, such as H. J. Lowe, used the pages of the *Class Teacher* to urge that the NUT organize itself as a union and join with other workers.[166] Similar views were expressed at the NFCT conference and at the 1907 conference the socialists came within 1000 votes of winning this position.[167] The arguments used then would reappear in the 1917 debates between civil service alignment and trade union participation.

Some attempts were made for the NUT conference to discuss the same issue: but only a handful of branches submitted motions for discussions in the pre-war years.[168] Even when the National Federation of Assistant Teachers (NFAT), as the NFCT was then called, agreed in 1912 to get the NUT conference of the following year to resolve the future direction of the union as a trade union, civil service branch, or profession, only one motion to that effect was submitted.[169] Nevertheless, within the Class Teachers' conference socialists prevented policy being adopted on a controlled entry profession[170] on the grounds that teaching would then become a (ruling) class preserve and that working-class people would be excluded from teaching.

There was a willingness, as I have shown, to engage in trade union activity, as exemplified by the West Ham dispute, when resignations were submitted, public meetings organized, and a shop-front office opened.[171] Such activity was seen in London in 1910. In response to growing teacher unemployment and continuing large classes in schools, an unemployed teachers campaign was set up, led by W. Nefydd Roberts, and financed by the NUT. Mass meetings were organized. Platform speakers included H. Elvin of the Clerks Union and George Lansbury, the Labour MP. Offices were hired in Holborn and leaflets were issued.[172] At NUT conference that year policy was passed condemning the indiscriminate manner in which the Board of Education controlled the number of certificated teachers and the serious waste of public money caused by unemployment. It was argued that the Board of Education was flooding the market and that consequently it had an obligation to pay sustentation allowances until teachers were suitably employed. The onus was placed on the Board of Education. An amendment calling on the NUT to issue its own diploma and regulate entrants was dismissed as unrealistic and impractical.[173] As a result of the registration of unemployed teachers many hundreds of teachers were placed to the satisfaction of the London Executive — at least — before the campaign was wound up as a success the following year.[174] But even this question of teacher unemployment was not discussed by the NUT in terms of its own *political* role: the focus was the Board of Education.

The Effects of the Feminists' Politicization of the NUT

The first major indication of a political approach occurs in the debate on parliamentary franchise, particularly from 1911–14. (I will deal at length with the work of the feminist teachers in the next chapter but here focus on the parliamentary franchise.) The specific relation which women teachers had with the state was not the same as that of their male counterparts. By reasons of gender they were barred from other professions and only allowed to stay in teaching if they remained unmarried. In exchange, they were paid less than their male colleagues for the same job — even when, on occasion, they worked in boys' schools. Thus, although the policies of the state had a special effect on their whole lives they were excluded from any — even 'fictive' — influence upon those practices by reason of their disenfranchisement. They were — as the feminists argued — expected to train new generations into citizenship while being barred from the exercise of the same citizenship themselves. It was not just that they adopted a political attitude towards their relationship with the state, but that a different political relationship with the state actually existed, from that of men teachers. This was eloquently stated by the NFWT thus:

> The fact is, we live, move, and have our being by Act of Parliament — *politics* — without having the only lever that will work the political machine. Our codes are framed by parliament; our inspectors are appointed and paid by parliament; parliament controls the size of our classes; it examines us, and grants or withholds our certificates; it can withdraw them too. It decides the amount of our pension, and forces us to contribute to the pension fund, whether we wish it or not; it says when our pension is to be paid, and *when it is not to be paid*; we cannot get a penny of it till we are sixty-five, but if we had an inspector's arduous life, we could draw our pension at sixty. Finally, it provides about half the money of our salaries. But politics are of no concern of the union! (Original emphasis.)[175]

What the feminist teachers brought to the union was a developed *political* consciousness particularly acquired from their campaigns in the WSPU and WFL *outside* teaching. To the NUT they brought their militancy, oratory, and organizational skills acquired from their speaking at street corner demonstrations, canvassing against the government, chalking on pavements and organizing demonstrations.[176]

The NUT included within its aims: 'To secure the effective representation of educational interests in parliament'. It endorsed the candidature of (male) teachers of all political persuasions and provided 5 per cent of election expenses of all endorsed candidates.[177] The feminist teachers were seeking an 'expression of sympathy' on the franchise so that they were not excluded from such an aim: 'That this conference expresses its sympathy with those members of the NUT who desire to possess and exercise the parliamentary franchise, but because they are women, and for that reason alone, are by law debarred from it.'[178]

Although the NUT executive adopted this position it did nothing to campaign for it and declined to present it to conference after 1914 on the grounds of the dissent caused amongst members.[179] Miss Cleghorn, the union's first woman president in 1911, also refused to address any meetings on the topic during her term of office, despite the fact that she had been elected with NFWT support.[180] The women teachers campaigned for associations throughout the country to adopt this position and organized fringe meetings on this at NUT conferences, as did the WSPY, WFL, NUWSS — and the anti-suffragists.[181] First and foremost parliamentary franchise was seen as a political issue which affected women teachers as women, rather than as a professional matter. It was *this* stance that the anti-suffragist reactionaries objected to. In their series of leaflets and speeches the anti-suffragists declined to debate the issue as such and concentrated on arguing against politics — ostensibly irrespective of what those politics actually were — being bought into the union.[182] Even one of the supposed supporters of the suffrage, the Liberal MP, former teacher, and general secretary of the NUT, speaking on the tactics to adopt (at a NUT conference fringe meeting) urged that the issue be treated as a union matter and not as a political question. He defined the question of the franchise as 'personal politics'. By making the franchise a union question, there could be greater parliamentary weight for the NUT.[183]

It is clear that the union was faced with the first national challenge to its own dominant ethos of 'neutrality'. It also served to highlight divisions inside the union. In particular, some male class teachers tried to portray the feminists as pursuing a cause which had no resonance with class teachers. Hostile articles appeared in *Class Teacher* referring to the oppression of men as a class — an argument to be developed in the 1920s by the breakaway National Association of Men Teachers.[184] However, other contributors did support women: the fact that conference had taken up political questions was a precedent they welcomed.[185] In a 1916 by-election for the executive in the East Ham area a series of leaflets was issued by the opposing candidates highlighting divisions in the union: Miss Hewitt, NFWT activist, head-teacher (and Labour supporter) and F. W. S. Gladwin, class teacher and signatory of an anti-suffrage leaflet (though this was not included in his publicity). He was supported by Whitlock, the local BSP teacher.[186]

In London there were acrimonious debates on parliamentary franchise, and subsequently equal pay, in the LTA. Huge meetings were broken up by rowdy men; rules were changed to prevent open discussion and referenda were forced on parliamentary franchise and equal pay with the LTA offices wording ballot papers and writing editorials in *The London Teacher* on their position.[187]

This brief account has been included here to indicate the importance of including the role of feminist teachers in any study of teachers' relations to the state in this period. Its omission *can* suggest that the debates of 1917 were simply a continuation of the earlier debates on trade union affiliation. Further, to omit a study of the role of organized feminists is to give a very partial account of 'politics'. In the year in which the franchise was first debated at NUT conference — 1911 — the year in which Lawn and Ozga describe growing militancy in the NUT — not one motion was discussed on TUC/LP affiliation (nor was it discussed in 1912, 1913, or 1914 when parliamentary franchise also aroused such heated debate).

The Nature of the Debate of TUC/LP Affiliation

In October 1913 the NUT executive debated using £100 of the union funds for the relief of children of striking Dublin transport workers.[188] Supporters referred to the need for trade union solidarity. The opposition argued that the union was non-political.[189] The opposition feared 'politics' as much as trade unionism within the union.

When the 1917 referendum on TUC/LP affiliation took place — a tactic surely adopted in the light of the success it brought to the LTA officers on parliamentary franchise and equal pay — the ensuing debate in *The Schoolmaster* focused both on the extension of educational provision advocated by the Labour Party and upon personal benefits teachers could hope to receive.[190] The call for this discussion arose initially from an unofficial salaries meeting attended by 250 associations who advocated TUC/LP affiliation as a tactic to improve low wages.[191] Some members counterposed that affiliation to the concept of a self-governing profession. However, the trade unionist strategy was not seen by most teachers as incompatible with the union's general strategies of alliances with the local state. Indeed the election of the Labour Party locally — and nationally — would help further this particular strategy.[192]

Nor was Labour Party affiliation necessarily opposed to professionalism. Lawn has seen guild socialism as a radical ideology influencing many teachers.[193] Teachers, such as Johnson, who advocated guild socialism saw this strategy as entirely compatible with the view of teaching as a profession.[194] During this period several teachers were moving towards the Labour Party because of its social policies. One enthusiastic teacher wrote to *The Schoolmaster* saying it was a pleasure to work in the East End. Labour would give 'better housing, higher wages, better sanitation, and the removal of slums, and with these [we] will see the obliteration of that social blot, the school nurse, and a sweetened atmosphere [will come] throughout the school'.[195] However, one of the leading advocates of Labour Party affiliation was Albert Maskelyne of Romford, a self-confessed Conservative, who nevertheless believed his interests as a teacher lay with the Labour Party.[196] It is also *this* period Crook refers to in his meeting with Baldwin, when he travelled around the country deflecting socialism.[197]

The TUC/LP debate took place in a period of general political and economic unrest in the country, but nevertheless the socialists were unsuccessful in their aims.[198] The Rhondda teachers, whom Lawn and Ozga believe were decisive in changing the character of the union, took little part in this debate at this time and appear to have done little to *organize* on the basis of their militant local experiences. Cove and William Harris were elected to the NUT executive for the South Wales area, in the wake of their success. On the executive, Cove argued against Labour Party affiliation and was critical of the feminists, particularly those in London, who continued their campaign for equal pay and opposition to cuts.[199]

Thus far I have explored the teachers' attitudes to the state educational and political strategies and analyzed the union's statist response. While accepting that the union was militant in the pre- and post-war years I have not shared Ozga and Lawn's view that teachers were any threat to the state in this period.[200]

The Effect of Burnham on Teachers' Organization

I now wish to look at the effect of the Burnham award upon teachers and the way in which this new pay structure was to change union organization and strategy. Prior to the introduction — and acceptance — of Burnham, separate salary scales existed in different local authorities. The outcome of pay levels was determined locally through militant action, as in the case of Rhondda, or lobbying and local political pressure. Henceforth a national structure comprised of local education authority representatives and the NUT (no representatives from other unions such as the separate NUWT were recognized) would determine salaries.[201]

There are three aspects to be emphasized. The first is that this partnership with local state representatives, backed up by the authority of the Board of Education, was what the NUT had sought for a number of years. It was also a structure which echoed that of the Whitley Councils which had also been welcomed by the NUT and government alike as providing a forum for the defusing of teacher/employer disputes. The Burnham structure was judged within a few months of its operation to be a success, according to Burnham writing to Fisher: '[It] has already succeeded in creating in the country at large a much clearer atmosphere and better temper, and has largely neutralised, in the province of public life, tendencies which at one time threatened not only to impair the efficiency of that service, but weaken its stabilising role in the critical period of reconstruction.'[202]

Secondly, the 'alliance' with the local education authorities was brought about in *opposition* to a trade unionist position. As I argued earlier, the NUT welcomed a partnership whilst continuing to discuss conditions of service, salaries action and TUC/LP affiliation as complimentary strategies. The Burnham agreement divided these strategies as mutually exclusive. Within the initial agreement it was stated that there would be no 'pressure' for an increase for two years in areas where equivalent scales already existed, for three years where scales were presently less, and four years where local education authorities were 'seriously affected financially'.[203]

Despite speeches from Rhondda delegates, the Burnham Report (to which amendments were not allowed by the NUT executive) was carried overwhelmingly at a special NUT conference, without even a card vote being called.[204] Thus, by the end of 1919 the NUT willingly dropped a strategy of union organization, albeit in local areas, in favour of a national scale achieved by 'negotiation' with local education authorities.

Thirdly, the Burnham salary levels were explicitly counterposed to the NUT policy of equal pay. Even in areas where feminist organization was strong, a national scale, which barred women from achieving more than four-fifths of men's salaries, was operative.[205] Prior to the agreement the NUT had sought to deal with the feminists in London by acceding autonomy in matters of scales of salary while *de facto* abdicating responsibility for implementing equal pay in national deliberations.[206]

A national scale administered by local education authorities and substantially financed by the central exchequer also meant that cuts could be easily effected on a national basis by the reduction of grants.[207] By creating an alliance with the local state the NUT was also in turn brought into a closer financial relationship with the central state. The action taken by the NUT served to cement the relationship with the state at the expense of rejecting any alternative positions of feminists and socialists alike. Within three years it would concede a 5 per cent wage cut, a decision welcomed by local education authorities as a 'public spirited action'.[208]

As a consequence in London in particular, union organization was very weakened. In the LCC there was a drop of nearly 8,000 in NUT membership with feminist and male teachers who were opposed to equal pay leaving the NUT to form respectively the NUWT and NAMT as autonomous unions. The feminists were no longer present at London or national NUT conferences.[209] The NUWT continued its militant opposition to Burnham in the face of NUT denunciations of them as 'foolish feminists'.[210] The NUT, throughout this period, declined to open the equal pay debate in its own ranks. Indeed *The Schoolmaster* defined equal pay as unessential for the 'real question' of pay.[211] The NUWT was also derided for its continued opposition to Burnham and the Geddes cuts; while the NUT welcomed the good humour shown by its members at conference as they voted for a 5 per cent wage cut.[212] However, as will be explained in the next chapter, the NUWT overestimated the willingness of the state to accede to its demands in the post-war period.

Influences outside Teaching on Teachers' Views

At the start of this chapter I indicated the importance of analyzing teachers' relationship to the state on the political and ideological level. The progressive policies of the NUWT and NFWT, unlike those of their male counterparts, had little origin in the debates of the Labour Party or the TUC. Nor can they be reduced to simply emanating from a trade union teacher consciousness. The existence of their political strategies, which I will develop in the next chapter, indicates the need for closer scrutiny of the debates inside the teachers' unions and recognition of the factors *outside* the educational state apparatus which influenced teacher and state strategies alike. Moreover, the starting point of this book in the strategies of the state, has served to indicate the lack of political and ideological autonomy of teachers. Lawn has suggested that the state did not develop policies for education which reflected the relationship between state and society until 1917.[213] This novel idea overlooks the very structures of education, in particular the financial relationship between the central and local state which led to the re-establishment in the Burnham arrangements of an organic relationship incorporating teachers into a statist framework. It also suggests that the state's incorporation of welfare reforms within the parameters of education were somehow unthought out or simply responses to teacher pressure. Teachers did express views in favour of educational reform, which were often similar to those of the Labour Party or TUC, but these were clearly within the framework set out by the state.

In the next chapter the relationship between the state and feminist teachers will be discussed in depth for it indicates how the operation of the educational state apparatus was situated by the state and feminist teachers within a broader perspective.

Notes and References

1 Seifert, *Teachers' Militancy: A History of Teachers' Strikes 1891–1987*, Lewes, Falmer Press, 1987, pp. 15–52.
2 Ozga and Lawn, *Teachers, Professionalism and Class*, Lewes, Falmer Press, 1981; Ozga and Lawn, 'Unequal partners: Teachers under indirect rule', in *British Journal of Sociology*, 7, 2, 1986, pp. 225–37; Martin Lawn, *Servants of the State: The Contested Control of Teaching 1900–1930*, Lewes, Falmer Press, 1987; Martin Lawn and Gerald Grace (Eds), *Teachers: The Culture and Politics of Work*, Lewes, Falmer Press, 1987.
3 Lawn and Grace, *op. cit.*, pp. vii–x.
4 *Ibid.*, pp. vii–viii.
5 Seifert, *op. cit.*, p. 31.
6 Ozga and Lawn (1981), *op. cit.*; A. Tropp, *The Schoolteachers*, London, Heinemann, 1957.
7 Ozga and Lawn (1981), *op. cit.*, p. viii.
8 *Ibid.*, p. 53.
9 Nicos Poulantzas, *State, Power, Socialism*, 1978, as quoted in Ozga and Lawn (1981), *op. cit.*, p. 154.
10 Bob Jessop, *Nicos Poulantzas, Marxist Theory and Political Strategy*, Basingstoke, MacMillan, 1985, pp. 149–90, esp. pp. 174–84; Ellen Meiksins Wood, *The Retreat from Class, a New 'True' Socialism*, London, Verso, 1986, p. 44; Bob Jessop, *Capitalist State*, Oxford, Blackwell, 1982, pp. 153–91, esp. pp. 156, 190; Ralph Milliband, 'State power and class', *New Left Review*, March/April 1983, 138, pp. 57–68; Ralph Milliband, 'Poulantzas and the capitalist state', in *New Left Review*, November/December 1973, 82, pp. 83–92.
11 Wood, *op. cit.*, p. 41.
12 Jessop (1985), *op. cit.*, p. 174.
13 *Ibid.*, p. 188; see Poulantzas, *Political Power and Social Classes*, London, NLB, 1973, pp. 69, 132–7.
14 See n. 9.
15 Lawn (1987), *op. cit.*
16 *Ibid.*, p. 86.
17 See Kean *State Education* (1988), p. 330 for a description of G. D. Bell's politics.
18 Chapter 1, pp. 20–1.
19 Lawn (1987), *op. cit.*, p. 63.
20 *Ibid.*, p. 74.
21 *Ibid.*, p. 161.
22 See Yoxall's comments to the Association of Headmasters (*The Schoolmaster*, 6

January 1909, p. 98). This reference is used by Ozga and Lawn to suggest that teachers opposed administrators' intentions to 'reduce teaching to a state function and teachers to state functionaries' (Ozga and Lawn (1981), *op. cit.*, p. 82). In fact Yoxall's remarks were made in opposition to teachers becoming civil servants and against the refusal of Morant to grant teachers a self-governing council. The NUT was not suggesting, for example, that the state did not fund training, nor that the NUT should control the nature of training. Concurrently the NUT was calling for increased state aid for local education authorities.

23 Ozga and Lawn (1981), *op. cit.*, p. 100.
24 *Ibid.*, p. 79.
25 *Ibid.*, p. 81.
26 Some contemporary NUT members argued that the teachers won because of the nature of the council rather than because of the teachers' campaign. Speaking at a LTA salaries demonstration Bentliff argued: 'If they had an LCC of trade unionists they might be as well off as Rhondda, where the union had secured a major victory' (*The London Teacher*, 30 May 1919, p. 132). Seifert (*op. cit.*, p. 30) also disagrees with Ozga and Lawn's line on the Rhondda strike. For details of the politics of the Rhondda see Stuart Macintyre, *Little Moscows*, Croom Helm, 1980, pp. 23–43; R. Page Arnot, *A History of the South Wales Miners' Federation 1914–1926*, Cymric Fed. Press, 1975; Hywel Francis and David Smith, *op. cit. The Rhondda Socialist/South Wales Worker*, founded in August 1911, often contains articles on educational discussions on Rhondda Council, for example, *Rhondda Socialist*, October 1911, November 1911, January 1912, 16 March 1912, etc. For coverage of miners' interest in education see South Wales Miners' Federation, *The Colliery Workers' Magazine*, 1923 etc., especially the women's page.
27 Ozga and Lawn (1981), *op. cit.*, p. 82; Seifert, *op. cit.*, p. 30.
28 Lawn (1987), *op. cit.*, p. 158.
29 Ozga and Lawn (1981), *op. cit.*, p. 84.
30 *Ibid.*, p. 98.
31 Ozga and Lawn (1986), *op. cit.*
32 *Ibid.*, p. 226. In his latest work Lawn has reverted to the concept of the local state. Lawn (1987), *op. cit.*, p. 159.
33 *Education 1900–1950*, Cmnd 5244, chapter 3, para. 1, HMSO 1950. *Education Act 1902*, HMSO, 1902.
34 See, for example, 'The Cost of Elementary Education: Review of the Board of Education Annual Financial Statement', *The Schoolmaster*, 4 March 1911, p. 450; 'The Cost of Education', *The Schoolmaster*, 20 January 1912, p. 135; 'Six-and-a-half million for London's education' and 'London's unanswerable case for increased state aid for education', *The London Teacher*, 20 February 1914, pp. 147 and 148; 'London's unanswerable case for increased state aid for education', *The London Teacher*, 27 February 1914, p. 172; presidential address of C. W. Hole, *The Schoolmaster*, 17 April 1909, p. 702.
35 Ozga and Lawn (1981), *op. cit.*, p. 118.
36 *Ibid.*, pp. 119–20.
37 Simon (1974) (1), *op. cit.*, pp. 212, 267–8.
38 See n. 118.
39 Ozga and Lawn (1981), *op. cit.*, pp. 85–6. They seem to have been misled by the terms of respect by which John Maclean has been described (see Chapter 2, nn. 83 and 84). See James D. Young, *The Rousing of the Scottish Working Class*, London, Croom Helm, 1979, pp. 117–19, 192.
40 See an account of S. F. Whitlock in Kean, *State Education*, 1988, p. 376.
41 Several ILP members, including H. J. Lowe from Wigan, contributed to the *Class Teacher*. Lowe was author of the ILP pamphlet on socialism for teachers. He argued at the NFACT conference of 1907 (*The Schoolmaster*, 5 October 1902, p.

580) and 1909 (*The Schoolmaster*, 2 October 1909, p. 741) for TUC/LP affiliation and for a strong sustentation fund. G. D. Bell of East London was another ILP member. I will deal with the left politics of the NUT more extensively in Chapter 6.

42 *The Plebs* was first issued in 1909. There is an editorial in issue June 1913, 5, 5, on elementary education. *Plebs*, 8, 10, November 1916, contains an article on 'What Labour Wants from Education', by G. D. Cole (not a teacher), and there is a letter from Cove in the same issue.

43 To cite John Maclean and James Maxton, Scottish teachers, in the context of a study dealing with a union operating exclusively in England and Wales is somewhat inconsistent. To imply that John Maclean, the political writer and orator, was politicized through his paid employment is a novel interpretation. (see n. 39).

44 Lawn (1987), *op. cit.*, p. 9.

45 The TSA was formed in 1907 (*Labour Leader*, 19 April 1907, p. 763, and *Socialism for Teachers*, ILP 'Pass on Pamphlet' no. 20, 1909). The TSA held a meeting at the 1907 NUT conference with Goldstone, future general secretary of the NUT and Labour MP, Hird of Ruskin College and Herbert Burrows, SDF member. Speakers at the 1908 fringe meeting of conference included Mrs Bridges Adams and Dr Haden Guest (*The Schoolmaster*, 18 April 1908, p. 766). The 1911 conference was addressed by Kier Hardie and was so well attended there was an overflow meeting (*The London Teacher*, p. 190). See Chapter 6, nn. 1–6.

46 Ozga and Lawn (1981), *op. cit.*, p. 73.

47 Lawn (1987), *op. cit.*, pp. 139–52.

48 See Chapter 5 for a full account.

49 See Garner, *op. cit.*; Constance Rover, *Women's Suffrage and Party Politics in Britain 1866–1914*, London, Routledge and Kegan Paul, 1967.

50 See nn. 26 and 27; *The Schoolmaster*, 22 March 1919, p. 412; *The Schoolmaster*, 19 April 1919, p. 584; Special Salaries Committee Minutes, NUT, 22 March 1919, 4 April 1919.

51 Ozga and Lawn (1981), *op. cit.*, p. 97. Lawn continues this line in Lawn (1987), *op. cit.*, pp. 56–7.

52 The TLL was not formed until 1923 (TLL newsletter no. 1, 1924). G. D. Bell in a letter to *The Schoolmaster* (17 November 1917, p. 552) says he had formed a Teachers' Labour Group. There are no references to the Rhondda teachers doing likewise.

53 See n. 52 and F. Harrison Bell, 'Teachers for Labour', in *Clarion*, 25 April 1924. The first meeting of the Rhondda Teachers' Labour League did not take place until 21 March 1924 (TLL newsletter no. 1, 1924).

54 *Daily Herald*, 31 December 1924 (by then he was an MP).

55 NUT circular denouncing the women who took the case to court from Yoxall to NUT branches. The NUWT was angry that the NUT would not support them (C8.49, May 1923, NUT archive).

56 Ozga and Lawn (1981), *op. cit.*, p. 99.

57 See James Hinton, *op. cit.*, pp. 119–47; Branson, *op. cit.*, pp. 1–15.

58 See Chapter 1, nn. 47–54.

59 Ozga and Lawn (1986), p. 228.

60 As described in Chapter 1, nn. 63–6. The Labour Party defined itself neither as a class party nor one seeking to challenge the state.

61 PRO: CAB 24/95 CP 329 and CAB 24/98 CP 605.

62 *The Schoolmaster*, 5 January 1923, p. 9; *Annual Conference Report*, NUT, 1918; *Annual Conference Report*, NUT, 1919; *The Schoolmaster*, 28 April 1919, pp. 627ff.; *The Schoolmaster*, 17 November 1922, p. 730.

63 See Chapter 1, n. 85; Chapter 3, nn. 12, 13, 17.

64 'The number of English teachers who are definite communists is very small: seven are known to this department and it is doubtful if there are many more' (PRO: Ed

24/1757: Minute from Special Branch to Home Office and thence to Board of Education 12 September 1925). A memo from the Assistant Commissioner Special Branch to Home Office, thence to Board of Education confirms that the Teachers' Labour League was under observation: 'As far as can be ascertained this body is the left wing of the NUT, which is deeply tainted with socialism. Attempts are being made to form a Communist Minority Group within this organization. Those connected with this movement are under observation' (Ed 24/1757, 18 May 1925).

65 Martin Lawn, 'Deeply tainted with socialism: The activities of the TLL in England and Wales in the 1920s', in *History of Education Review*, 14, 2, 1985, p. 33. Again no details are given.

66 Lawn (1987), *op. cit.*, p. 129. Dan Griffiths wrote a regular column for the *Swansea Labour News* during 1921. He describes the support he received against victimization and his successful reinstatement: 'The overwhelming mass of the people and their schoolboys are absolutely with me. Mothers have already come to the school asking what they can do for my defence, and big strong men with clenched fists and with tears in their eyes have stopped me in the streets to cheer me on my way denouncing the traducers' (*Swansea Labour News*, 12 November 1921; see 3 December 1921 for an account of his reinstatement). Marjorie Pollitt, who taught at St John's Road school in Hoxton, was fined £50 for publishing a strike workers' bulletin. She lost her job with the LCC, despite Mrs Lowe's attempts to refer back her dismissal (minutes of Teaching Sub-Committee, LCC, 23 June 1926, p. 410, and 7 July 1926, p. 465). The Labour Party ACE refused to support her (*Education*, 4 June 1929; *School Government Chronicle*, 10 July 1926; *ACE Minutes*, 15 November 1926). She wrote an article in *Communist Review*, 7, 1, May 1926, on the class struggle in schools. She seems to have taken no further interest in education. Harry Pollitt in *Serving my Time*, (1940, London, Lawrence and Wishart, p. 280) refers to her working as a secretary in an advertising firm. Miss Clarke was a secondary teacher in Birmingham. Her certification was withdrawn. Her case was with the legal department at NUT for a year and she received no sustentation. Eventually she was partially reinstated but as an elementary teacher. She later taught in West London (*Educational Worker*, May 1927, September 1927, etc.).

67 David Capper, 'The British teachers and the General Strike', *Teachers International*, June 1926.

68 Fisher, *An Unfinished Autobiography*, London, Oxford University Press, 1940, pp. 97 and 105; Percy, *Some Memories*, London, Eyre and Spottiswood, 1958, p. 103.

69 Ozga and Lawn (1981), *op. cit.*, p. 146.

70 A view which Lawn seems to accept: Lawn (1987), *op. cit.*, p. 161.

71 As quoted in David Reeder, 'A recurring debate: Education and industry', in *Education and the State*, vol. 1, Dale, Esland, ergusson, MacDonald, (Ed.) Lewes, Falmer Press, p. 182.

72 Reeder, *op. cit.*, p. 183; Percy, *op. cit.*, p. 108.

73 Note by Fisher 'The growth of expenditure on education', PRO: CAB 24/98, CP 605, 10 February 1920.

74 Kean (1981), *op. cit.*, pp. 53–7.

75 'Draft Report on Margate Conference Resolution', ACE, Labour Party, 1927. This was in response to the motion moved by TLL member H. Wheate at the previous year's Labour Party conference (*Annual Report*, Labour Party, 1926, p. 264).

76 'Education and the Empire', in *Empire Review*, 37, June 1923, pp. 581–2.

77 Percy, *op. cit.*, p. 93.

78 *Ibid.*, p. 108.

79 *Ibid.*, p. 103.

80 *Ibid.*

81 *Ibid.*

82 PRO: Ed 24/1758. Letter from A. Somerville of Wimbledon to Percy, 7 February

1926, describing unrest at a local Conservative Teachers' Association meeting. Percy's letter in reply to Herbert Bain, principal Conservative agent, 7 June 1926.
83 Speech to London CTA, 19 May 1927, as printed in *The Times*, 20 May 1927.
84 Editorial, 'Notes of the Week', *The Schoolmaster*, 21 May 1928, p. 808: 'The nation is justly proud of itself; its self control; its moderation; its humour.' Percy had written to teachers thanking them that 'they [had] contributed materially to the stability and orderliness which have so happily characterised the past few days' (*ibid.*). In the same issue, 'London Education' (p. 816) states that in the East End no more than twenty teachers were absent and in no one school were there more than three teachers absent. In appreciation of this sterling work Percy had granted them an extra three days holiday. A week later *The Schoolmaster* (28 May 1926, 'Notes of the week', p. 848) expanded its themes attributing calm in the country to the professionalism of the teachers: 'In the school today teachers pride themselves on the habits of self government which they are inculcating in their pupils; the fact that strike meetings and processions were conducted all over the country without conflict with the police... shows that the self governing instinct is being strongly developed...' ('See also 'London education', *The Schoolmaster*, 28 May 1926, p. 854, which describes prefects organizing prayers when teachers were late during the strike.) David Capper (*op. cit.*) also admits 'the mass of teachers were not drawn into the class struggle during the nine days that the strike lasted'. However, he says sympathy was displayed. The examples he gives are few: some teachers read the *British Worker* in the East End and in one school a teacher attempting to join volunteers was frustrated by another teacher's protest. Such Conservatism was evident even before 1926. In November 1924, for example, Stanley Baldwin was guest of honour at the LTA annual dinner, invited before he had become Prime Minister (Stanley Baldwin, 'Teachers and Taught', speech given at the annual dinner of the LTA, 28 November 1924, in *On England*, Philip Allan and Co., London, 1926, p. 160). Like Percy, Baldwin appealed to the 'common sense' of teachers: 'The primary concern of those who have such a sacred trust as you have is the unfolding of the child's personality, and not the victory of party' (Baldwin, *op. cit.*, p. 165).
85 Speech of Lord Percy to CTA, 19 May 1927, in PRO: Ed 24/1758.
86 Report of reply to a parliamentary question from Sir Basil Peto, *The Times*, 18 February 1927.
87 'Teachers and politics', in *The Times*, 7 January 1927.
88 'Frankly I am afraid that I have very little patience with the whole business of oaths of allegiance... I confess... that I am horrified by your assumption that teachers are to be regarded as state servants... anything more alien to the whole public school tradition of this country cannot be conceived... the best safeguard against such regularities is to give teachers a sense of reasonable independence and not to subordinate them too much either to a central or a local authority' (PRO: Ed/1753, letter to Sir Charles Yate, 25 January 1927).
89 Charles Trevelyan, 'The Broad High Road in Education', Labour Party, 1924.
90 'Draft Report', ACE, *op. cit.*
91 PRO: Ed 24/1736, Memorandum to Selby Bigge, 31 January 1917.
92 *Ibid.*
93 This point was made some years later by Michael Sadler addressing a meeting of the Association of Assistant Masters in Secondary Schools (*Morning Post*, 6 January 1923). Interestingly, an editorial also opposing civil service status for teachers cites the greater cost to taxpayers, and greater influence of the NUT. It does not mention any 'red menace' which the civil service concept would help combat (*Daily Telegraph*, 8 January 1923).
94 The same memorandum (Ed 24/1736) also makes specific reference to London teachers who were opposed to the idea on financial grounds. The state would have

to construct salary scales; teachers would ask for the highest scale presently existing and the treasury would level this down. London teachers would lose out financially. In fact the LTA did attempt to reach agreement with the LCC prior to the acceptance of Burnham partly because they thought any such scale would have a 'prior claim'. See nn. 201–8.

95 PRO: Ed 24/455 1910.

96 Letter to Sir Robert Morant from a Board of Education employee, 27 October 1910, in Ed 24/455.

97 Letter to Sir Robert Morant regarding the demonstration of 29 October 1910 (Ed 24/455).

98 Ed 24/422: 'Teacher Immorality'. The files contain several examples of women who have had illegitimate children and who subsequently have been boycotted for misconduct and punished by having their certification suspended or cancelled. Supplementary teachers in such a position were sacked. It should be remembered that local education authorities (or governing bodies of voluntary schools) retained the power to remove teachers. The Board of Education action was unnecessary in ensuring that teachers were not employed; but it was necessary to maintain notions of acceptable behaviour.

99 Ed 24/1757. This file contains a series of newspaper cuttings on Labour candidates. G. D. Bell, TLL activist, standing in Southwark in 1922, repudiated 'direct action' and had no desire for 'revolutionary upheaval', but nevertheless a *Daily Telegraph* clipping (1 November 1922) was kept on him. The cutting of the same date on G. F. Johnson of Norwich includes handwritten notes ascertaining who he is and where he teaches.

100 Ed 24/1757 includes copies of TLL literature, reports from the Home Office and Special Branch minutes. A note from the Special Branch to the Home Office (forwarded to the Board of Education, 25 February 1927) refers to £12 contributed to the EWI, instead of the £2,500 required by Moscow. It includes accounts of correspondence between the TLL and EWI on the position to be adopted on the Labour Party after its expulsion from the party. I will expand on this in Chapter 6.

101 See n. 64.

102 Simon (2), *op. cit.*, p. 73. Ozga and Lawn (1986), p. 228.

103 *The Schoolmaster*, 20 November 1920, p. 884. This includes an article 'Creating little Communists in schools', on the spread of Bolshevik teaching in Proletarian schools. *The Schoolmaster* urges teachers to write to papers pointing out that these are not elementary schools. That is, the NUT *itself* recognized that the communist threat did not exist *inside* schools. A similar recognition is found in the *Swansea Labour News*, a Labour Party paper. Commenting that the aims of the Seditious Teaching Bill are laudable, an editorial adds: 'We hope they will not have as much trouble as we think they will in finding such schools' (*Swansea Labour News*, 20 May 1922).

104 Ozga and Lawn (1981), *op. cit.*, pp. 87–8.

105 Deputation, 20 November 1923, in PRO: Ed 24/1757. Its first annual report was issued in 1926. It had been set up in February 1924 from a meeting at the central Conservative Party offices (Ed 24/1758).

106 He addressed a meeting of the first AGM of Lancashire and Cheshire Teachers' Circle in February 1927 (*Manchester Guardian*, 28 February 1927, in Ed 24/1758).

107 A leaflet was prepared in August 1928 in the run up to the general election, called 'Education advance: A hundred years retrospect; What the Party has done'. Over half of the positive features recorded are on the nineteenth century. There is one sentence on 1922 and one on 1925. There is a record of a meeting between Percy and the CTA central advisory committee, 14 July 1928. This may suggest that the advisory committee did not exist properly before this as there are no references to an earlier meeting. The honorary secretary was Alderman Sainsbury, the chair was

Miss Faithful (principal of Cheltenham Ladies College). The committee included Miss Conway, NUT executive member and former NUT president and Miss Robinson, Lewisham member and president of the LTA in 1921 (Ed 24/1758).

108 Letter, 17 November 1923, from Crook MP to Capt. Jessel includes the following: 'I was ex-president of the NUT at that time (1917) and spent the greater part of the following year at meetings all over the country in opposition to this movement.' In a deputation to Baldwin (20 November 1923) Jessel expressed alarm at teachers turning away from the Conservatives in 1917 because of the increased cost of living then. This disaffection had continued, he said, because of Geddes cuts, Burnham not being enforced, large class sizes, and the dismissal of married women teachers. In the same file there is a memo from Selby Bigge to Wood dated 20 November 1923 (then President of the Board of Education) on a discussion he had with Baldwin. Baldwin wanted to know why teachers were going over to Labour: 'I said of course they were afraid of a reduction in salaries and they thought that they could get more protection from the Labour Party than from anyone else; but apart from this they were probably influenced by the view that the Conservative Government was reactionary and that the Labour Party was the only one fully committed to the progressive development of education. As he gave me an opening I took the opportunity of telling him that in the enforcement of economies we had really had the devil of a time, and that we felt that it was good policy to relax the pressure where we could' (Ed 24/1757).

109 For example *The Schoolmaster*, 28 December 1912, 'News and comments', p. 1108, argues for equal opportunities on the grounds of the nation's good, while identifying teachers with this aim: 'It will be well for the state when it is generally recognized that the ploughman's son has as much right to develop his natural abilities as has the son of a duke. Society is the loser in not availing itself to the fullest extent of the capacity of all its members.'

110 *The Schoolmaster*, 5 February 1921, 'The Fight for Education', p. 242, example of weekly column devoted to implementing the Fisher Act. Series of articles in *The Schoolmaster*, 1909: for example, 'Notes and Jottings', 30 January, p. 791; 'The Children's Charter', 27 March, p. 543; 'Notes and Jottings', 3 April, p. 592; 'Notes and Jottings', 24 April, p. 754; 'Notes and Jottings', 1 May, p. 794: 'We have always contended that the child who is compelled to attend our elementary school is absolutely entitled to proper nurture, else the expenditure on his mental training will be largely wasted.'

111 Teachers were expected to explain the nature of the Empire. After marching around the playground and saluting the flag, children received a half day holiday. A typical lesson on Empire Day is described by an Infants' teacher in 'A day in an infants' school', *The Schoolmaster*, 31 August, 1907, p. 364. *The Schoolmaster*, 17 August 1912, Editorial 'Empire and the schools', in support of the Imperial Education conference: 'There are some teachers in English schools who jeer at Empire Day — sometimes, perhaps, for party reasons; there are some others who wave the flag too vigorously — perhaps, again, for party reasons... [However], children should be taught the glorious record of the race and of the Empire.'

112 'Are the elementary and special school teachers less patriotic than their colleagues, or is the sense of Empire less keen among the working classes, who supplied the men who fought, bled, and died on the battlefields of South Africa?' (*The London Teacher*, 16 May 1913, Editorial, p. 387.)

113 *The London Teacher*, 16 May 1913. There are two letters critical of Empire Day on the grounds that it was not true patriotism and that a largeness of mind was needed. In the issues of 23 and 30 May there are letters in response, for example: 'I am a flag waver. I love the sight of the Union Jack. I glory in the name of Britain. I wish in my turn to protest against the shameful rubbish which 'A London Teacher' contributed to a recent issue' (*The London Teacher*, 30 May 1913, p. 488). The question of

imperialism was raised by the TLL in the 1920s, but the focus here was upon parental and children's activity. I will discuss this further in Chapter 6.

114 'The Imperial Education Conference decisions', *The Schoolmaster*, 11 and 27 July 1923, p. 132; 'The place of Imperial Studies in education', *The Schoolmaster*, 30 May 1924, p. 992. The LTA committee's report on the British Empire Exhibition does contain teacher criticisms: of the queues and lack of drinking water! (*The London Teacher*, 23 May 1924).

115 Report of the LTA AGM in *The London Teacher*, 20 December 1912, p. 1018. Minutes of London Members Committee, NUT, vol. 2, 23 November 1911. There was opposition to the cadet corps specifically on the grounds that this might lead to pressure on teachers to run them.

116 Lawn, *op. cit.*, p. 9, sees such actions as being of a radical nature: 'Teachers involved themselves with political organisations that fought for these welfare facilities [meals and health provision] — at this time, this had to mean the ILP or SDF or Trades Council groups opposed to ratepayer domination of local councils.'

117 This point is also made by Brian Simon (1), *op. cit.*, p. 212.

118 Ozga and Lawn (1981) p. 71, cite this as occurring in 1908. In fact the 1907 conference (*The Schoolmaster*, 6 April 1907, p. 698) supported a motion on class size of forty, relating this to the size of classrooms and the health of pupils. Further, large classes meant children were 'inadequately prepared for the battle of life'. An addendum was moved by Dakers and Bentliff, of the NUT executive (from Newcastle and London respectively) which was accepted by the mover and seconder: 'To endeavour to secure the co-operation of the Trades Congress, the LRC, the ILP, the Co-operative societies, trades unions and any other organisation interested in the educational welfare of the children, to bring about this urgent reform.' Links with the Co-op were no new phenomenon. The NFAT national committee (*Minutes*, NFAT National Committee, 27 October 1906, NUT archive) agreed, on Steer's recommendations, that the Co-op be asked to run a study session on 'Conditions of Primary Education in England' about the effects of large classes. It was agreed to approach local co-ops and to obtain the names of local teacher 'co-operators'. Delegates were regularly sent from the NUT executive to Co-op conferences. The discussion on class size continued at the 1908 NFCT conference. Bell argued: 'He had now got inside the labour movement and urged teachers to drop their snobbishness and class consciousness and ally themselves with the workers' (*The Schoolmaster*, 3 October 1908, p. 552). The LTA committee, on receipt of a letter from the ILP promoting the physical welfare of children and increased imperial aid, endorsed the ILP position (*The London Teacher*, 1 June 1909, p. 183).

119 *The Schoolmaster*, 22 April 1911, pp. 804ff.

120 *The Schoolmaster*, 13 April 1912, pp. 709ff.; *The Schoolmaster*, 20 April 1912, pp. 764ff.

121 *The Schoolmaster*, 24 October 1921, pp. 446ff.

122 'News and Comments' in *The Schoolmaster*, 28 September 1912, p. 491: 'We deplore the advocacy of a "practical training" which aims at earmarking the children of any class for a particular calling regardless of fitness. To do so is to foster, rather than prevent, "industrial unrest" which is so much deplored.' See article by Steer, 'Whither are we going?', in *Rhondda Socialist*, 17 August 1912. He opposed the craze of motor activity in order to make competent workers. Children should be trained for something higher than manual dexterity.

123 *The Schoolmaster*, 6 October 1906. NFAT conference: Coad of West Ham and Bell of East London moved an amendment in favour of secular education (p. 604). This was largely defeated. The NUT conference of 1906 passed a motion in opposition to creed tests and carried a motion that teachers should not be required to attend Sunday Schools and places of worship (*The Schoolmaster*, 21 April 1906, p. 854). An editorial opposed the TUC decision ('Notes and jottings', *The Schoolmaster*, 14

September 1907, p. 436): 'The resolutions . . . are drastic and unmistakable and imply the banishment of the Bible from our schools . . . "free and secular education" apparently is the accepted solution of the educational question by the workers, and if the supporters of religious teaching are not alert and tactful the workers will have their way . . . ' Candidates stood for election to the NUT executive on platforms of secular education, for example (*The Schoolmaster*, 22 February 1908, p. 379): A. C. Burgess of Cardiff CTA called for complete secular education to avoid 'the religious wrangles'. There were also articles in the *Class Teacher* on this issue, for example January 1907, by H. J. Lowe. The NUT was subsequently involved in disputes with Swansea and West Riding councils who refused to pay the same salaries to teachers in non-provided schools as their counterparts in state school as this would involve subsidizing denominational beliefs. See *The Schoolmaster*, 'Notes and jottings', 23 January 1909, p. 148; 20 March 1909, p. 504; 15 May 1909, 'Notes and jottings', p. 872. The issue still aroused controversy in the 1920s, for example LTA conference (*The London Teacher*, 26 November 1926, p. 410). David Capper moved an amendment to a motion at NFCT conference 1929 calling for the complete removal of all forms of religious education from the curricula of schools which were publicly funded. It was defeated. In his speech, reprinted in *The Teachers' International*, October–December 1929, he also mentions Dan Edwards, South Wales executive member, advocating this position on the executive.

124 A pioneer of this work was the reactionary, anti-suffragist, Mrs Burgwin. See Tropp, *op. cit.*, p. 214, and *The Woman Teacher*, 7 November 1911. NFCT conference 1908 (*The Schoolmaster*, 3 October 1908, p. 551) supported the extension of the Provision of Meals Act funded by the Imperial Exchequer. It also accepted an amendment moved by Crook that it was not a teacher's job to serve meals or to have meals on the premises. *NUT London Members Minutes*, NUT, vol. 2, 21 October 1906, agreed that the feeding of paying children should not be encouraged; that is, feeding should be for the necessitous only (*Minutes*, 7 July 1910). The feeding of children in school halls had been opposed and now the LCC had implemented it the situation was being monitored by the teachers (*London Members Minutes*, 7 July 1910). 'Feeding the schoolchildren', *The Schoolmaster*, 25 June 1910, p. 1171, made it clear that under the PMA legislation no teacher was obliged to serve meals or to collect money. All these caveats were within the following general framework: 'We have always contended that the child who is compelled to attend our elementary schools is absolutely entitled to proper nurture, else the expenditure on his mental training will be largely wasted' (*The Schoolmaster*, 'Notes and jottings, 1 May 1909, p. 794).

125 Bentliff, Labour supporter and president in 1912, addressed conference calling for the need for popular control of schools (*The Schoolmaster*, 13 April 1912, p. 694). Dakers, president in the following year, spoke on 'equality of opportunity, regardless of rank, fortune or social status' and argued 'the interests of the worker's child are our interests' (*The Schoolmaster*, 29 March 1913, pp. 632–42). Kenward, president of the NFCT for 1913, addressed conference on the 'physical fitness of children: the first condition of education' (*The Schoolmaster*, 4 October 1913, p. 602). Powell, president of the NFCT in 1917, called for a 'common school for children of all classes' and 'a broad highway of educational opportunity' (*The Schoolmaster*, 6 October 1917, pp. 356–9 and p. 362).

126 For motions on imperial aid see for example *The Schoolmaster*, 17 April 1910, p. 702; *The Schoolmaster*, 2 April 1910, p. 605; *The Schoolmaster*, 7 January 1911, p. 38; *The Schoolmaster*, 28 December 1912, p. 1126.

127 *The Schoolmaster*, 17 November 1922, 'Union election platform', p. 730: 'The union points out the danger of national physical deterioration; of children being deprived of opportunities for obtaining higher education, and thus the loss of intellectual, industrial and commercial efficiency by the nation; all these at a time when the

present can only be amended by the future and brightened by the full use of the nation's capacities, and by encouraging this in the young.'

128 Women were needed to teach girls because they understood them. The modern line about the identification of girls with women teachers as an incentive for academic achievement was not prevalent (*The Schoolmaster*, 4 January 1908, pp. 11–12).

129 There seems to have been little debate at NUT conference. Perhaps this was because the president prevented debate — see letter from Eleanor Mardon (NFWT member) in *The Schoolmaster*, 8 May 1909, p. 844, saying women had tried to make policy at conference in 1907 and 1908 and had been prevented from doing so. There was strong feeling too against mixed schools. A full report of the discussion on mixed schools and combined departments is found in the report on the women's conference (*The Schoolmaster*, 4 January 1908, pp. 10–14). There NFWT members argued, unsuccessfully, that a man accepting appointment as the head in a girls/infants department should be found guilty of unprofessional etiquette and should be expelled from the union.

130 It was agreed to send a deputation to the Board of Education concerning derogatory comments on the ability and enthusiasm of teachers made by Mr Watkins, HMI for West Ham. Local NUT and CTA branches had already passed motions on this (*London Members minutes*, vol. 2, 30 June 1910). The LTA position of calling for women HMIs to be appointed from elementary schools was endorsed by the Ladies' Committee (*Ladies' Committe minutes*, 5 November 1909). Women HMIs who were appointed had a brief for needlework or domestic training rather than for a particular geographical area. See Hilda Martindale, *Women Servants of the State 1870–1938: A History of Women in the Civil Service*, London, G. A. Unwin, 1938, pp. 36ff. The LTA opposed the appointment of a direct inspector who had no experience at all in elementary schools. This follows on from the LTA AGM decision of 1909 which opposed the appointment of two assistant inspectors who were inexperienced and not Londoners (*The Schoolmaster*, 5 February 1910, p. 216). An editorial of *The London Teacher*, 2 May 1913, 'The unrest in the schools', p. 339, complained about the pressure upon teachers by the administrators: 'Today uniform requirements of the code have been replaced by the multitudinous suggestions of the inspectorate, athwart [sic] all are the drive and grind and hustling of the administrative machine.'

131 See *Hansard*, fifth series, 1911, vol. xxiii, 21 March. The Holmes-Morant circular dated January 1910 complained about the inspectors who were ex-elementary teachers. It went on to criticize elementary teachers: 'as a rule uncultured and imperfectly educated, and many ... if not most of them are creatures of tradition and routine'. These remarks particularly incensed the National Association of Certificated Teachers. These were teachers who were qualified and certificated but had not attended training colleges to obtain their qualifications. They worked within the NUT on a policy of the elimination of distinction between qualified teachers. They campaigned for opposition to the Holmes-Morant circular at NUT conference and succeeded (*Brief History of the Association*, NACT leaflet in NUWT archive). The LTA condemned the circular as it reflected the view of the 'ruling classes' on the way other classes should behave (*The Schoolmaster*, 6 May 1911, p. 934). A protest meeting was held at the Royal Albert Hall jointly with the civil service unions. The protest included opposition to their exclusion from the inspectorate and the promotion of those already there only if educated at public schools and the older universities (*The Schoolmaster*, 2 May 1911, p. 1028). The NUT conference condemned the circular as discrediting teachers and scholars who didn't belong to a certain social class (*The Schoolmaster*, 22 April 1911, p. 314–22).

132 *The Schoolmaster*, Editorial, 17 January 1920, p. 91, 'Whose impudence?'. See also *The Schoolmaster*, 3 May 1913, 'Madame Montessori and existing teachers', p. 902:

'How many teachers has Madame Montessori seen and how many of these were not Italians?' In a memorandum produced by the education committee of the LTA, Walter Sherman notes that Montessori had two trained teachers and a helper for a school of thirty-five pupils: 'The "finest in the world" is so because first of all it is staffed three times as generously as the ideal infants school in the LCC.' It would be impossible for them to adopt such methods given the poor pupil–teacher ratios that existed, he said. Her methods were described as far-fetched and fanciful. Apparatus for distinguishing the difference between hot and cold was scorned: 'This apparatus is to be used by children who have passed through at least two Winters and Summers, who have been fed hundreds of times and bathed and washed many times. By means of "apparatus" they are taught "hot" and "cold" more effectively' ('Madame Montessori and her English disciples', *The London Teacher*, 3 April 1914, pp. 292–3).

133 The substance of Holmes' *What is and What Might Be (op. cit.)* was criticized both because of the abstract nature of his ideas and because of the views the same author had displayed towards teachers in his infamous circular.

134 Some classroom teachers did become enthusiastic. A LCC conference for teachers (*The Schoolmaster*, 11 January 1913, p. 70, and *The Schoolmaster*, 1 February 1913, p. 211) warned teachers to be cautious over 'Montessoriana'. *The Schoolmistress*, 2 March 1911, p. 430, reports a series of LTA meetings on education, full to overflowing, the majority being women. The Montessori system was used to attract teachers to visit Rome on their holidays (*The Schoolmaster*, 23 August 1913, Travel Column, p. 312). The NUWT organized various meetings on progressive educational topics: 'The new methods of the progressive schools of America' (*The Woman Teacher*, 1 October 1926). The London Unit organized an exhibition on individual work and then published 'Individual Teaching Apparatuses and Schemes of Work' (NUWT, 1923). Two leaflets were also written by Miss Coombs on individual teaching with vertical classification and with under-5s. Speaking at the NUWT conference in 1920 Miss Croxson said: 'I have never found that I could get my local association of the NUT to discuss real educational questions' (*The Woman Teacher*, 4 June 1920).

135 'The Dalton Plan', in 'Women's supplement', *The Schoolmaster*, 25 February 1922, p. 314. See Helen Pankhurst, *Education on the Dalton Plan*, London, Bell and Sons, 1922. A variation of the scheme was written for secondary schools by Dr O'Brien Harrison, TLL member in Clapton, *Towards Freedom: The Howard Plan of Individual Timetables*, London, ULP, 1923.

136 Editorial, 'Freudism in schools', *The Schoolmaster*, 24 April 1920, p. 823. An editorial the following year headed 'Anarchy in education', *The Schoolmaster*, 6 August, 1921, p. 191, stated: 'The child is making a bad start at school and with the express connivance of teachers obsessed by Freudian and Montessorian concepts.' See Kean (1981), *op. cit.*, pp. 25–38.

137 'If children can be trained to form these ideas [new ones] correctly by viewing the pictures then we ought to welcome the advent of the cinematograph in to the educational world, but if not . . . the ideas formed are mainly erroneous' ('Children and the cinema', *The London Teacher*, 31 October 1913, p. 834).

138 'Child and the cinema', *The Schoolmaster*, 24 November 1922, p. 786. The general secretary of the NUT joined with other luminaries in signing an open letter which concluded that as a means of popular entertainment and instruction, the cinema constituted 'a grave danger to public morality' (*The Schoolmaster*, 2 August 1913, p. 201). This grave threat was created by the content of the films and their showing in badly ventilated rooms which were not closely supervised by adults. Subsequently the LCC, LTA, Victoria League and National Commission on Public Morals all set up sub-committees to investigate the cinema and its educational role. All bodies expressed concern about the detrimental moral effects upon their children. Teachers

were specifically concerned about the lack of influence in this growing pastime. A 1919 report of the LCC, for example, indicated that 92 per cent of London children went to the cinema more or less frequently and those children who supported the teachers' moralistic attitudes were few (*The Schoolmaster*, 5 July 1919, p. 32). When reports, such as that of the Victoria League in 1919, did suggest how films could be used in schools their emphases were on supplementing the existing school syllabus, rather than altering or replacing it, and on ensuring that the content of the films shown would have a morally correct influence (report from Crook, NUT representative on the Victoria League, *The Schoolmaster*, 13 September 1919, p. 418). They stressed the need to ensure that 'the truth' was maintained and that good moral influences were achieved through the portrayal of noble deeds in the lives of the great men and women ('Film lessons for school children', *The Schoolmaster*, 13 September 1919, p. 418). The interests of the pre-1920s seemed to have waned by 1926 when a LCC report, endorsed by the LTA, stressed that the finance was not available to extend work on the cinema and that the cinema was limited as an educational medium (*The London Teacher*, 12 November 1926, pp. 376 and 384). Even amongst the more adventurous teachers, such as those on strike in Lowestoft who took children to the cinema three afternoons a week to see educational films, there was a standard approach to the nature of the films shown. There was no attempt to refer to the cinema as a form of popular culture or entertainment or to analyze the images produced in an imaginative way. The overwhelming consideration was whether the films portrayed reality and whether they were instructive (*The Schoolmaster*, 21 December 1923, pp. 971 and 975).

139 The NUWT was the only British body to send delegates to the European conference in the Hague on educational films. It wanted the state regulation of films for children. The British Board of Film Censors wasn't such a body, because it was connected with the film trade. Instead they wanted films with wholesome influences (Grace Cottell, 'Films for children', *The Vote*, 4 January 1929, p. 5). See Kean, *Deeds not Words*, (1990), *op. cit.*, Chapter 3.

140 On the suggestion of Miss Bonwick the central committee wanted a deputation to the Board of Education on the teacher training input of sex education to deal with questions arising in teachers' daily work (*Central Committee minutes*, NFWT, 8 December 1917). The NFWT education conference of 1918 passed a resolution in favour of sex hygiene in schools (*Annual Report*, NFWT, 1918). It organized discussion classes on sex hygiene and produced a pamphlet on how to teach the subject in school. Theodora Bonwick, to whose work with the ELFS on sex hygiene I referred in Chapter 2, n. 113, was a leading proponent: 'Long before a child reaches the age of fourteen, much harm has already been done.' See Kean, *Deeds not Words*, *op. cit.*, Chapter 3 for a full description of the life and work of Theodora Bonwick.

141 Editorials at the start of the war indicate their feelings: 'Our place in the firing line' (*The London Teacher*, 4 September 1914, p. 655); 'The nation's rally and ours' (*The London Teacher*, 11 September 1914, p. 671). All NUT associations were affected. In London alone the deaths were as follows: East Lambeth 26, Hackney 27, Finsbury 22, East London 18, West London 18, North West London 14, West Lambeth 27, Westminster 6 (*NUT War Record 1914–1918*, NUT, 1919).

142 'They offered themselves freely . . . they did their duty and the service of education is the richer for their practice and exemplification of those principles of civic duty and patriotism which in times of peace they taught . . . by precept and exhortation' (*NUT War Record, op. cit.*, p. 9).

143 *Ibid.*, p. 10.

144 A conference was called on 30 December 1915 on economies in education. It was mainly attended by educational unions. It agreed unanimously that teachers should be paid no less than the minimum grade to which they belonged as laid down in the

scale of the local education authority (*The Schoolmaster*, 8 January 1916, pp. 34–8). The executive motion to the 1916 conference was: 'While recognising the need for national thrift and agreeing that the full resources of the nation should be available for the purpose of obtaining complete success over the forces of Germany and its allies, conference regards it as vital to the future of the nation that the educational efficiency of the schools should be maintained' (*The Schoolmaster*, 11 March 1916, p. 330). There was an amendment demanding that 'the whole state and municipal expenditure on education should be administered as to secure that the opportunities for education should be equally available for all the children of the nation' (*The Schoolmaster*, 29 April 1916, p. 564). Neither referred to any action, not even a deputation to the Board of Education. See also a motion passed at conference unamimously accepting certain economies during the war but 'the status quo must be restored at the earliest possible moment' (*Annual Report*, NUT, 1916).

145 This was an issue on which the NFWT and NUWT felt strongly. Agnes Dawson supported an unsuccessful amendment at NUT conference 1916 condemning the executive for doing nothing about the employment of unqualified teachers (*The Schoolmaster*, 6 May 1916, p. 600). Subsequently at an LTA conference (*The Schoolmaster*, 13 May 1916, p. 634) Agnes Dawson and Miss A. K. Williams successfully moved a motion saying that further supplementary teachers should only be employed after available certificated teachers had been employed.

146 *Report*, NUT, 1916, p. xxxv.

147 See for example *The Schoolmaster*, 22 April 1916, p. 532, letter from Dan Edwards (no address) regarding conscientious objectors who were imprisoned even though education was on the list of alternative services of national importance. The executive should get the imprisoned members back in the schools. *The Schoolmaster*, 13 May 1916, p. 640, includes a letter from Edgar S. Player (Stoke Newington) saying Mr Ernest Everett of St Helens had been imprisoned for two years hard labour. There were also several letters against this stance.

148 See n. 84.

149 *The London Teacher*, Editorial, 'The triumph of reaction', 21 January 1921, front page.

150 *The Schoolmaster*, 1 February 1924, pp. 1169–72.

151 *The Schoolmaster*, 'Looking ahead', 3 April 1925, p. 607.

152 Throughout this period NUT conference supported increased imperial aid for local education authorities, for example see *The Schoolmaster*, 17 April 1909, pp. 702ff.; presidential address of Jackman and imperial aid motion, *The Schoolmaster*, 2 April 1910, pp. 592ff.; 'Six-and-a-half million for London's education', *The London Teacher*, 20 February 1914, p. 147. An editorial of 1919 ('The new LCC', *The London Teacher*, 7 March 1919, p. 57) said the state should 'recognise the value of their services to the state and *to the safety of the state* and their desire for fair treatment' from the local state. NUT conferences of 1922 and 1924 called for involvement in the administration of the local education authorities ('The Annual Conference', *The Schoolmaster*, 2 May 1924, p. 743).

153 NFCT conference of 1912 agreed that there was 'no wiser expenditure of public money than on education: the children in primary schools, by developing intelligence and building up character and imparting knowledge; it is therefore desirable in the interests of the state and of the localities to obtain the best possible teachers for the schools' (*The Schoolmaster*, 5 October 1912, p. 574). In his presidential address Cove argued that education was a national investment and that the state needed schools to direct individual initiative. Only national capital could finance national business. 'Education is a social service and the school is a social agent' (*The Schoolmaster*, 22 April 1922, pp. 664–8). Underdown in his presidential address in 1917 said that 'efficient men and women are the best permanent capital that the state possesses' (*Report*, NUT, 1917). An editorial, 'London and the budget', in *The*

London Teacher, 26 June 1914, p. 531, argued that education should be two-thirds financed from the state as a national service combined with local control and initiative.

154 *Annual Report*, NUT, 1907, p. lxix. The West Ham Council was condemned for retrospective cuts in the scale of salaries 'all for the sake of saving an amount equivalent to one penny in the pound on the rateable value'. For details of the West Ham case see *Annual Report*, NUT, 1908; *Report of the Tenure Committee* and *The Schoolmaster*, 16 February 1907, p. 304; 16 March 1907, p. 520; 13 April 1907, p. 752; 11 May 1907, p. 920; 18 May 1907, pp. 959–60; 20 April, p. 731; 27 April, p. 827; 4 May, p. 873; 11 May, p. 919 (and photograph of strike office); 25 May, p. 999; 1 June, p. 1035; 8 June, p. 1105; 15 June, p. 1159; 22 June, p. 1209; 27 July, p. 180; 10 August, p. 253; 21 September, p. 466, for the terms of the settlement.

155 'Town Councils as education authorities: Are they a success?' by Cllr. Waddington (and NUT executive), *The Schoolmaster*, 31 August 1907, p. 362. Editorial, 'The Annual Conference', in *The Schoolmaster*, 2 May 1924, p. 743.

156 *Reconstruction Problems 18. Industrial Councils: The Whitley Scheme*, Ministry of Reconstruction, 1919, p. 11. Prior to adopting Burnham as a distinct educational body the NUT engaged in talks with NALGO concerning a public sector triple alliance. See Spoor, *White Collar Union — 60 Years of NALGO*, Heinemann, London, 1967, pp. 68–9.

157 *The Schoolmaster*, 26 April 1919, p. 648.

158 *The Schoolmaster*, 10 April 1920, pp. 726–8. The NFWT also opposed Whitley and favoured advisory committees: 'Women teachers are strong enough in themselves to make a thoroughly self-governing profession. Can we afford to give over all we have won at this moment?' (*Central Committee minutes*, NFWT, 7 June 1919).

159 'The Annual Conference,' *The Schoolmaster*, 2 May 1924, p. 43: 'We have always desired co-operation but too often in the past the desire for co-operation has not existed in administrative quarters. The spirit of suspicion has now gone.'

160 'Teachers in public life', *The London Teacher*, Editorial, 25 October 1912, p. 815. 'We often have evidence of the value of the work performed by teachers elected on public bodies, and without distinction of party, we wish success to all those who are now seeking municipal office.' Teachers were elected to councils in East Ham, West Ham and Hornsey (*Minutes*, London Members Committee, NUT, vol. 2, 1 November 1909). There was an attempt to get teachers to stand for election in educational authorities with NUT backing as a strategy for favouring teachers' interests (*Minutes*, London Members Committee, 29 November 1909). A similar decision was taken regarding Urban District Council elections (*Minutes*, London Members Committee, 14 March 1910). The Middlesex teachers were lobbying prospective candidates on their positions of teacher co-options (*Minutes*, Middlesex subcommittee of London Teachers Committee, vol. 4, 24 February 1913). The Finance and General Purposes committee agreed to 5 per cent of the election expenses of any (male) teacher standing for Parliament, who was a NUT member.

161 The NUWT sent questionnaires to candidates in elections before deciding whether to support them or not. They stressed they were not party political but nevertheless needed a 'politically minded membership'. The members should elect 'men and women of honest purpose and high ideals, whose chief desire is to serve the best interests of the whole community, no matter to what party they belong' (Circular from Ethel Froud, general secretary to parliamentary secretaries, 25 October 1922, in NUWT parliamentary file).

162 *The Schoolmaster*, 11 May 1907, p. 920. The teacher candidate C. W. Truelove got 634 votes which would ordinarily have been sufficient to elect him, but he was beaten by Best with 1023 in Upton ward. In Lowestoft in 1923, Mr F. J. Ratcliffe, 'The Teachers' Leader', stood. The Labour Party candidate withdrew in his favour. He was defeated by 1596 to 1119, the highest vote ever in a municipal election in

Lowestoft (*The Schoolmaster*, 5 May 1923, p. 906, 1 June 1923, p. 946). See *The Schoolmaster*, 4 May, p. 770; 11 May, p. 819; 8 June, p. 1002; 6 July, p. 10, for coverage of demonstrations, parental support and welfare centres run by teachers in their campaign.

163 Tropp, *op. cit.*, pp. 216–17, talks of a militant 'forward movement' taking over the union. The NUT had to 'accustom itself to the new environment of co-operation and partnership'. Ozga and Lawn (1981), *op. cit.*, pp. 3–4.

164 'Executive report', *The Schoolmaster*, 11 October, 1913, pp. 650ff.

165 Todmorden CTA was affiliated to its trades council and Bradford had formed a separate association to do this ('News and comment', *The Schoolmaster*, 12 August 1911, p. 240). Jason Hope was the Trades Council secretary in Carlisle and a member of the Class Teachers Association (letter in *Class Teacher*, November 1903). Southampton was affiliated (*Class Teacher*, November 1903), Swansea CTA had been affiliated since *c*.1900, Cardiff CTA joined the LRC, and Merthyr, Darwen and Blackburn affiliated to the trades council *c*.1900 ('Teachers Associations and Trades Councils', *Class Teacher*, September 1906). Keighley affiliated *c*.1892 (letter to *Class Teacher*, January 1908). Veysey, the secretary of Hackney Collegiate Class Teachers' Association, (CCTA) was the assistant secretary of the trades council. Hackney CCTA had been affiliated since 1910 (*London Class Teacher*, June 1911). Rhondda CTA affiliated in 1913; the *Rhondda Socialist* was pleased that teachers finally recognized that they were workers (*Rhondda Socialist*, 15 March 1913).

166 H. J. Lowe, 'Teachers associations and the Trades Council', *Class Teacher*, September 1906; letter of George Clementson, Carlisle CTA (and trades council) in support, *Class Teacher*, November 1906; H. J. Lowe, 'Teachers and the Labour Party', *Class Teacher*, September 1907; letter from Horner, *Class Teacher*, January 1908; 'The case for trades unionism', *Class Teacher*, July 1908, and September 1908.

167 Motion moved by Bell and Buckley: for – 6120; against – 7389 (*The Schoolmaster*, 5 October 1907, p. 558).

168 *The Schoolmaster*, 8 January 1910, p. 68, Barking: 'That this conference is of the opinion that, as the interests of teachers are intimately bound up with the interests of workers and that as demands for increased educational facilities from that section of the community must inevitably tend to the benefit of the teaching profession, the time has now arrived for considering the advisability of the NUT uniting with the Labour Party in parliament . . . ' *The Schoolmaster*, 9 January 1909, p. 62, motion from Staffordshire North regarding reorganizing the NUT as a trade union; *The Schoolmaster*, 11 January 1908, p. 72, from West Ham on same lines.

169 *Minutes*, NFAT, 21 December 1912. A motion had been moved by Harry Smith at Leyton CTA, and passed at the Annual Conference of the NFAT. But the only motion submitted for NUT conference was the same one from Leyton (*The Schoolmaster*, 28 December 1912, pp. 1122ff.).

170 *The Schoolmaster*, 2 October 1909, p. 741. Previous question was moved by Coad and J. T. Davis (Plymouth). Coad opposed teachers paying for their own training. For him this would have been on a dock labourer's pay.

171 See n. 154.

172 'News and comment', *The Schoolmaster*, 29 October 1914, p. 114; 'Unemployed teachers demonstration', *The Schoolmaster*, 22 October 1910, p. 680; 'News and comment', *The Schoolmaster*, 5 November 1910, pp. 754 and 772; 'London's unemployed teachers', *The Schoolmaster*, 11 March 1911, p. 494; article on the campaign by W. Nefydd Roberts in *London Class Teacher*, February 1911. PRO: Ed 24/455 for reports on the demonstrations of 27 and 29 October. This file contains the pamphlet issued by the unemployed teachers with a photograph of the Holborn office. *Minutes*, London Members Committee, 29 June 1911, vol. 2, NUT: The names of 700 unemployed teachers to work at supply jobs or who had applied for work had been turned down were sent to the education officer (22 October 1910).

An office was opened and financed by the union (6 October 1910). By 15 December 1910 it was reported that practically all the unemployed had obtained supply or permanent jobs. By 25 May 1911 the figures were reduced further.

173 *The Schoolmaster*, 2 April 1910, pp. 592ff.

174 *Minutes*, London Members Committee, NUT, vol. 2, 29 June 1911. The offices were closed and the issue was incorporated into the union's own work. A letter written by F. Jehu, the treasurer of the joint council for ex-students to the Board of Education (14 November 1910) thanking them for the action taken on large classes and asking for their view of the employment of trained teachers at unqualified rates (PRO: Ed 24/455).

175 NFWT leaflet, 'Women's suffrage and the NUT' (n.d.). A similar line is advocated in 'Why the women's suffrage resolution is legitimate NUT business', WTFU (n.d.). See Kean (1990), *op. cit.*, Chapter 2.

176 For an introduction to the work of the WSPU and WFL see Les Garner, *op. cit.*, and Constance Rover, *op. cit.*; A. J. R. (Ed.) *The Suffrage Annual and Women's Who's Who*, Stanley Paul, London, 1913. This includes autobiographical accounts of individuals' suffrage activities, including those of NFWT and WTFU members.

177 See n. 160. Aims as in, for example, *Annual Report*, NUT, 1911, no. v.

178 Motion submitted by seventy-five associations for 1912 conference. See *The Schoolmaster*, 13 April, 1912, for conference discussion, pp. 718ff.

179 *Minutes*, Ladies' Committee, NUT, 21 November 1914. It first agreed to recommend to the executive that it postpone the motion for the 1916 conference. Subsequently it agreed (*Minutes*, Ladies' Committee, 18 November 1916) to submit for 1917 conference: 'Whenever the franchise is again before parliament the claims of women in this matter ought to receive just consideration.' But it agreed (*Minutes*, Ladies Committee, 17 November 1917) not to recommend it for 1918 conference. Although it was not discussed at the 1916 NUT conference there was still a feminist presence campaigning for it (*The Vote* 5 May 1916; 850 copies of *The Vote*, were sold).

180 *The Woman Teacher*, 17 June 1927, p. 280.

181 See, for example, *The London Teacher*, 4 April 1913, p. 244; *The Vote*, 17 April 1914, p. 413; 24 April 1914, pp. 3–4; 5 May 1916, p. 1025.

182 'The attempt to capture the NUT by Women Suffragists', issued by Arthur Gronno; 'Some Facts Concerning the Conference of the NUT and the Women's Suffrage Resolution', issued by Arthur Gronno, 2 April 1914, 'The fourth attempt by suffragists to capture the NUT conference', with various signatures (1914): 'We do not wish to see the NUT changed from an educational body to one divided into political camps. [We should] put it out of the power of the suffragists to wreck our meetings and waste our time . . .' (in NUT archive in unmarked file in tea chest).

183 *Minutes*, Ladies' Committee, NUT, 20 May 1911. There is a lengthy verbatim report of speeches at NUT fringe meetings attended by 400 members.

184 R. H. Roberts, 'Women's suffrage and equal pay', *London Class Teacher*, December 1912: 'No sensible person will deny that men as a class have more responsiblities than women as a class . . . nature has given him his ability.'

185 William Hurden, 'Women's suffrage and equal pay', *London Class Teacher*, December 1912; 'Impression of conference by a delegate', *London Class Teacher*, June 1911.

186 Hewitt's leaflet quotes the *Class Teacher*'s leaflet: 'Your choice lies between West Ham Class Teacher and East Ham Head Teacher.' She refers to the fact that there is already one class teacher on the executive for the area, Harry Smith (a suffrage supporter and socialist from Leyton, who'd signed up during the war). Altogether, they issued three leaflets each. Gladwin was elected (leaflets in NUWT archive, unmarked file).

187 WTFU pamphlet 1, 'The Referendum'; WTFU leaflet on plebiscite; WTFU

Women's Suffrage and the LTA; *The London Teacher*, 28 June 1912, p. 544; 20 September 1912, p. 699; 29 November 1912, p. 952; 20 December 1912, pp. 1022–4; 31 January 1913, pp. 90–91; 7 February 1913, p. 101; *The Schoolmaster*, 1 February 1913, p. 204; 8 February 1913, p. 258, etc.

188 The campaign was set up by women in the labour movement. See Dora Montefiore, *From a Victorian to a Modern*, London, E. Archer, 1927, pp. 156–9; Margaret Blunden, *The Countess of Warwick*, London, Cassell, 1967, pp. 228–35; Emmeline Pethwick-Lawrence, *My Part in a Changing World*, London, Victor Gollancz, 1938, pp. 300–301.

189 *The Schoolmaster*, 11 October 1913, pp. 630–1. Rather than use the union funds as such, £100 was sent from the reserve fund to be replaced when the collections came in from the schools. The executive launched the campaign and in weeks after *The Schoolmaster* printed lists of schools donating. There were also series of letters for and against the collections.

190 For examples of different arguments in favour of Labour Party affiliation see: *The Schoolmaster*, 10 February 1917, p. 172. In a deputation to the executive from the organizing conference, Tasker, president of the London CTA, chair of the LTA finance committee (and future member of the London Schoolmasters' Association) referred to the elementary schools as 'simply class schools ... being the schools for the workers' child. Unfortunately, the control of education was in the hands of the upper classes.' *The Schoolmaster*, 21 April 1917, p. 498, G. D. Bell spoke at NUT conference for affiliation on the Labour Party's record on child welfare.

191 *The Schoolmaster*, 10 February 1917, p. 170.

192 The executive counterposed the two concepts on the ballot paper (report of *ad hoc* committee, *The Schoolmaster*, 15 September 1917, pp. 265ff.) and later (*The Schoolmaster*, 8 April 1921, p. 691) an editorial argued that political affiliation and self-governing professions were incompatible.

193 Again no references are given in Ozga and Lawn (1986), p. 229.

194 Letter from G. F. Johnson (*The Schoolmaster*, 19 January 1918, p. 88). Labour Party affiliation, according to guild socialists, meant a self-governing profession.

195 For example, *The Schoolmaster*, 23 March 1918, letter from John Megins.

196 Letter in *The Schoolmaster*, 22 December 1917, p. 208. Also letter from Bell, *The Schoolmaster*, 11 November 1917, p. 532, referring to Maskelyne as a lifelong Conservative.

197 See n. 108. Meanwhile in his own association, Tottenham, Crook was less popular. In a letter from Miss Sims, NFWT, to Ethel Froud, 23 September 1917 (letters A–M, 1917, in NUWT archive, in unnumbered file) she says: 'He is getting badly out of favour with our men I fear and this is his association.' A later (undated) letter says: 'On Tuesday as you see Mr Crooks comes to his home association and I think he will get a warm reception. The women will not vote for him on the executive — that I feel sure about.' (This latter point refers to his position on equal pay and the War Aid fund.)

198 *The Schoolmaster*, 6 April 1918, p. 438: for – 15, 434; against – 29, 743. The ballot paper linked TUC affiliation with Labour Party affiliation.

199 Executive discussion on TUC affiliation, *The Schoolmaster*, 10 July 1920, pp. 57–9. Cove said: 'If he thought this step bound them to the Labour Party he would vote against it ...' On election to the vice-presidency (*The Schoolmaster*, 2 April 1921, p. 636) Cove argued that his election gave him the 'complete and effective answer to the secessionists'. See Betty Vernon, *Ellen Wilkinson*, London, Croom Helm, 1982, pp. 219–21, for another, unsympathetic reading of Cove's radicalism. William Harris, secretary of the local trades council, died the following year. See *The Schoolmaster*, 20 September 1919, p. 462, for his obituary.

200 Ozga and Lawn (1981), p. 118.

201 *Board of Education Report of the Standing Joint Committee on a Provisional Minimum Scale of Salaries for Teachers, etc.*, Cmnd 443, HMSO, 1919. Out of twenty-two teacher representatives, only two were women: Florence Dunn and Evelyn Phillips. The NUWT protested against their own exclusion as well as at the findings of the report. They held a special conference to protest against the report (*The Woman Teacher*, 9 January 1920). They also protested to the Board of Education from the inauguration of the Burnham inquiry (PRO: Ed 24/1783) and forwarded the Board of Education a motion from their county hall meeting (*The Woman Teacher*, 24 October 1919, pp. 7–38).

202 As printed in *Report of the Standing Joint Committee on the Standard Scales for Teachers, etc.*, Board of Education, HMSO, 1920. Letter dated 13 October 1920. For debates on Whitley see *The Schoolmaster*, 10 April 1920, and 26 April 1919, pp. 627ff. Also *Reconstruction Problems 18, op. cit.*, pp. 726–8.

203 Cmnd. 443, *op. cit.*, para. 15. This was extended in 1920. Board of Education, 1920, *op. cit.*, para. 24.

204 *The Schoolmaster*, 3 January 1920, pp. 8ff. Cove, H. J. Ridley and William Nicholas spoke against the removal of the right to strike.

205 Cmnd. 443, *op. cit.*, para. 2. For example: Certificated master two years college trained: Min. £160. max. £300. Certificated mistress two years college trained: Min. £150, max. £240.

206 This was carried in a national referendum by 35,004 votes to 15,039 (*Minutes*, Special Salaries Committee, NUT, 26 July 1919). The committee agreed to take no part in enforcing the then agreed national scale. In response to a complaint from Miss Ellis of Newcastle that it was 'illegal' to put forward differentials locally and that it should be the union scale, the committee said that differentials should be reduced (not eradicated). This was reaffirmed by the executive (*Minutes*, Special Salaries Committee, NUT, 20 September 1919). Prior to the Cheltenham conference ratifying the equal pay referendum the LTA had rejected equal pay in a referendum counterposing it as a paper policy to an already negotiated agreement with the LCC before the NUT conference decision had taken place: 'A bitter struggle', *The London Teacher*, 30 August 1918 (front page), LTA account of NFWT action; *The London Teacher*, 23 August 1918, p. 237; 'A salaries homilectic', *The London Teacher*, 26 April 1918, p. 49; and 'Equal pay', *The London Teacher*, 2 May 1919, p. 105.

207 PRO: Ed 24/1783. Correspondence between Major Hills (a supporter of the NUWT) and Fisher on equal pay. Hills accused Fisher (22 July 1921) of letting down teachers. Fisher replied that the government did not pay salaries, but the local education authorities did. If a local education authority agreed to pay equal pay the Board of Education would only pay three-fifths of the *Burnham* rates, not of any sum agreed locally. Hills argued: 'What teachers want is to put before you their right for freedom to negotiate with the local education authorities, a freedom which the present action of the government denies.'

208 *Report of the Board of Education 1922–23*, Cmnd. 2179, para. 129, p. 67, HMSO, 1924. Local authority representatives at Burnham, 5 January 1923: (p. 67, para. 129).

209 'London education', *The Schoolmaster*, 17 April 1920, p. 769. No woman spoke at the NUT conference from London. There was one less executive seat for London members because of the numbers. The LTA AGM reported the decline (*The London Teacher*, 30 January 1920, p. 23). Although Lawn has recently made an attempt to recognize that feminists organized inside the NUT, he fails to understand the nature of the splits that occurred and when they took place. Thus he fails to highlight (Lawn (1987), p. 139) the fact that Miss Conway's comments on endowment of motherhood were *opposed* by the feminists and takes at face value (Lawn (1987), p.

143) Goldstone's assertion that large numbers of women attended the NUT conference in Cheltenham when there was, in fact, a large decline due to the absence of the NFWT feminists (*The Schoolmaster*, 3 May 1919, p. 698).

210 Editorial, *The Schoolmaster*, 14 February 1920, p. 295; Editorial, *The Schoolmaster*, 18 December 1920, p. 1063.

211 Editorial, 'The London scale', *The Schoolmaster*, 15 May 1920, p. 363. Women would not get equal pay until there was a family endowment. This view was also expressed by Miss Conway, 'The Burnham Award from a woman's point of view', in *The London Teacher*, 8 February 1925, p. 166, and she said that women should not leave the NUT. The Ladies' Committee reaffirmed Burnham (*Minutes*, Ladies' Committee, NUT, 16 February 1923).

212 *The Schoolmaster*, 5 January 1923, p. 6 (Editorial on the special conference): 'In nearly every respect a model conference . . . [The seceders have] drawn off ill humours from the union body politic.' *The London Teacher*, 3 April 1925, p. 113, recognized that women were worse hit than men by the cuts in increments but added: 'We are sure London teachers will take a broad and reasonable view of the award.'(!)

213 Lawn (1987), *op. cit.*, p. 213.

Chapter 5

Feminist Teachers' Views on the State

If the relationship between the NUT and the central state in this period has been given scant attention, the role of organized feminist teachers has been almost ignored. In some respects this is surprising, for the feminist teachers had a significant effect upon debates inside the NUT in the period immediately before the First World War. They continued their opposition to the state's sexist practices inside and outside the educational state apparatus with a fierce tenacity of purpose which they celebrated in their own publications.

However their feminism, as opposed to their other progressive policies, has served to isolate them from the concerns of educational historians. Although Tropp describes the feminists' activities as a 'success' in that women teachers gained influence,[1] he fails to describe in any depth their perspectives and strategies. Their activities have been ignored by Simon and dealt with by Ozga and Lawn as those of a pressure group which can be traced to factors *inside* the NUT.[2]

The treatment that the NUWT has received more recently at the hands of feminist historians has tended to be conceived primarily in response to this absence within the discourse. That is, detailed attention has been given to the specific arguments developed by the feminists, especially when they were organized independently of the NUT; but analysis of the particular relationship between women teachers and the state has received less consideration.[3] As I shall argue in this chapter, the particular attitudes the NFWT/NUWT developed towards the state and education — and towards the NUT — were formed by its members' politicization. This occurred both as a result of their particular economic and political relationship with the state as women teachers, but also as a result of their politicization as feminists outside the NUT.

My study of the role of feminist teachers in this period will look at their particular relationship with the NUT. I do not do this simply because the NUT was the union to which the majority of unionized elementary teachers belonged or because the feminists worked within the NUT with varying degrees of enthusiasm for most of this period. To ignore this relationship with the NUT, before the feminists split to form the National Union of Women Teachers, is to suggest an organizational strength commensurate with their commitment, as they put it, to 'the cause'. Such an argument would overestimate their influence and is one I reject. As a consequence of this, I will pay little attention to *The Story of the NUWT*, written by one of the last activists, Miss Pierotti, in the 1960s.[4] While this labour of love sums up the enthusiasm and commitment of feminist teachers who saw themselves dedicating their lives to the cause of feminism it does little to provide us with a sober assessment of the political and organizational weakness the NFWT — and NUWT — suffered.

What was the Relationship between Women Teachers and the State?

As stated in the previous chapter, the specific relationship which women teachers had with the state was not the same as that of their male counterparts. Women had few opportunities to enter other professions in the first few years of the century. As a delegate eloquently explained to the 1911 NFAT conference this meant that many women resented the fact that they were teachers.[5]

Other feminists, including those active in the NUWT, spent much time and energy acquiring additional qualifications in the hope of being successful in other careers.[6] Further, women were generally only allowed to stay in teaching as long as they remained unmarried. Thus women teachers' personal liberty was severely curtailed.[7] As I shall explain later it was not necessarily the case that women teachers *wished* to marry but that irrespective of their choice the state was encroaching upon their personal lives outside their paid employment. In fact, as Mrs Ridge, one of the London NFWT members, argued, the marriage bar would not necessarily lead to more teacher vacancies.[8] Even when married women were not barred from teaching they were excluded from being considered for positions within the local inspectorate.[9]

Women teachers, of whatever grade, were paid less than their male counterparts. This proved particularly frustrating to older women at the top of salary grades who could see younger — and less experienced — men earning more money than them: 'Why should capable women teachers be compelled in many cases to serve under semi-capable headmasters, to work twice as hard and receive half their pay and, almost as galling, receive less pay than assistant masters of the same grade?'[10] Women were also more likely than men to be paid as supplementary teachers, that is as unqualified poorly paid 'helpers'.[11] However, such women were excluded from membership of the NUT and NFWT/NUWT alike. The NFWT was vigorous in its opposition to the introduction of additional 'teachers' of this type, 'guinea girls', which the LCC tried to employ during the war.[12]

Older women were also particularly affected by the state's refusal to grant early optional retirement, for they were more likely than their male counterparts to suffer mental or physical breakdown.[13] Although several leading members of the NFWT were headteachers, most, like their counterparts in the NUT, were classroom teachers, mainly in elementary schools and often in inner city areas. Like their colleagues they complained about their difficult job:

> We desire strongly to combat the idea that teaching in the primary schools is easy work, to be performed as a 'pocket money' task by an educated or partially educated person. On the contrary, it is exhausting both to mind and body, although the hours of actual teaching are comparatively few. It is, moreover, frequently carried on in the cities, amid the most disheartening conditions of dirt, poverty and disease, and in the country in almost complete isolation from social and educational advantages . . . [14]

In addition to the sexism operated by the state in their working lives, all women teachers, irrespective of their qualifications or status were barred by reasons of their gender from the vote. They were thence excluded from any direct influence, however 'fictive', to refer again to Perry Anderson's comment in Chapter 1, upon the parliamentary processes which would deliberate the conditions under which their paid employment was to take place. These circumstances materially affected all women teachers. As will emerge through a discussion of the feminists' politics in this chapter, what divided the members of the NFWT from the women of the NUT, who were not members, was their conscious feminism and the way in which they organized around that feminism inside and outside the NUT.

Similarities to, and Differences from, the NUT in Respect of Strategies for State Education

In the last chapter I argued that teachers accepted the framework for educational debates which were provided by the state. Teachers' *differences* with the state were not determined by sharp ideological questions but by the specific classroom tasks they were required to undertake. Although the feminists supported the progressive measures of the NUT and labour movement in respect of the raising of the school leaving age or increased welfare provision,[15] their views on general education policy differed from the NUT in three important respects. First, the feminists attached great importance to the discussion of curriculum issues and the *structure* of educational provision. This was not so much because they were more 'professional', but because the structure of educational provision had a direct affect upon their own pay and working conditions. That is, their concern was based, in part at least, upon their objective location within the education service. Because of this, the NFWT took a keen interest in the question of mixed schools and combined departments. From the earliest publications of the Equal Pay League it is clear that the feminists favoured separate departments.[16] Such a system ensured that women were not deprived of the possibilities of promotion up to and including that of a headship of a girls' department in an elementary school.[17] However, it also ensured that girls were taught by women and were not placed in the position of having to compete against boys who had more opportunity to study given the domestic duties with which girls were encumbranced.[18]

The corollary of this position — which the feminists did not dispute — was that boys should be taught by men teachers.[19] The NUT adopted the view that in the few areas where boys were taught by women, the teachers should obtain equal pay. This was strongly opposed by the Equal Pay League: it suggested both that it was more valuable a task teaching boys and that women could not obtain fair wages without competing with men.[20] By the 1920s this position of the NUT was cited as an example of why women should not join the NUT. By arguing for partial equal pay on the grounds of *who was taught*, the NUT was encouraging the view that the education of girls was inferior to that of boys.[21]

The second way in which the NFWT differed from the NUT in its response to the state's educational policy depended upon the feminist consciousness women teachers brought into the classroom. The role and content of girls' education within the curriculum was the focus for much debate. The feminists questioned the state's educational practices when they militated against girls' progress. This was particularly noticeable in the attention they gave to the teaching of domestic subjects and to the education of very young children, which was still considered by the state to be the remit of mothers.

There was not a homogeneity of opinion on such issues amongst women teachers. Miss Cleghorn, a Conservative, who only nominally supported the NFWT,[22] was scornful of educational thinking which would have working-class girls learning how to make hydrogen rather than how to scrub floors.[23] Even other, feminist, teachers also supported the view that since a majority of girls in their care would become mothers then they should be taught housecraft skills.[24] However, in common with the current of opinion inside the National Union of Women's Suffrage Societies (NUWSS), which was hostile to domestic training,[25] and the views of working-class socialist women as expressed, for example, in the *Rhondda Socialist*,[26] several NFWT members advocated removing domestic training to the last few years of a girl's elementary education.[27] Some went as far as suggesting that boys be taught fathercraft in line with the new thinking on 'sex equality' which was apparently indicated by the campaign for the parliamentary franchise.[28] It was not that any feminist teacher was advocating the entire removal of domestic training from the school but rather that a feminist perspective was brought to bear upon this area of the curriculum.

There was also a feminist response to nursery education and to the age of admission of young children to infants' classes. As a debate at the 1908 NUT women's conference indicated, NFWT members were conscious of the effect that exclusion from school had upon the mothers of small children.[29] They were also keen to reject the view advocated by the Labour Party, as expressed by Tawney, that nursery education was only for the children of the most deprived and negligent of parents.[30] Rather, as Agnes Dawson argued, nursery education should be available for all who desired it.[31] It was not just that they identified with mothers out of feminist concern. By placing an emphasis upon the need for fully qualified staff they were also hoping to raise the status of women teachers who formed the entire staffs of the nursery and infants schools.[32]

The third difference the feminists had with the NUT in respect of broad education policy was in their attitude towards the Progressives. In the last chapter I referred to the hostility to the work of Holmes and Montessori. The NFWT, however, saw in Montessori's educational philosophy the 'spirit of freedom'[33] which was embodied in their own feminism. Far from viewing her work as an intrusion upon their classroom expertise they welcomed her emphasis on independent learning, which found a resonance with their own practice of self education.[34]

These three different ways of seeing educational practices were linked by the feminists' own perspective on the role of education in facilitating social change. I mentioned at the start of this chapter their desire to obtain more qualifications and hence alter their own position in society. But the desire for education was also interpreted more widely than this. In Chapter 2 I explained how many socialists held the view that knowledge *per se* would lead to a change in society and the arrival of socialism. The feminists took the view that education of the right sort would assist women and girl pupils attaining equality in society. It was for such reasons, rather than an abstract professionalism, that they prided themselves in their interest in education. They tackled reactionary attitudes to girls' education,[35] and promoted particular subjects, such as PE, in the interests of girls.[36]

The Specifically Political Aspects of their Curricular Concerns

The feminists' political experiences outside the educational state apparatus also directly influenced their attitude to what education should be given in schools. The NFWT and NUWT worked closely with the umbrella group the British Council for Social Hygiene, and in particular with the Association for Moral and Social Hygiene (AMSH). Like the feminist teachers the AMSH was in favour of equal rights. Specifically it sought to secure 'equal standards for morality for men and women . . . It [aimed to] oppose and seek to overthrow all forms of official recognition and commercial exploitation of vice . . . to encourage the highest public and private morality.'[37]

Accordingly, the NFWT argued that instruction in sex education and moral standards of behaviour for girls and boys should be given in schools. It issued a pamphlet of lesson materials for teachers.[38] However, the NFWT was unable to win the support of the Board of Education (or the NUT) for its positions,[39] even though it had evidence that parents wanted such instruction given in schools, as evidenced by the response to Theodora Bonwick when she broached the topic with parents:

> She became aware of the futility of leaving all the gaining of the knowledge of sex to chance, so she called a meeting of the parents in which she discussed with them the danger of ignorance and the possibility of the facts either being given by parents or by teachers. The parents with no uncertain voice, begged her to take on the work and for a period she did so . . . but the Education Authority decided against this method of imparting knowledge regarding the facts of life, and forbade it to be used in schools.[40]

On the suggestion of Miss Bonwick the NFWT sent a deputation to the Board of Education to advocate that sex instruction be provided in the teacher training syllabus to enable teachers to deal with questions arising in their daily work.[41] They organized their own classes to discuss the topic and continued to pass conference motions in support of their position.[42]

Such activities were specifically directed towards the state. It was the state, they argued, which had the responsibility for the education of children in moral matters. It was not that they were arguing that the state had no part in the 'private' life of individuals, but rather that it had a responsibility, which it was not fulfilling, to encourage a particular moral standard.

The NFWT adopted a similar attitude towards the cinema. It expressed concern about the physical and mental well-being of children in cinemas. Its central committee deplored the character of many films passed for exhibition to children. Children under 14, they argued, should not be admitted to a cinema after 6 p.m. because of the unhealthy atmosphere. There should be 'children only' areas made safe through women patrols: 'All plays [sic] suggestive of criminal or immoral actions, and scenes of a coarse and terrifying nature should be excluded.'[43] It called upon the state to regulate films for children to ensure that such films were of 'wholesome influences'. The British Board of Film Censors could not be relied upon since it was connected with the film trade.[44]

Attitudes to the State

Earlier I argued that the NUT viewed the role of the state as a positive force for good. A similar view was reflected by the NFWT in its demands that the state act as a moral force for the good. Here it was calling for an extension of the state's *ideological* activities into the arena of morality. Despite their own exclusion from the state as women, in the period before 1918, nevertheless they demanded the extension of state powers. In some ways women teachers, as state employees, were in an anomalous position. On the one hand they were worse paid than their male colleagues, yet better qualified than other women workers. The function they provided in relation to state education was the same as that of their male colleagues but their treatment at the hands of the state was different. It was not that they were the same as other women workers but that their position as women performing a function within the state was treated differently to that performed by men.

In advocating the NFWT's demand for equal pay at the NFAT conference of 1911 Miss Wood noted that women teachers formed the aristocracy of women workers because of their relatively better wages.[45] Yet despite their often excellent qualifications,[46] the crowding of women into one profession resulted in lower pay levels.[47] This situation was exacerbated during the war when there was an increase in the numbers of women teachers employed to replace the 17,500 men teachers in the war.[48] Although women were fulfilling a state service, they were excluded from wartime regulations that provided some hope of increased pay to women workers employed by the state, for example, in the munitions industry.[49] This is not to argue that such regulations *did* benefit women but rather that women teachers were excluded from a state 'provision'.[50] By the end of the war, however, women were leaving teaching at the prospect of better paid jobs, despite their particular qualifications.[51]

The effect of this objective financial and political position coupled with their position as feminists led the NFWT to place much emphasis upon the state in altering their position in society. This position is well summarized by Miss Byett in her presidential address to the NFWT conference of 1918: '[As] members of a democratic state, women must claim for themselves equal opportunities of service, and to that end they must have equal opportunities of training, equal advantages of education.'[52] She then argued that equal pay was needed not just because women teachers were a 'sweated group of workers' but because the work they did training girls, was as important as training boys. In describing the work of the NFWT to date she said: 'Our association together in the Federation has aroused in us not merely a keener consciousness of ourselves as a distinct body in the state, but also a keener vision of our work in relation to the state.'[53]

This consciousness of the particular role of women in relation to the state was elaborated in their explanation of their own 'civic consciousness'.[54] They believed that because they were denied full citizenship, as voters, yet were nevertheless employed to teach the state's future citizens, they were more conscious of their own role as citizens and of that which would be played by the girls they taught. Their 'citizen spirit' was expressed in this willingness to stand for positions in local authorities. I have already explained that the NUT attached great importance to the election of teachers to local education authorities, irrespective of the particular political positions of teacher candidates. The NUWT/NFWT did not demonstrate so much confidence in the abilities of teachers *per se* to advocate their views. They gave no automatic support to teachers standing for election in the NUT,[55] nor to any candidate — male or female — in a municipal or parliamentary election. All candidates were circulated with questionnaires ascertaining their present and past positions and actions on matters of importance to women teachers before it was decided to offer support.[56]

Several NUWT members stood for election, sometimes successfully, to local councils: Miss Fannie Thomas, NFWT president elected on an explicitly suffrage platform in 1912, was returned in 1919 in Pontycymmer. Her platform made a particular appeal to working-class women and called for their involvement in discussions on the design of future council housing.[57] Miss Kenyon was elected in Oldham achieving the position of mayor by the 1960s.[58] In London Ethel Froud, the NUWT general secretary, stood unsuccessfully on a Labour platform for St Pancras Council in 1925.[59] In the same year Agnes Dawson, a former NUWT president, relinquished her position as a headteacher of an infants school and became a Labour member for the LCC area of Camberwell, with the financial backing of the NUWT. Although her particular platform made no reference to the position of women teachers it did discuss the need for extended educational provision for working-class children and for improved health and welfare provision in working-class areas. Nevertheless there was NUWT support for her education and she herself on election regarded her role there as carrying out 'the cause', a commonly held view in the NUWT.[60] Feminist teachers elected as councillors were not seen as representatives of teachers but as representatives of the feminist cause. The NFWT/NUWT, keen to ensure that a woman's perspective was evident in local councils, campaigned for equality of representation between men and women on the committees of councils.[61]

After the partial extension of the parliamentary franchise to women over 30 in 1918, the NFWT immediately urged all members to register and set about trying to stand several feminist candidates in support of the NFWT's positions. Here the broad nature of the central council's politics was to make the backing of candidates difficult. Miss Bathurst expressed herself willing to stand in support of the women teachers on an independent platform, which created dissent amongst members unsympathetic to her position on Ireland, and finally declined to put herself forward.[62] Miss Phipps, the secondary headteacher from Swansea, stood as the sole NUWT candidate on an independent platform against Sir Samuel Hoare in Chelsea where she obtained a credible vote.[63] The NUWT made links with supporters on local councils such as Mrs Lamartine Yates, or with sympathetic MPs such as Major Hills who was to prove invaluable in their lobbying for equal pay and representation on Burnham.[64]

In addition to working with sympathetic MPs and councillors the women teachers saw Parliament as a focus for their own actions. It was to Parliament that they addressed their 100,000 signatures on a petition against the Geddes cuts and it was to Parliament as well as the Board of Education that they addressed their demands for equality.[65] For the feminists Parliament was the embodiment of the state and although they were employed by the state as represented in the Board of Education it was to Parliament they looked for the achievement of their own demands and those of women outside the educational state apparatus.

In the first decades of this century the NUT was the only union representing qualified elementary teachers. The overwhelming majority of NFWT members — on their own admittance — were members of the NUT and, in London, of the LTA.[66] But in the first few years of this century few of the feminists took any active part in the work of the NUT. The first annual report of the Equal Pay League, the NFWT's predecessor, listed the national membership by name. It totalled less than fifty.[67] Yet the women who joined the NFWT and who campaigned vigorously for the NUT to support the franchise and equal pay were not young teachers new to the profession. Leading members of the NFWT, such as Miss Byett, Miss Phipps, and Miss Agnes Dawson were all teachers before the turn of the century.[68] I have argued that the NFWT and NUWT had trust in the state to be responsible for education even though it denied the existence of women for electoral purposes. It was this same confidence in the state which led the feminists in the first years of the century to rely on the state to give them equal rights with men. When they realized that their demands for equal pay and the parliamentary franchise were unlikely to be acceded to without a strong campaign, then they decided to start working within the NUT in a vigorous way. Reflecting on their actions many years later, Nancy Lightman, a class teacher in Hackney, and a WSPU speaker, explained: 'The suffrage resolution came first, and when they [LTA officers] refused that, we told them equal pay would be fought for in the association as they wouldn't help us to get parliament to act.'[69] A similar expression of the NFWT's orientation was expressed by Miss Phipps in a contemporary letter to Miss Froud: 'Cheer up. We have got the vote without the "expression of sympathy" from the NUT. That was what I wanted.'[70] In other words, the NUT was seen as a vehicle to assist women in achieving political rights *within the state*.

In analyzing the way in which feminists worked inside the NUT and the issues they took up it is important to look briefly at the different feminist organizations to which they belonged, for it was such a political background which influenced their actions inside the NUT. I agree with Schwarz and Hall,[71] when they argue that 'the intellectual forces of feminism may have drawn from the socialist tradition as well as from liberalism, but they were primarily constituted by women's distinctive histories and concerns.' However, I do not accept their view that the feminist suffrage movement was 'positioned . . . *against* the state and existing institutions of power' (my emphasis).[72]

The suffrage organizations, militant and constitutionalist alike, were all orientated to demands upon the existing state for the inclusion of women within its existing parameters. Although violent acts may have been committed which were against the law, these were carried out with the intention of leading to women's incorporation within the state. Further, such actions ceased when the WSPU perceived its first allegiance to lie with the state in time of imperialist war.[73] Those feminists who took their demands for equality beyond that encompassed by the state were few in number and small in influence. Further, the actions of the feminist suffrage movement were totally directed to change being effected through political institutions. Industrial *action* organized by trades unions played no part in this campaign. The character of the militancy was such that it was acceptable to women from different classes in society and not simply those economically oppressed.

Many members of the NFWT/NUWT were Labour Party members. But it was the feminist movement organized outside the Labour Party in the suffrage campaigns which provided the impetus for their politics. Labour Party members such as Agnes Dawson, Ethel Froud, Misses Conway and Hewitt,[74] were active in the suffrage movement rather than in the Women's Labour League (WLL) of the Labour Party. This was not an explicitly feminist organization. Most of its members were married women and the work of the organization was geared to providing support to married women unable to attend meetings because of childcare responsibilities and to supporting the Labour Party's campaigns on social and welfare issues.[75] The Hackney branch of the WLL did submit a motion to the 1914 conference supporting equal pay for teachers, but this was unusual. When education was discussed this was usually in the context of provision rather than improving the position of women teachers and girl pupils.[76] Few members of the NFWT seem to have been members of the non-militant suffrage organization, the National Union of Women's Suffrage Societies (NUWSS). Indeed at a celebration dinner for the achievement of the full franchise in 1928, Agnes Dawson suggested that such women were something of a rarity in the NFWT. Reminiscing upon her early suffrage activities she commented that her colleagues often 'had thought fit to twit [sic] me on occasions that I was a constitutionalist, a law abiding suffragist.'[77]

Several NFWT and WFTU members were supporters of the WSPU.[78] Such teachers proudly described their activities on behalf of the WSPU chalking pavements, speaking at Hyde Park corner and at street corner meetings, organizing and attending demonstrations.[79] However, what is perhaps more significant in explaining the NFWT's activities inside the NUT is the involvement of many NFWT members in the Women's Freedom League.[80] The WFL, an organization which has received much less attention than the WSPU,[81] characterized itself as a militant organization which also operated democratically.[82] Its focus for militancy was entirely upon the state. However, as Emmiline Pethick-Lawrence wrote in her account of her activities in the WFL, it was not simply concerned with political rights but also with economic and social equality.[83] These were to be achieved through political campaigns.

It was the WFL which initiated the women's tax resistance campaign.[84] It was also responsible for the campaign for women to stay away from home on census night 1911 on the grounds that such state activity should not be recognized when the state refused to recognize the existence of women as voting citizens.[85] The Women's Freedom League members played a prominent part in fund raising for the children of the Dublin Transport Strikers, a cause, as has been stated in the last chapter, which was supported by socialists inside the NUT.[86] The Women's Freedom League was far more sympathetic to the Labour Party and Labour Movement than the WSPU. Although the WSPU had had its origins in the ILP and working-class organisations in Manchester it became increasingly estranged from this social milieu. However, those women who split to form the WFL remained firmly committed to working with working-class women.[87] Unlike the WSPU, which refused to support parliamentary candidates on the Labour Party platform, the WFL decided to give support to them in three-cornered contests 'as a more effective weapon against a government that denies justice to women'.[88] In addition to its orientation to working-class women and the labour movement, the WFL may also have attracted feminist teachers by its methods of organization. As a result of their opposition to the increasingly autocratic methods of Christabel and Emmeline Pankhurst, those who left the WSPU and formed the WFL placed great emphasis on internal democratic procedures.[89] There were annual elections for officers and a committee, voted for by every member. By every member having a vote in the organization they had 'an opportunity of becoming conversant with the methods and procedures of representative government'[90] presently denied them as disenfranchized citizens. Continuing its campaigns during and after the war the WFL saw the achievement of the franchise in 1918 as a starting point for further campaigns aimed at changing the state's attitude towards women. The NUT was to continue to work closely with the WFL in the 1920s on campaigns against double standards in the courts and other institutions which penalized women.[91]

I have mentioned the importance the WFL attached to its own democratic procedures because these practices were to inform the feminists' own demands within the NUT for democratic rights for the membership. This was reflected in the two objects the WTFU adopted at its inception:

1   To get fair play for women teachers in the educational world.
2   To organize women teacher suffragists and sympathizers so as to make their point of view felt in their own organisations.[92]

It was also reflected in the democratic processes the NFWT adopted for its own organization. Annual elections took place to the central council, and election platforms (and the minutes of the central council meetings) were published in the *Schoolmistress*.

The Effect of Feminist Politics inside the NUT

Although a majority of the teaching profession (and the NUT) were women, the NUT paid little attention to their specific needs. Women were expected to be interested in working for the Benevolent and Orphan fund, a charitable fund run by the NUT, yet were denied equal access to any financial benefits paid to needy teachers, even though their subscriptions were the same as those of their male colleagues.[93]

Women were not expected to involve themselves in the mainstream of union affairs: 'We women are not wanted by the men either at Russell Square [NUT headquarters] or in the local associations (except, of course, to prepare tea!) but our subscriptions appear to be required . . . fellow women members, let us determine to have more representatives at Russell Square, and a woman president as a start.'[94]

It was against such a background that the NFWT members — increasingly radicalized by their experiences in the suffrage movement — involved themselves in the NUT. Women were urged to attend their local association meetings and to ensure that they were well organized and businesslike.[95] Both the NUT Ladies' Committee and the NFWT welcomed Ladies' Committees in local associations,[96] to encourage women's involvement. The NFWT, in keeping with its emphasis on women's self-organization to achieve representation, argued for the equal representation of women and men in the electoral areas for the executive.[97] This was supported albeit most cautiously by the NUT Ladies' Committee.[98] The Ladies' Committee of the NUT believed that it was women's fault that men rather than women were elected to the executive: 'Women are apathetic, too easily swayed by the wiles of men, who persuade them to smile and look pleasant, while they assimilate as many of the plums of the profession as possible, and accept with pleasure the woman subordinate, rejecting the woman co-ordinate.'[99] However, unlike the Ladies' Committee, the NFWT took it upon themselves to organize for the election of women to the executive.[100] The Ladies' Committee showed itself less willing to oppose the existing state of affairs inside the union. For example, although it realized *The Schoolmaster* was not read widely by women teachers, it rejected any suggestion that the women's page should be made more responsive to women.[101] The committee issued recruitment leaflets aimed at women which failed to take a stance in favour of equal pay (or the franchise) and which stood back from campaigning for existing NUT policy against combined departments.[102]

The Ladies' Committee saw the women in the NFWT as a threat. As early as 1908 they were referred to as a menace by Miss Cleghorn, the future

NUT president.[103] In order to ward off this feminist threat the Ladies' Committee called a women's conference in January 1908.[104] The feminists were hostile to this initiative because it was not open to all women, nor was it open to local associations to elect their own representatives. Men also attended the conference. The 'delegates' to the conference were hand picked by the Ladies' Committee who rejected many NFWT members in the process.[105] Subsequently the London branch of the NFWT wrote in complaining that the conference was not representative, it was called a women's conference but men spoke and voted; it was not open to non-selected NUT members to attend and hear the debate. They wanted to know who had elected the delegates and on what basis.[106] The detailed résumé of the conference as printed in *The Schoolmaster* is of interest in showing at this early stage the splits between the feminists and the majority of women inside the NUT on combined departments and mixed schools, the age of admission of children to infants schools and the seriousness with which men's 'unprofessionalism' towards women was considered by the feminists.[107]

The Ladies' Committee and the 'mainstream' of the NUT were anxious to diffuse the different perspective offered by the feminists. Editorials in *The Schoolmaster* attempted to distance the feminists from their colleagues. Those who called for the election of women candidates in women's interests were defined as guilty of sex prejudice: *The Schoolmaster* welcomed the election of an overwhelming majority of men to the NUT executive in 1909.[108] This showed, it argued, that there was no sex prejudice in the union. A different example of this same distancing tactic is revealed in a later editorial of January 1910,[109] in which women were warned for appearing to be too clever, for such behaviour would be seen by men as unfeminine and would alienate them from the male sex.

These particular examples are mentioned — in addition to the points made earlier about the way in which feminists perceived their treatment inside the NUT — to show that before the NFWT started to organize in earnest for the franchise in 1911 there was still great opposition to feminists inside the NUT. Part of this opposition was revealed in the way that undemocratic procedures were used, especially in the LTA, to prevent the feminists' view being heard. It is likely that the experience of the WSPU and WFL split outside the NUT caused feminists inside the NUT to be most conscious of the type of organization and procedures adopted by the NUT. The feminists were at the forefront of campaigns for democratic decision-making in the NUT. Within the LTA they led the campaign to retain general decision-making meetings open to the entire membership to take decisions on a quarterly basis.

In the LTA the feminists had achieved some success in getting equal pay agreed as LTA policy and losing the parliamentary franchise question by a respectable amount at such general meetings.[110] Such meetings were very well attended and, in the case of the franchise discussion, overflow meetings had to be held in adjacent halls.[111] In response the LTA officers, however, called for referenda on these matters on the grounds that they would be more representative and democratic and thereby ensured the defeat of the equal pay principle.[112] To counter this, leaflets were issued by the NFWT and WTFU. These argued that a referendum was undemocratic in that it could not reflect *strength* of feeling. It also militated against free speech, in that people could vote without hearing arguments. The LTA was seen to be acting in an analogous way to the state: excluding women's participationn in the decision-making process.[113]

Because of such experiences the activity of the NFWT and WTFU came to be directed as much against the NUT for their undemocratic practices as against the state. Women were enraged that male delegates to annual conference did not follow mandates of their local NUT associations,[114] and were shocked that within a professional organization their views could not be seriously heard.[115] For some NFWT members their first militant suffrage action was not directed against the state but against the NUT. Stella Newsom vividly remembered her 'first militant action' taken shortly after she started teaching in 1910. Attending a branch meeting of the Leicester NUT she was amazed that the meeting refused to discuss the franchise issue: 'I was so furious I dashed onto the platform and demanded my subscription back. And got it! I can still see the chairman — an old fellow with a beard — turning out his trouser pockets to find 2/6d while the meeting sat stupified.'[116]

Such experiences led the feminists, in London at least, to set up a specific single issue campaigning organization on the suffrage question alone, the Women Teachers Franchise Union (WTFU), with the intention of forcing the NUT to campaign for what was the executive's policy: the franchise. It was the political experience of such women *outside* the union which led to their consciousness of different methods of organization to those favoured by the NUT. It also led them to increased militancy[117] and to an increasing estrangement from the NUT.

Debates inside the NFWT about its Relationship with the NUT

Although the decision finally to secede from the NUT or, as the motion to the central council put it, to declare a 'distinct severance',[118] was not taken until 1919 it had been an issue which the feminists had previously discussed. It must be stressed that when they finally left the NUT before equal pay was endorsed by a referendum of the membership, this was done in the belief that equal pay *would be carried*. However, they also recognized that the NUT — in the light of their previous experience — would be unlikely to campaign for its own policy if it was of a feminist character. Moreover, it was clear that the NUT would not be a ready vehicle for the transmission of their demands upon the state: 'We were convinced that, *whatever the result*, the NUT would do nothing to make equal pay practical politics, and that, on this question, as on all others, women must work out their own salvation'[119] (my emphasis).

In considering the different analyses of women in the NFWT to their female colleagues outside the Federation, it is important to realize that there *were* areas of agreement between the feminists and women teachers in general. The NFWT, for example, did not advocate that women within the NFWT *only* vote women to positions of office. They supported men who were sympathetic to their aims such as Allen Croft, who had been a supporter of suffrage at 1911 conference,[120] and opposed those who had proved hostile to feminism.[121]

The feminists in fact had a particular 'orientation' towards men, recognizing that men had had different experiences to them. In reporting the debate on the franchise at the West Lambeth Teachers' Association, Miss A. K. Williams argued that it was not men's fault that they were hostile: 'They had not such practical experience as was necessary to enable them to realise what it really meant.'[122] The WTFU expressed similar sentiments: 'More propaganda is still necessary in the teachers' organisations if full liberty is to be secured to those that come after us . . . no . . . difficulty shall deter the WTFU from proceeding towards its goal — the freedom of women, which will *encompass man's perfect freedom.*'[123]

The feminists believed that there was a distinctive women's point of view which needed to be voiced particularly on educational matters which primarily involved women, such as the teaching of domestic subjects, or of young children in nursery classes.[124] Although the feminists believed that women had particular experiences which resulted in different perspectives to men, they did not hold the view that they should be treated differently to men. The line of their argument for equality was entirely counterposed to the positions of Mrs. Burgwin, one of the leading members of the Anti-Suffrage League inside the NUT. Arguing that women as a sex were different to men she used this to maintain that the vote for women was unnecessary.[125]

The nature of their feminism becomes clearer when one considers the NFWT members' attitudes to women. Their identification with, and empathy towards, women *teachers* depended on the political views of the women concerned. From reading the minutes of their meetings and private correspondence it is clear that the feminists were particularly scathing towards women who feigned sympathy with the feminist cause while declining to organize on that basis inside the NUT.[126] Their belief that men could be sympathetic to women's cause and also that women as a sex could not necessarily be relied upon to act in their own interests informed the debates on secession from the NUT.[127] Some members argued against secession on the grounds that in local associations men, rather than many women, supported the feminists' arguments.[128] For their part men sympathetic to the feminists' cause were mindful of the consequences of secession for trade union organization and argued that equal pay, for example, should be supported in the cause of union unity.[129]

The Campaigns of the NFWT prior to Secession

There are three campaigns I wish to highlight here which indicate the feminists' perceptions of the state and their relationship to it. The first is the campaign for NUT support for the parliamentary franchise, which had its origins *outside* the educational state apparatus in the political relation between women and the state. In taking their argument into the NUT the feminists made explicit links between their role as women teachers and their political role in society. What distinguishes their argument from those of unsympathetic colleagues is their explicit recognition of the political content of education, and of the political relationship between the state and teachers. A leaflet issued by the WFTU in support of their campaign within the LTA indicates the way in which their view of the political relation to the state as disenfranchised women, and as teachers, underpinned their whole argument. Seven points are made in favour of their case:

1 Politics govern the whole of their professional life . . .
2 Education is essentially women's work . . .
3 Education aims at making the best possible citizens; women are denied the rights of citizenship . . .
4 Women teachers care for the work of the school clinic, and would hasten on its development . . .
5 Women teacher suffragists believe in equal pay for equal work . . .
6 The married women's position is assailed . . .
7 The Teachers' Provident Society will not accept any women as first class lives, and yet women have to pay more than men for superannuation with less benefits because it is said that women live longer.[130]

The leaflet ends with a call to all women: 'We stand to lose professionally, educationally, and as women if we still leave the control of the LTA and the NUT in the hand of such reactionaries as those who would not "play fair" . . . '[131]

It is not simply that the women were calling for the NUT to take a stand in support of their rights as citizens but that the NUT itself by its own rules and policies was *de facto* aligning itself with the state in its political exclusion of women. That is women members, like the men, paid a parliamentary levy in their membership to contribute to the pay of men teachers elected to Parliament with NUT support. Yet through their lack of franchise women themselves were unable to benefit directly from this scheme.[132]

The franchise debate inside the pages of *The Schoolmaster*, the local associations and annual conference covered two areas: the desirability (or not) of women achieving the franchise and the role of the NUT in ensuring this (or not). Thus in the pages of *The Schoolmaster* one reads letters from feminists advocating the suffrage position to an audience deemed to be needing to be educated on this matter. In particular one finds letters justifying (or attacking) the WSPU's attacks on private property.[133] The feminists used the pages of *The Schoolmaster*, like any other platform open to them, to express their general political opinions as feminists. They also discussed the specific role of the NUT on this question, in particular the parliamentary levy and the tactics used by respective factions within the NUT.[134]

As stated in the previous chapter much of this debate centred on the nature of *politics* and the NUT support for political activity. Thus the union's donation to the children of the Penrhyn quarrymen over ten years before was used to show that the union already had adopted political positions.[135] From 1910 feminists organized within local associations to ensure that parliamentary franchise motions were forwarded by local associations for discussion at NUT conference. The first conference at which the franchise was debated, 1911, took place against growing activity of the suffrage movement outside the NUT,[136] and the increasing influence of women and feminists within the NUT.[137] The feminist campaign was well organized. In 1912, for example, over seventy identical motions appeared on the preliminary agenda thus ensuring that the topic would certainly be discussed.[138] This is not to suggest that such motions passed through associations as non-contentious business, but rather that the feminists took organization within the NUT seriously.[139]

The NUT conferences were a focus for the suffrage organizations themselves to hold fringe meetings and to sell their literature. Open air meetings were held in the conference towns, rooms were hired by the different groups and women teachers paraded around the town with sandwich boards advertising their respective meetings and stating their demands.[140] During an Anglican church service held at 1914 conference, for example:

A woman offered up a public prayer from the steps of the altar for a woman and for the Cause of woman. The congregation was so staggered that the woman's prayer was distinctly heard; having offered it she walked straight out of the church. Her sisters, however, were brutally treated; they were literally thrown from the church; several were seized by the throat and in one case, a girl's spine was injured.[141]

When Lord Haldane, the Lord Chancellor, attended NUT conference in 1913 as a guest of the executive he was lobbied by suffragists (and anti-suffragists) and heckled when addressing the conference.[142] However, despite the vigorous campaigns of feminists inside and outside the NUT, the NFWT and WTFU never succeeded in obtaining NUT backing for the parliamentary franchise. The tactics of their opponents suggest that this was not because the majority of the NUT necessarily opposed the *suffrage* for women but because many of the more reactionary members realized the precedent this would set for other organizations, particularly the socialists, to operate within the NUT. Accordingly the feminists met fierce opposition.

In London the anti-suffragists sought to 'eliminate the question of women's suffrage entirely from the objects of the Association'.[143] On several occasions at NUT conferences the reactionaries adopted the procedural tactic of moving the 'previous question' once the parliamentary franchise was moved. This motion meant that the previous position of the union should stand, that is, that there should be no position on the franchise. Ostensibly the anti-suffragists did not seek to express any view on the suffrage question, but rather to express the view that it was outside the educational aims of the NUT. This supposed neutral position of the anti-suffragists did not stop one of the leading women opponents, Mrs Burgwin, seizing the opportunity when addressing conference to accuse the WSPU of attempting to take over the union and to denounce women teachers for their militant tactics in fiercely political language.[144]

The feminists' initial defeat was used to positive effect. A special meeting was called for women delegates after the franchise debate. This was attended by about four hundred women who heard Miss Cleghorn say: 'We have many more suffragists in Aberystwyth today than if [the debate] had not taken place.'[145] They went away in buoyant mood: 'Every woman will go home from this conference a missionary.'[146]

This missionary work was to be carried out by the NFWT and the WTFU, formed in 1912, and not by the official structures of the NUT. The feminists rejected the advice given them by Sir James Yoxall, the union's general secretary and Liberal MP, who had warned them not to approach the issue as a political question, but as a union one.[147] As previously stated, for the feminists the NUT was not important *per se* but was a vehicle for the achievement of their demands. So, they continued to prioritize the *politics* of the suffrage and also to pursue equal pay within the union. In these campaigns they frequently met with hostility from male colleagues but realized this was an inevitable effect of their campaigns.[148]

The second campaign, for equal pay, pre-dated the franchise campaign and had been the basis of the formation of the Equal Pay League in 1904.[149] However, equal pay was raised again within the NUT both because of the opportunities opened by the franchise campaign and because of the feminists' own perceptions of the relationship between the franchise and their economic position in society. These links were described in *Votes for Women* thus:

> Perhaps nothing better could be expected of men [in turning down the suffrage motion at NUT conference in 1912] who so calmly pocket a monetary award for being men. They know perfectly well that their qualifications and their work being in no way superior to the work of women teachers, they are not entitled to receive a higher salary ... The decision of the teachers' conference is more nicely calculated than anything else could be to arouse this powerful band of women workers in action in defence of their rights.[150]

In addition to political and economic arguments, the feminists also placed their demands within an ideological framework. In her pamphlet written for the NFWT, Helena Normanton argued that to deny women teachers equal pay was to suggest that the education of girls was less important than the education of boys:

> Our present education system is not one calculated to foster much originality in either men or women but the fact that an enormous number of women working in mixed departments have practically no hope of promotion, and that those who do obtain a headship are always responsible to a committee overwhelmingly masculine in composition, does most likely tend to restrain women's initiative.[151]

The kernel of their argument was that teachers — all teachers — should be paid for the job of teaching rather than on their circumstances outside paid employment. Despite what was said to the contrary they recognized that men teachers did not get paid more because of any dependents they might have but because of their sex and the higher esteem in which their work was held.[152] Conscious of the fact that teaching was increasingly seen as a suitable profession for women, the feminists realized that if men were driven out of teaching altogether this would seriously affect pay levels. Pay differentials, they argued, exacerbated this situation by threatening men's employment in boys' schools. If women could be paid less by the state for doing the same job it would result in worse pay levels for all teachers, men and women alike. To this, many men countered that equal pay would itself result in a lowering of pay levels for all.[153]

The NUT executive, including several of its women members, opposed equal pay. As in the case of the suffrage campaign the feminists recognized that their own activity was necessary: 'There is little doubt, judging from the tone of the Aberystwyth meetings, that the men of the local associations will fight the motion, and it will take all the enthusiasm and energy of the friends of the feminist movement to carry it through.'[154] Although the issue was lost at the NUT conference of 1913,[155] there was greater progress in London. The feminists succeeded in getting the LTA to adopt the principle of equal pay,[156] only to have this overturned by a referendum of the entire London membership which the officers insisted on calling.[157]

The feminists continued to organize within the NUT and LTA until after the war, but with a growing sense of the futility of this course of action. Emily Phipps, for some time a NUT executive member from Wales, declined to stand for re-election in 1917, although nominated, on the following grounds:

> I find myself utterly at variance with the entire policy of the executive in its attitude towards women teachers' salaries, as shown, one, in the attempt to make compulsory through the Board of Education a scale of salaries which differentiates between the

payment of men and women teachers of the same professional status and experience; two, in the apparently joyful acquiescence, through the pages of *The Schoolmaster*, in the local scales of salaries which increase rather than diminish the already existing differences. The situation has developed so rapidly during the last few weeks that I feel any influence that I may possess would be more useful off the executive rather than on that body. I cannot silently consent to what appeared to me to be a monstrous injustice to women.[158]

When equal pay was finally accepted as a demand by the NUT in 1918 it was accompanied by the retrogressive view that the state should give grants for 'wifehood' and 'motherhood'.[159] Thus although equal pay was acceded it was not on grounds sympathetic to the feminist case but was directly opposed to the arguments they had conducted against payment based on personal circumstances rather than upon the job in hand. This acceptance of equal pay as an interim measure until wifehood or motherhood was financially rewarded was based on the view that women *were* different to men and not equal as citizens. Such a position had always been resisted by the NFWT as antithetical to feminism. This line of argument became widely accepted within the NUT in the 1920s. It also became a central feature of the National Association of Schoolmasters (NAS) and the London Schoolmasters' Association (LSA) arguments *against* equal pay.[160] In some respects there was a difference in the campaign on equal pay and on the franchise. In the latter campaign the feminists saw the NUT as a vehicle for assisting them in putting pressure upon the state for political equality. It was a focus for activities because of the 'access' it provided to a body of opinion. In the case of the campaign for equal pay the NFWT and WFTU realized that NUT was the body which had direct responsibility for negotiating with the local education authorities and for placing demands upon the educational state apparatus in respect of teachers' pay and conditions. The NFWT as a group within the NUT was denied any direct and independent access to these state institutions. As I shall elaborate, the feminists realized they needed direct access to the state in pay negotiation for the NUT was a *barrier* to their demands.

The third campaign I wish to highlight is the feminists' opposition to the sacking of married women teachers as permanent teachers. The move by local authorities to sack married women teachers was particularly strong in the 1920s in response to the Geddes cuts and numbers of unemployed teachers.[161] But it had also been considered by the LCC in 1909. In response the LTA immediately rallied in opposition to this and was able to preserve the *status quo*.[162] This action was perceived as a threat to the personal and economic rights of women in general.[163] At the same time as demanding their *political* involvement in the state through the franchise, the feminists were seeing the same state institutions *excluding* them from an economic role if they married. Here again the feminists recognized the role of the state which went beyond the educational state apparatus. The campaigns which they undertook focused on the political rights of women teachers rather than upon specific instances of women being sacked. This is partly because many NFWT members had taken the conscious decision to remain single and had difficulty in understanding why individual women should wish to give up this right.[164]

A pamphlet was issued shortly after the war defining the rights of married women teachers. This was written by an unmarried woman, Miss Byett, a former NFWT president, on behalf of the Federation. She argued that women, irrespective of their marital status, should have equal citizenship. Whether women wished to return to teaching after having children was a question, she argued, for women themselves to decide. What is of particular interest in the pamphlet is Miss Byett's surprise that women should *want* to get married:

> The fact of being married is, as some of our bright young women begin to perceive, a decided drawback, so great a drawback that many, not the least intelligent, deliberately choose single life. Whether this result is foreseen by our sapient councillors is doubtful. They deplore delayed marriage and lowered population, and at the same time render marriage and motherhood more difficult and less honoured.[165]

The NUWT was to campaign forcefully for the rights of married women teachers in the 1920s and 1930s. Nevertheless the choice of many members was to stay unmarried, a feature which caused them to be derided as inadequate women by the LSA and to be estranged from women teachers who were not feminists and who did not share their personal cultural lifestyles.[166]

In these three campaigns one notes an awareness and a political perception lacking from the NUT strategies in this period. Feminist teachers questioned the existing practices of the state and examined them critically and consciously from a feminist political perspective. It was this awareness of their role and the part that they themselves had to play in challenging it that differentiated their strategies most clearly from the dominant NUT practices. It was the feminists' analysis of the state as well as of the role of the NUT which led to their decision to leave the NUT.

The Decision to Become an Autonomous Union

By the end of the war the state made a concession to the feminists by granting the suffrage to women over 30. This political shift had been accompanied by a shift in economic positions in that the state had shown itself willing during the war to intervene directly within the economy. The NFWT formed the opinion that it would be possible to wrest economic gains from the state in the same way as political gains had been achieved.[167] In a leaflet the NFWT issued to education committees it referred to the recommendations of the War Cabinet Committee on women in industry as justification for women teachers also receiving equal pay. Given that this had been conceded in principle by the state and, they explained, local authorities had received increased funding from the treasury, then the principle of equal pay should apply as soon as possible to the teaching profession. Their line of argument was directed exclusively towards the state, opposing 'the inference of the inferiority of women and women's service to the state implied by lower pay'.[168] The feminists approached the task of convincing the state of the justice of their cause with optimism. The NFWT was convinced of its own strength: 'Women teachers are strong enough in themselves to make a thoroughly self-governing profession. Can we afford to give over all we have won at this moment?'[169]

Their discussions were increasingly focusing upon the pressure that feminists could place directly on the state. In this their debate reflected the mood of the times. Their militancy was not only a 'throwback' to their militancy of the suffrage campaigns before the war but reflected that of the contemporary period in the industrial sector. Addressing the 1919 NFWT conference as president, Agnes Dawson expressed the times thus:

> They had today to regard very seriously three other R's, and to acknowledge they are initial letters of significant words . . . rebellion, reconstruction, revolution . . . she submitted that those who have taken . . . upon themselves any responsibility in education should especially turn their attention to the causes which have brought these words into such extraordinary significance today . . . If the Education Act of 1918 were rightly administered by wise administrators, whose love of country was more to them than the hoisting of the Union Jack or the singing of 'Rule Britannia', if the people of Britain could be prevailed upon to put an ounce of thought in the approaching elections, and we could have each clause of the new Education Act intelligently put into operation, and alongside that, a real reform in the housing of the workers, the results would mean revolution writ large without blood, and some of them who would be privileged to see the new generation of children grow into manhood and womanhood would see this thing . . . [170]

This speech was not just rhetoric for the presidential occasion. Shortly after, on Agnes Dawson's recommendation, the feminist teachers engaged in militant activity and agreed to take strike action and to set up their own sustentation fund in pursuit of the actions that they were taking against the refusal of the LCC to agree to equal pay.[171]

By November 1919 the NFWT had already organized a mass meeting at the Royal Albert Hall, supported by nineteen other organizations, on equal pay,[172] and collected ten thousand signatures on a petition on the same topic within a few days.[173] However, such militant action, while winning the support of thousands of women teachers in London, had not been successful in winning equal pay from the LCC.[174] Further, this action had been vociferously opposed by the LTA and NUT in London who condemned the NFWT for taking matters into their own hands and creating disunity in the profession. A reading of *The London Teacher* editorials and reports of LTA meetings makes it clear that the LTA had no intention of implementing the equal pay policy passed at the national NUT conference. The LTA appears to have little understanding about the *way* in which the feminists regarded equal pay.[175] It was not simply a question of their economic situation, but of the way in which their 'services' were regarded by the state. A *London Teacher* editorial sees the issue in a very different manner: 'We know that opinions are sharply divided upon the question of equal pay for equal work. Men hold strong views for and against; so do women. We believe that the desire for the permanent improvement of the position and status of the teacher will guide us through this controversy . . . '.[176]

By the time that the central council of the NFWT in November 1919 agreed to recommend to the membership that a 'distinct severance' be taken from the NUT,[177] the feminists had already organized thousands of women teachers independently of the NUT on equal pay and thus had seen their own strength, as well as the apathy of the NUT. Its own London Unit, which by 1918 was the combined organizations of the London NFWT and WFTU, had already held a meeting in March 1918 and agreed 'that this meeting of the London Unit of the NFWT advises its members to concentrate their energies upon their own organization'.[178] It was also evident that many women were simply not renewing their memberships to the NUT, irrespective of any decision taken, or not, by the central council.[179]

The NFWT had discussed for some years its relationship to the NUT and had formed the conclusion that the NUT, irrespective of the pressure the feminists brought to bear upon it, would not campaign in their own interests.[180] The NFWT did *not* secede from the NUT until it had judged both that the state was capable of making conclusions *and* that the Federation itself was capable of organizing forms of trade union action in addition to political action. This organization consisted of lobbies, petitions and demonstrations aimed at the local education authority, backed up by the threat of strike action.[181]

The NFWT/NUWT as an Independent Union

Initially the NFWT was able to recruit many members especially in London,[182] and the Ladies' Committee of the NUT was obliged to take some steps to involve itself in campaigns on behalf of women teachers because the NUWT was presenting itself within organizations, such as the National

Council for Women, as the only representatives of women teachers.[183] These belated attempts to concern themselves with women's needs were treated disdainfully by the NUWT. When the Ladies' Committee approached the Six Point Group with a view to affiliation this was opposed by the NUWT representatives.[184] However, the Ladies' Committee refused to adopt an equality perspective on the issue of women's representation and discontinued even the women's meetings at NUT conference.[185]

Such moves did nothing to convince the NUWT that the NUT was an organization they should rejoin. In the early 1920s members who were also NUT members were ineligible to stand for the central council.[186] By the conference of 1927 it was agreed to scrap joint membership in its entirety.[187] This independent fight for equality was to take place against the state's new structures for pay of teachers and against the state's refusal to recognize the feminist union as worthy of inclusion on the consultative committee which agreed the Burnham pay structure. Thus, although the Board of Education received separate deputations from the feminists on sex hygiene or on the position of married women teachers, the NUWT was excluded from any consultative processes which involved the NUT. Their role was not seen as that of a *union* negotiating with employers but as a pressure group campaigning on certain (peripheral) issues alone.

The NUWT's autonomous role, then, was to take place against a change in the relationship between the central and local state in the determining of teachers' salaries. The national structure of Burnham excluded the possibility of equal pay being conceded in areas where the feminists were well organized. It also meant that as a new organization, just setting up legal and welfare services,[188] it was being challenged in effect to compete with the NUT nationally, in a changing political arena. The energies of the new organization were simultaneously directed towards achieving equal pay and recognition under Burnham and recruiting teachers into its membership. Outside London this was not an easy task. At a council meeting in March 1920 Agnes Dawson reported that they were not making sufficient headway, although as president she had been to meetings around the country to 'preach the gospel of independence'.[189]

By the early 1920s, as was noted in the last chapter, teachers were working in an increasingly hostile climate. However, in addition to the general economic effects of the Geddes cuts, women teachers were specifically affected by the decision of many local education authorities to sack married women teachers. In Chapters 1 and 3 I described the state's offensive against socialist policies in the 1920s. It must also be recognized that there was an increasingly hostile climate towards feminism. In addition to the economic attacks on women there was ideological opposition to many of the views feminists had campaigned for within the suffragette movement. What distinguishes the NUWT from its counterparts in the NUT in the 1920s is its maintenance of critical attitudes towards the state and its adherence to an equal rights perspective. In the face of hostility from the state, NUT and, increasingly, the NAS,[190] the feminists maintained their objects of equality with men,[191] and took this demand into the National Union of Societies of Equal Citizenship (NUSEC), of which it was a founder member,[192] and into the Six Point Group.[193] It continued to organize lobbies, demonstrations, and mass meetings in conjunction with such groups.[194] It also maintained its increasingly isolated position on equal rights of men and women in the moral field through its work in AMSH.[195] Its emphasis on political autonomy and its experiences of working in mixed organizations,[196] made the NUWT very wary of closely aligning itself with the Labour Party. It was such *feminist* responses which led to this decision. The NUWT members continued to define themselves as women *workers* and to support other women workers: 'We demand that women shall be paid as workers and not as workers paid as women. We demand equal pay between men and women teachers, because we demand that women teachers shall not be paid as women, but as workers . . .'.[197]

The feminists had debated Labour Party affiliation at the same time as the NUT and rejected it on the grounds that, as far as the political franchise went, 'no special guarantee of help from Labour any more than from other political parties' was offered.[198] One of the main protagonists against Labour Party affiliation was Labour Party member Agnes Dawson. She used her influence, in particular, on the central council to dissuade members against either Labour Party or TUC affiliation. She argued that 'women in the Labour Party and in the TUC were, and would be, swamped'.[199] This stance did not prevent the union giving full financial and political support to Agnes Dawson when she stood, successfully, for the LCC on a Labour Party platform in 1925.[200] She was regarded as the NUWT's representative, rather than the Labour Party's, on the LCC. Indeed it was through her role on the LCC that the NUWT was successful in achieving an end to the marriage bar in the 1930s.[201]

The sceptical attitude to the Labour Party may well have been justified. By the late 1920s the Labour Party, together with a section of the NUSEC, had rejected the concept of equal rights in favour of one emphasizing a separate and distinctive role for women within the family.[202] Despite the NUWT's unwillingness to submerge its own politics within those of the TUC or Labour Party it did send 'delegates' to the Labour Party's Advisory Committee on Education. These were offered to the NUWT (and NUT) by the Labour Party in an individual capacity.[203] However, despite the NUWT's conscientious attendance little attention was paid to their demands. The NUWT's 'representatives' faced hostility from Labour Party and NUT members alike on the committee, especially in respect of equal pay.[204]

None of these comments on the NUWT's attitude to the Labour Party should be seen to suggest that they were unsympathetic to progressive causes. On the contrary, the NUWT supported the peace pilgrimage, organized by the Women's International League;[205] it involved itself in fundraising for the children of striking miners;[206] it adopted a sympathetic stance towards the treatment of animals;[207] and it sent a delegation on the educational trip to the Soviet Union, organized by the TLL.[208] It was proud to assert its explicitly political stance:' Outside the union, criticism has been levelled at the NUWT for its political activities; but members have fully realised the necessity for establishing the fundamental right of women to full citizenship, and have splendidly responded to the many calls made upon them to assist in the struggle.'[209]

By the mid 1920s the NUWT was aware that its campaigns for political and economic equality within the state were long-term issues. However, it was increasingly hostile towards the NUT and saw it as a barrier to equality rather than as a potential ally. Some of its bitterest attacks were reserved for women attempting to work inside the NUT:

> Probably they had no previous experiences of the earlier phases of the fight, and like others who had never tried it, thought they had only to work hard and systematically in order at least to get the NUT to make equal pay its policy. They *should* know better now ... People who are wise will not continue the same tactics indefinitely without any success: they will change their methods.[210]

They issued a series of leaflets aimed at women members of the NUT in which they reiterate their commitment to political self-organization: 'Equal pay will only be secured by work — unremitting, earnest, courageous; not by diplomatic shelving of the question. It will be won just as soon as all women teachers desire it and work for it.'[211]

The NUWT's organizational autonomy coupled with its recognition that the achievement of political and economic rights were long term campaigns led it to organize its own cultural activities to reaffirm a feminist identity in a difficult political period. At the NUWT's social events, dinners and teas,[212] a feminist 'lifestyle' was celebrated, in the same way as one saw socialist organizations developing their own alternatives in the Socialist Sunday Schools' activities. Flower arrangements were made in the NUWT's colours: green and gold. Singing, usually led by the NUWT choir, included the NUWT song 'The Awakening'.[213]

This cultural activity, which had its origins in the suffragette organizations of the pre-war period, was also reflected in the way in which the NUWT organized its demonstrations. For the 1921 demonstration on equal pay and equal opportunities a bannerade (sic) competition was held, which was won by the St Pancras branch with its slogan 'Women Arise, the Dawn is Here'.[214] For the 1927 demonstration jointly organized with other women's organizations the banners included the following slogans: 'Who would be free herself must strike the first blow' (the national NUWT motto); '*Non mihi, non tibi, sed nobis*', accompanied by a dove and an olive branch; 'Woman's cause is man's: they rise or sink together' (Woolwich); '*Laborare est orare*' (Willesden); 'Liberty, justice, equality' and 'No question is ever settled until it is settled right' (West Ham).[215]

For the demonstration on equal political rights in 1926, the disenfranchised under-30s were asked to wear green dresses made from green silk. A bulk purchase of silk had been made for the occasion from John Lewis. Another contingent were graduates wearing cap and gown; another group was organizing a Montessori class on a lorry as part of the procession. Bicycle riders, who were to take messages during the day, were to wear green and yellow ribbons. All members were expected to walk. Cars would be available, but it was stressed that these were only for those with infirmities.[216]

The NUWT leaders in the 1920s continued to be those women who had been politicized by the suffrage campaigns and who had adopted their political stance and lifestyle for 'the Cause'. This stood them in good stead in a hostile environment. Writing of her experiences as one of the only two NUWT teachers in Grimsby and of the local NUT hostility Miss Hurley wrote: 'Of course it made no difference to my actions. I took my individual course as usual — I was a suffragette.'[217] This relation between politics and lifestyle continued in this period and helped reinforce their own commitment and involve younger teachers in their feminist cultural traditions:

> My thoughts flashed back to Miss Pringle at Buxton and your helping Miss Kenyon in the snow. Miss Froud at the café near the British Museum when I reported on the Dartmouth conference with Miss Phipps, Miss Crosby, Miss Cooper in Dartmouth Naval College. The train journey to Blackpool soon after Nancy Parnell had been to the House to represent the under-30s. Oh! How we talked! . . . The tea Party at 39, Gordon Square in the 1920s, Miss Dawson's country dinner at Newport, etc. etc. Memories just tumbled forth and culminated in the photos of the Pankhursts which my father collected and his Oxford friends who inspired me to feminism when I was seven years of age. It seems incredible when I look back over the years but at that age I had heard many notable speakers at meetings — for my father took me everywhere with him — Cripps, Snowden, MacDonald, Thomas, Despard, Lansbury and all interested in social reform he travelled to hear often carrying me on his shoulders.[218]

In particular the relationships they formed with each other formed a valuable source of strength in maintaining their political commitments.[219]

The Weakness of the NUWT's Strategies

In the last chapter I argued at some length that any assessment of the relationship between teachers and the state needs to be situated within the context of the political, ideological and economic relation between the two, both inside and outside the educational state apparatus. The relationship between women teachers and the state in this period was different to that of men teachers. This was partly because of the role of the educational state apparatus in determining pay levels and conditions of service, and, in particular excluding married women teachers from the workforce. It was also due to the broader relationship between women and the state as characterized by women's disenfranchisement. What made the NFWT /NUWT different from the NUT in its response to these material factors were first its awareness of the role of the state particularly in the political arena and secondly its belief that changes were needed in state strategies which were to be undertaken by teachers in explicitly political campaigns.

The weakness of the NUWT's strategies can be attributed to three main areas. The first was its size. The organization was small; a fact which its enthusiastic organization often belied. It also had much less influence in the 1920s after the split from the NUT.[220] The second area was the NUWT's perception of the state's willingness to accede to its economic demands. The feminists saw the partial gaining of the franchise, a political gain, as the first step towards economic equality. In doing so, it severely underestimated the effects of the restructuring of the relationship between the central and local state as embodied in the Burnham committee. The third area was the feminists' estimate of their own organizational capacity in a changing ideological climate. The politics of the suffrage movement was based on political demands on the state. However, the disintegration of the suffrage movement during the war meant that it was not possible simply to recreate that movement in the new ideological climate of the 1920s.

Despite these weaknesses in the feminists' strategies it is clear that they were both conscious of the role of the state in different aspects of their lives and were more critical of it than their NUT counterparts. Moreover, unlike the NUT, the feminists did evolve strategies which incorporated the ideological, the political, and the economic

An omission of a study of the feminists' organization in this period gives a distorted view of teacher politics and fails to highlight the ways in which the state, outside the educational state apparatus, was able to have such a direct effect upon teachers' lives.

Notes and References

1 Tropp, *op. cit.*, pp. 157–8.
2 Ozga and Lawn (1981), *op. cit.*, p. 73.
3 Sarah King, 'Feminists in teaching: The National Union of Women Teachers 1920–1940', in Lawn and Grace, *op. cit.*, pp. 31–49; Alison Oram, 'Sex antagonism in the teaching profession: The equal pay issue 1914–1929', *History of Education Review*, 14, 2, 1985, pp. 36–48; Alison Oram, 'Serving two masters? The introduction of a marriage bar in teaching in the 1920s', in *The Sexual Dynamics of*

History, London Feminist History Group, London, Pluto Press, 1983, pp. 134–48; P. Owen, 'Who would be free herself must strike the blow', in *History of Education*, 17, 1, March 1988, pp. 83–100.

4   A. M. Pierotti, *The Story of the NUWT*, NUWT, 1963.

5   Unsuccessfully moving an amendment in favour of equal pay Miss Wood berated the delegates: 'Surely no-one supposed they went out into the world to earn their feeble wages because they liked it?' (Report of NFAT conference, *The Schoolmaster*, 7 October 1911, pp. 608–9). Some feminist writers of the period have described the relief they felt on leaving teaching. Margaret Nevinson, for example, a leading WFL activist stated: 'The worst of all my struggles after knowledge was the fact that for young women of my day there was nothing but teaching' (Margaret Nevinson, *Life's Fitful Fever*, A. and C. Black, London, 1926, pp. 58–9).

6   The law proved attractive to many teachers. Helena Normanton, first English woman QC, and WFL member, was asked to write a pamphlet for the NFWT on equal pay on the grounds of her legal qualifications (H. F. Normanton, 'Sex differentiation in salary', NFWT, 1914). In the 1920s, Miss Phipps, the editor of *The Woman Teacher* and headmistress of a girls' secondary school in Swansea, achieved her ambition by qualifying as a barrister. Even when honorary degrees were awarded by some universities to teachers of high standing in the NUT women were barred from receiving them. Thus Miss Conway, the NUT president in 1918 when the conference was held in Oxford, was prevented from receiving an honorary degree from the town's university, as was the custom for incoming NUT presidents. Oxford and Cambridge did not give honorary degrees to the women the NUT nominated. Instead, three men were selected for this honour: the former treasurer, retiring president, and the defeated presidential candidate (*The Vote*, 5 April 1919, quoting an article on this written by Miss Cutten, NFWT member, in *The Schoolmistress*).

7   Margaret Nevinson, 'The legal wrongs of married women', WFL, 1923. Various arguments, including that of personal liberty, were given by Mrs Tidswell on this topic to a meeting of the National Council of Women (*Ladies' Committee Minutes*, NUT, 20 October 1922).

8   '. . . the bringing in of a rule — non-retrospective — will not create vacancies . . . it will possibly result in a decrease of the marriage rate among teachers . . . ' (interview with Mary Ridge in *The Woman Teacher*, 16 January 1912, p. 333).

9   The Ladies' Committee of the NUT passed a motion protesting against the refusal of the LCC to allow married women teachers to apply for inspectorate posts (*Ladies' Committee Minutes*, NUT, 21 November 1914).

10   Editorial, *The Woman Teacher*, 12 September 1911, p. 38.

11   Tropp, *op. cit.*, pp. 117–18.

12   Motion moved by Miss Dawson and Miss Williams at the LTA conference 1916 (*The Schoolmaster*, 13 May 1916, p. 634) and see also *Central Council Minutes*, NFWT, 3 February 1917. Ozga and Lawn (1) *op. cit.*, pp. 96–7, state that the NUT agreed to admit unqualified teachers into membership in the wake of the 1919 Rhondda action. However, in London, the LTA voted to exclude such teachers from membership at its conference in 1919 (*The London Teacher*, 14 November 1919, p. 285).

13   In the second leaflet of the Equal Pay League (n.d., 1905(?) in the NUWT archive) there is the demand for the retiring age for women teachers to be considerably lowered and the allowance very much increased. Further, in recognition of the 'frequent breakdowns' of women teachers there is the call for the provision of 'Homes of Rest'. Early optional retirement was not favoured by the NUT executive arguing that optional retirement ages would soon become compulsory and older women teachers would be compulsorily replaced by younger teachers. NFWT members argued that the alternative to early optional retirement would be disability pensions which lacked dignity and relied upon possibly conflicting

medical opinion. At the conference called for women in the NUT in 1908 this topic was fully debated. Early optional retirement was agreed at NFWT conference, for example in 1911 (*The Schoolmistress*, 4 April 1911, p. 84). However the NUT was reluctant to even open the pages of *The Schoolmaster* to consideration of the question (letter from Miss Mardon in *The Schoolmistress*, 14 March 1912, p. 420) and thus the debate was continued in the pages of *The Schoolmistress* especially during the first months of 1912.

14 Extract from a letter from the NFWT to the Board of Education requesting a deputation to present the case for equal pay (*Central Council Minutes*, NFWT, 3 March 1917).

15 See for example report of NUWT conference in *The Vote*, 13 January 1928, p. 13; article by Miss Neal (NUWT member) in support of raising the school leaving age in *The Vote*, 18 October 1929; report of NUWT education conference in *The Vote*, 18 May 1928, p. 157; Agnes Dawson, 'Nursery Schools', NFWT, n.d., 1919(?).

16 'The abolition of the office of headmistress and the subordination of all departments to a headmaster have been subjects for resolution to conference after conference; yet the evil not only continues, but increases, and it is now time women teachers took the matter into their own hands and gave careful consideration to the means for the cessation of this practice' (Equal Pay League and NFWT leaflet, 1905(?), NUWT archive).

17 Successive conferences of the NFWT came out against the amalgamation of departments, for example, the NFWT conferences of 1909 (*The Schoolmaster*, 17 April 1909, p. 721) and 1911 (*The Schoolmistress*, 20 April 1911, p. 41).

18 The relationship between the domestic duties of girls and the position of their women teachers is covered in a pamphlet *The Spirit of Citizenship*, WTFU, 1913: 'When the boy's school hours were over he was free to go and play with his campanions. In the girl's case the home claimed her.' The pamphlet continues by describing the different duties of men and women and argues that because of this women are nearer to the 'citizen spirit' yet they are denied the vote.

19 Debate at NUT conference 1909 on combined departments (*The Schoolmaster*, 17 April 1909, p. 706). At the NFWT meeting at the NUT conference 'most delegates agreed it was a man's job to teach boys' (ibid, p. 721).

20 The second Equal Pay League leaflet (n.d., 1905(?)) recognized that if the position of equal pay for women teaching in boys' schools was 'left to stand alone [it] will be dangerous, as it only improves women's salaries where they enter into direct competition with men.'

21 See a series of articles in *The Woman Teacher*, 29 April, 1927, p. 232; 6 May 1927, p. 240; 20 May 1927. p. 256; 27 May 1927, p. 264; 10 June 1927, p. 272; 17 June 1927, p. 280. The debates which took place within the NUT and NFWT on mixed schools also focused upon the career opportunities for women teachers, for example *The Schoolmaster*, 30 April 1910, p. 814; 22 April 1911, p. 888.

22 As the Ladies' Committee minutes show: 'I can quite see some future good in the Women's Federation, whereas now it is a menace' (*Ladies' Committee Minutes*, NUT, 20 June 1908).

23 Miss Cleghorn speaking at NUT conference 1909 (*The Schoolmaster*, 17 April 1909, p. 706).

24 NFWT meeting at the 1910 conference listened to a paper read by their new president, Miss Dix, on domestic subjects and went on to debate the right age for learning the subject (*The Schoolmaster*, 2 April 1910, p. 626).

25 'Slaves should break their chains and they who want women to be free should help in the chain breaking and not try to rivet the links closer by advocating domestic teaching for all schools for all girls, fostering in the minds of girls that simply because of their sex they must inevitably some day be ready to cook a man's dinner and tidy

up his hearth' (Ada Neild Chew, the NUWSS full-time organizer 1911–14, writing in *The Common Cause*, 1913, as quoted in Les Garner, *op. cit.*, p. 20).

26 *The Rhondda Socialist*, 26 October 1912 (Women's Column) carries a criticism of a lecture given by Mrs Snowden, wife of Philip Snowden MP, in Treherbert when she encouraged the teaching of domestic duties to girls: '. . . an absurd proposal . . . a retrograde step . . . we have to recognise the fact that the ignorant motherhood of the country arises from the class of neglected, over-worked, over-burdened girl children who have been kept at home to mind the baby and help mother when they ought to have their proper share of mental training, and to have enjoyed free hours for child play.' The article continues by pointing out that if it had been suggested that boys should carry firewood and coal or imitate the workings of the colliery it would have been apparent to everyone that such a position would be retrograde.

27 Miss Palmer at the busines meetings of women teachers at NUT conference, 1913 (*The Schoolmaster*, 5 April 1913, p. 724). In her presidential speech to the NFWT conference in 1918, Miss Byett argued that continuation schools should not be mainly about domestic training for girls (Miss Byett, L.L.A., 'Women in Education' in 'Presidential Address', NFWT, 1918).

28 *The Schoolmaster*, 5 April 1913, p. 724.

29 *The Schoolmaster*, 4 January 1908, p. 13.

30 'Brief on nursery schools', memorandum no. 3, October 1918. Advisory Committee on Education, Box 1–60, Labour Party archive. See Kean (1981), *op. cit.*, pp. 53–7.

31 Agnes Dawson, 'The lower age limit of compulsory attendance', *Conference Papers*, LTA, 1917. 'Our first demand is that they [nursery schools] must be opened just where they are needed' (Agnes Dawson, 'Nursery schools' NFWT, n.d., p. 4); Hilda Kean and Alison Oram, 'Who would be free herself must strike the blow', *South London Record*, 3, 1988, pp. 40–53.

32 Agnes Dawson, 'Nursery Schools', *op. cit.*, p. 6. See Kean, *Deeds not Words*, (1990), *op. cit.*, Chapter 3.

33 *Central Council Minutes*, NFWT, 6 September 1919.

34 The first editorial in *The Woman Teacher*, 29 September 1919, p. 2, said: 'In purely educational matters we have always been in the forefront.' The education conferences which the NUWT held at least annually were concerned with broad educational issues and were not confined to classroom practice. See for example report of 1927 conference in *The Vote*, 20 May 1927, p. 157.

35 See, for example, an account of a meeting of the Portsmouth Education Committee at which a councillor had stated that girls did not need to be taught maths because they would be dock labourers' wives: 'We used to read in our younger days that the fairies did all the work provided we were very, very good. We suggest girls should be taught to be good and no doubt modern fairies of labour-saving domestic appliances will relieve girls of requiring any education whatsoever' (*The Woman Teacher*, 3 October 1911, p. 84).

36 See article by Miss Burls advocating equal opportunities in sports training in *The Woman Teacher*, 9 September 1927, p. 345. Her own interest was reflected in the speech she gave at 1931 NUWT conference on equal pay: 'We are living in 1931, not in 1831. Women have given up vapours and megrims for athletics, running and swimming . . .' (*Southend Pictorial*, p. 1, 2 January 1932). The feminist interest in sport for girls was such that a separate suffrage organization for gym teachers had existed before the war A. J. R. (Ed.), *The Suffrage Annual and Women's Who's Who*, Stanley Paul and Co., London, 1913, p. 40). The NUT Ladies' Committee was less enthusiastic and did not support swimming for girls until after there had been extensive consultation with the local NUT associations (*Ladies' Committee Minutes*, NUT, 20 February 1915).

37 See Chapter 4, nn. 138–40, and Sheila Jeffreys, *The Spinster and her Enemies. Feminism and Sexuality 1880–1930*, Pandora, 1985, pp. 73–4.

38 Edith Cooper and Mary Mason, *The Teaching of Sex Hygiene*, NFWT, n.d.
39 An editorial in *The London Teacher*, 15 May 1914, p. 387, backed the LCC's decision in banning this from schools. The Ladies' Committee of the NUT agreed that it was neither desirable nor practicable to be introduced as a subject into elementary schools (*Ladies' Committee Minutes*, NUT, 20 December 1915).
40 *The Woman Teacher*, 23 November 1928, p. 50. A brief survey of the life work of Miss Theodora Bonwick.
41 See n. 140 in Chapter 4 and *Central Council Minutes*, NFWT, 8 December 1917.
42 *Annual Report*, London NFWT, 1918, describes the discussion classes held and includes the motion passed at the NFWT education conference.
43 *Central Committee Minutes*, NFWT, 3 March 1917.
44 Grace Cottell, 'Films for children', *The Vote*, 4 January 1929, p. 5; and n. 138 in Chapter 4.
45 *The Woman Teacher*, 3 October 1911, p. 93.
46 *Suffrage Who's Who, op. cit.*, for details, provided by the teachers themselves, of their own qualifications.
47 This point was made by the NFWT themselves, for example, as expressed in Emily Phipps, 'Equality of opportunity', NUWT, n.d.
48 NUT War Record, 1914–18, *op. cit.*, p. 37.
49 See Arthur Marwick, *The Deluge — British Society and the First World War*, London, Bodley Head, 1965, pp. 91ff.
50 See Sylvia Pankhurst, *op. cit.*, pp. 157–62. During the war the ELFS, WFL and NUWSS issued manifestos demanding the vote and insisting that a woman who did a man's work should get a man's pay. These damands on behalf of the women in the munitions industry were placed by Sylvia Pankhurst before Lloyd George in 1916.
51 Editorial, *The Schoolmaster*, 30 June 1917, p. 791.
52 Miss Byett, *op. cit.*
53 *Ibid.*
54 Address of NFWT President, Miss Thomas, to NFWT conference 1912. *The Schoolmistress*, 11 April 1912, p. 22; 'The NUT and the women's suffrage', WTFU, n.d. (1913?).
55 The Central Council decided who would have the support of the NFWT in elections. See for example *Central Council Minutes*, NFWT, 13 February 1915.
56 Circular from Miss Froud to NUWT parliamentary secretaries, 25 October 1922, in NUWT unnumbered parliamentary file, NUWT archive. In the same file there is a typed note which describes the position of the London Unit in the 1923 election. It urged its members to work for eight candidates, six Labour and two Liberal, only one of whom was a woman, Susan Lawrence, who successfully defeated the Conservative, Crook, the former NUT president.
57 A copy of Miss Thomas's platform in the Local Government file, number 48 in box 69, NUWT archive, includes: 'In the past men have built houses, but now the opportunity is given, by Act of Parliament, for women to have a voice in their construction, position and aspect.' A similar view was expressed by Miss Byett, *op. cit.*, when she argued that women should be in all professions, including architecture. Blocks of flats had been designed without lifts, by men, because it had not occurred to them that there were problems dragging prams up flights of stairs.
58 According to the *Oldham Evening Chronicle* of 23 July 1931 (in NUWT pictures file) she had been a magistrate involved in the action against the dismissal of married women teachers in Oldham. See also letter from Miss Kenyon as Mayor of Oldham, 8 June 1961, in unnumbered brown box file, NUWT archive.
59 Copies of election literature in Local Government file 48 in box 69 in NUWT archive.
60 See election address in Local Government file 48 in box 69, and letter of thanks from

Agnes Dawson to her supporters. For details of her work on the LCC see Hilda Kean and Alison Oram, *op. cit.*, and Kean, *Deeds not Words*, (1990), Chapter 5.

61 *Central Council Minutes*, NFWT, 3 March 1917. The Ladies' Committee of the NUT consistently opposed the position of parity between men and women on public bodies (*Ladies' Committee Minutes*, NUT, 15 July 1921 and 2 September 1921).

62 Letter from Miss Bathurst to Miss Froud, and vice versa, 9 March 1920, in NUWT parliamentary file in NUWT archive.

63 She obtained 2,419 votes (*The Vote*, 3 January 1919). The London Unit of the NFWT contributed £300 towards the election expenses (letter to Miss Ferrari from central office, 10 January 1919, thanking her for her donation, NUWT parliamentary file). There was some controversy over her candidature. The NUWSS opposed her standing in an unwinnable seat, although subsequently thought the vote received was most encouraging (letter to Miss Froud from Ray Strachey, 19 December 1918, in NUWT parliamentary file). Miss Phipps seems to have been somewhat jaundiced by her experiences and in a letter to Miss Froud dated 4 February 1920 she stated: 'Holding the views I do, I shall never secure election, as I should antagonise every party; and we have proved already that it is useless to count on the women's vote under the present franchise' (in box 69, NUWT archive). See Kean, *Deeds not Words*, (1990), *op. cit.*, Chapter 5.

64 Several of the local council links were facilitated through the WFL. Mrs Lamartine Yates advocated equal pay on her platform (*The Vote*, 28 February 1919, p. 98). Most of her election workers in 1919 were NFWT members (*The Vote*, 14 March 1919, p. 117). See also Emmeline Pethick-Lawrence, *My Part in a Changing World*, London, Victor Gollancz, 1938, pp. 323–49; Nevinson, *op. cit.*, pp. 251–60; for Hill's work on the feminists' behalf see PRO: Ed 24/1744, Ed 24/1783, Ed 24/1784.

65 Petition presented 1 November 1922 (NUWT parliamentary file and PRO: Ed 24/1783).

66 The LTA did not formally join the NUT until 1922. In practice it was a semi-autonomous body of the NUT.

67 EPL leaflet n.d. (1904?), NUWT archive.

68 Agnes Dawson was born in 1875 (see Kean and Oram, *op. cit.*). Miss Byett recalled attending a suffrage meeting in Birmingham in 1885 (*The Woman Teacher*, 5 October 1928, p.3). *The Woman Teacher*, 9 April 1912, contains photographs on p. 104–6 of women delegates to NUT conference 1912. Most of them seem to be in their late 30s or 40s.

69 Letter from Nancy Lightman, 31 May 1964, to Miss Pierotti, in unnumbered brown box file (faint 7–11) in NUWT archive.

70 Letter from Miss Phipps to Miss Froud, 8 February 1918, in members' correspondence file 1918 in NUWT archive.

71 Schwarz and Hall, *op. cit.*, p. 15.

72 *Ibid.*

73 Christabel Pankhurst, *op. cit.*, p. 283. The NUWT was to support the Women's International League, a pro-peace feminist organization, in the 1920s (Bussey and Tims, *Women's International League for Peace and Freedom*, London, George Allen and Unwin, 1965; Helena M. Swanwick, *I Have Been Young*, London, Victor Gollancz, 1935; see Introduction to Catherine Marshall, C. K. Ogden and Mary Sargant Florence, *Militarism Versus Feminism*, (Eds. Margaret Kamester and Jo Vellacot, London, Virago, 1987). See Kean, *Deeds not Words*, (1990), *op. cit.*, Chapter 4. The NFWT was critical of the NUT War Aid Fund to which NUT members contributed, because funds were issued on a discriminatory basis to war victims and their dependants (*Central Council Minutes*, NFWT, 9 June 1917).

74 See entries in Kean, *State Education*, (1988) Appendix; *Central Council Minutes*, NFWT, 6 March 1920; 'Portrait' of Miss Hewitt in *The London Citizen*, East Ham

edition, Labour Party, June 1922. WFL suporters in the NUWT also tended to be Labour Party supporters.

75 See Dr Marion Phillips, 'How to do the Work of the League', Women's Labour League, Labour Party, n.d. From the annual reports it is clear that many members were married often to men active in the Labour Party. Its approach is typified by one of its publications, 'My Favourite Recipes', by the wives of Labour MPs.

76 The motions submitted by Hackney supported mixed schools under the joint headship of a man and woman, with equal pay for equal service. Hackney also submitted motions to the same conference calling for maximum class size of thirty in elementary schools and for physical education to be taught in elementary schools (*Conference Agenda*, 26 January, 1914, Women's Labour League).

77 *The Woman Teacher*, 5 October 1928, p. 3. *The Suffrage Who's Who, op. cit.*, lists no NFWT members as a London branch secretary of NUWSS. However the NUWSS (as well as the militant bodies) did organize activities at the NUT conference (*The London Teacher*, 24 April 1914, p. 317).

78 See Kean, *State Education*, (1988), Appendix, for details. Activists included the Townsend sisters in Lewisham, who also helped found the Women Teachers' Franchise Union; Nancy Lightman and Theodora Bonwick, Hackney teachers; Miss Froud, the future general secretary. NFWT members who were WSPU secretaries included Mrs Cocksedge in Tooting and Balham, Miss Bonwick in Hornsey, and Miss Cutten in Putney and Fulham (*Suffrage Who's Who, op. cit.*, pp. 11–20).

79 *Suffrage Who's Who, op. cit.*

80 The Hackney secretary was Mrs Pierotti, whose daughters were to become active teachers in the NUWT; the Highbury secretary was Miss John, a NFWT member, and the Tottenham secretary was Miss Eggett (*Suffrage Who's Who, op. cit.*). Several Swansea women teachers including Miss Phipps and her friend Miss Neal were members.

81 Rowbotham, *op. cit.*, p. 87, has stated that 'the WFL has never received the attention and publicity of the WSPU because it quietly organized tax and census resistance'. That is, Rowbotham suggests that the difference between the WSPU and WFL was primarily based on the tactics they adopted. However from a reading of the WFL's *The Vote*, and Pethick-Lawrence (one of the founders of the WFL), *op. cit.*, and Linklater, *op. cit.*, it is clear that the differences were based on different politics and internal democracy. Kean, *Deeds not Words*, (1990), *op. cit.*

82 *Suffrage Who's Who, op. cit.*, p. 113.

83 Pethick-Lawrence, *op. cit.*, p. 171: 'The WFL developed many interesting new forms of militancy approved of in conference by all members; it stood four square in all vicissitudes, carried on even during the years of the Great War, and is still pursuing its undeviating purpose to win not only political equity but complete social and economic equality for women.'

84 This resulted, amongst other things, in the imprisonment of a Hackney male school teacher for refusing to declare the tax returns of his wife. Nevinson, *op. cit.*, p. 210 on Mark Wilks: 'His headmaster was naturally indignant and kept sending protests to the government to release an innocent and necessary man, whilst overworked teachers wrestled with overcrowded classes.'

85 There are several witty accounts of census night in *The Woman Teacher*, 5 October 1928, pp. 2–4. Miss Phipps, WFL member, recounted spending the night in a cave off the Swansea coast, while Miss Agnes Dawson recalled that she sat up all night on a hardbacked chair at a friend's house — one of her only militant acts.

86 See Chapter 4, nn. 188–9; Pethick-Lawrence, *op. cit.*, p. 301; Montefiore, *op. cit.*, p. 156.

87 Subsequently when the split occurred it was in working-class districts of the East End and Glasgow that the WFL was to have its largest branches (Linklater, *op. cit.*, p. 133).

99 *Suffrage Who's Who, op. cit.*, p. 108.

89 Linklater, *op. cit.*, pp. 120ff.; Pethick-Lawrence, *op. cit.*, pp. 280–82.

90 *Suffrage Who's Who, op. cit.*, p. 112.

91 Linklater, *op. cit.*, pp. 245–9, for an account of the WFL's campaigns against prostitution, child marriage and female circumcision, especially during the early 1930s. These issues were also taken up by the AMSH, the secretary of which was Alison Neilans, also a member of the WFL (Jeffreys, *op. cit.*, pp. 74, 80, 164).

92 *Suffrage Who's Who, op. cit.*, p. 134.

93 It was this injustice that led Miss Lane to campaign for a women's organization within the NUT — the Equal Pay League (Phipps (1928), *op. cit.*, pp. 1–3).

94 Letter from an 'old stager', *The Schoolmaster*, 25 May 1907, p. 1020.

95 Letters in *The Schoolmaster*, 8 June 1907, from 'Harfat', p. 1129, and from Mrs Read, p. 1130; letter in *The Schoolmaster*, 15 June 1907, p. 1188, from Eleanor Mardon.

96 *Ladies' Committee Minutes*, NUT, 20 June 1908. Letter from Tate in *The Schoolmaster*, 4 May 1907, p. 897, where he mentioned Miss Lane advocating Ladies' Committees at the meeting for women delegates at NUT conference (as reported in *The Schoolmaster*, 13 April 1907, p. 736).

97 *Ibid.*

98 In an article 'Women at conference' the NUT executive women recognized the threat of the NFWT but also advocated greater representation of women (*The Schoolmaster*, 13 April 1907, p. 751).

99 *Ibid.*; Miss Broome on the same issue at 1909 conference in *The Schoolmaster*, 17 April 1909, p. 722, and 24 April 1909, p. 756.

100 Letter of Eleanor Mardon urging women to stand for the executive in *The Schoolmaster*, 8 May 1909, p. 844. The NFWT stood candidates over a period of years for the executive and urged support for them through the pages of *The Schoolmistress*.

101 They preferred to read *The Schoolmistress*. It often provided a column for the NFWT to explain and advertise its affairs under its own editorial control. In the article on women at NUT conference, the executive women stated: 'We refuse to accept the position that the NUT has passed resolutions against combined departments and done nothing more' (*The Schoolmaster*, 13 April 1907, p. 751). The Ladies' Committee recognized the 'great dissatisfaction among the mistresses throughout the country, as they feel the union has not done all that it might have to protect the interests of the woman teacher, and it is feared that unless some step is soon taken to show the women members that they are being considered and their interests are our concern, we shall have our ranks largely diminished' (*Ladies' Committee Minutes*, NUT, 17 September 1910).

102 *Ladies' Committee Minutes*, NUT, 3 June 1910.

103 *Ladies' Committee Minutes*, NUT, 20 June 1908.

104 *Ladies' Committee Minutes*, NUT, 22 June 1907. This meeting agreed that attendance would be by invitation only.

105 The Ladies' Committee rejected, for example, NFWT members Miss Jane Dinning, Miss Hogan and Miss Titcombe (*Ladies' Committee Minutes*, NUT, 19 October 1907). See various letters to the Ladies' Committee, for example from Miss S. Keen of Hackney, protesting strongly against the use of NUT funds because the conference was neither representative nor for women only (*Ladies' Committee Minutes*, NUT, 18 January 1907 and 22 February 1907).

106 *Ladies' Committee Minutes*, NUT, 20 March 1907.

107 *The Schoolmaster*, 4 January 1908, pp. 9–14.

108 *The Schoolmaster*, 8 May 1909, p. 635.

109 'Intellectual women: Clever women are unpopular', *The Schoolmaster*, 29 January 1910, p. 165.

110 *The Schoolmaster*, 29 January 1910, p. 165: a wrecking amendment was defeated by 377 to 269.
111 *The London Teacher*, 20 September 1912, p. 701. A wrecking amendment was carried by 660 to 598.
112 *The Schoolmaster*, 8 February 1913, p. 258; *The London Teacher*, 20 September 1912, p. 701.
113 'Women's suffrage and the LTA', WFTU, (n.d. 1913?); 'The Referendum', WFTU pamphlet no. 1, n.d. (1913?).
114 The women teachers meeting at NUT conference agreed that the refusal of male delegates to vote for association policy was 'in opposition to all rules of honour' (*The Schoolmistress*, 11 April 1912, p. 24).
115 On occasion this was also the case literally. See for example the report of the franchise debate in *The Schoolmaster*, 5 April 1913, pp. 714–16. Recalling the 1911 debate Miss Byett said that the 'mere attempt to move the resolution . . . in the words of *The Times*, "caused conference to degenerate into a howling mob" ' (*The Woman Teacher*, 5 October 1928, p. 3). The Association of Headmistresses, representing women headteachers in private and secondary schools, had passed motions on the franchise and organized a parliamentary petition as early as 1909, yet the NUT would not even listen to them (Nonita Glenday and Mary Price, *Reluctant Revolutionaries. A Century of Headmistresses 1874–1974*, London, Pitman, 1974, p. 68).
116 Letter from Stella Newsom to Miss Pierotti, 7 June 1964, in unnumbered brown box file in NUWT archive.
117 Letter from Emily Davison in *The Schoolmaster*, 30 September 1911, p. 564; *The Woman Teacher*, 5 September 1911, p. 29; *The Schoolmistress*, 4 January 1912, p. 255.
118 Moved by Agnes Dawson (*Central Council Minutes*, NFWT, 15 November 1919).
119 Ethel Froud, 'Women teachers and equal pay', in *The Vote*, 2 April 1920, p. 4. The central council had voted to take no central part in the referendum on equal pay inside the NUT (*Central Council Minutes*, NFWT, 27 April 1918).
120 They welcomed his advice on how they should campaign for their motion to be accepted. (*The Woman Teacher*, 23 January 1912, p. 350).
121 Letter from Eleanor Mardon opposing support for Bentliff as vice-president (*The Woman Teacher*, 30 March 1911).
122 *The Woman Teacher*, 3 October 1911, p. 113.
123 *Annual Report*, WTFU, 1915. Similar sentiments were expressed later in the NUWT to the effect that men needed educating and it was women who would do it (one of the slogans on the equal pay demonstration banner, *The Woman Teacher*, 12 November 1920, p. 58). Kean, *Deeds not Words*, (1990), *op. cit.*, Chapter 2.
124 Eleanor Mardon in *The Schoolmistress*, 6 April 1911, p. 6. See nn. 24–32.
125 *The Woman Teacher*, 16 April 1912, p. 116. *The Schoolmistress*, 18 April 1912, p. 37.
126 The correspondence from Miss Froud to Miss Robson, 22 November 1917, explains the basis of NFWT support for candidates. 'It is . . . our policy to require more than *promises*, we also desire to know what a candidate has *done* or tried to do to further our interests . . . most of the women on the executive have done little or nothing to establish the principle of equal pay — according to our point of view. We, as a Federation, cannot work for the election of anyone (not women even) unless they are prepared to subscribe to the objects of the Federation and to do their utmost to establish them in practice.' In the same file there is a letter from Miss Phipps to Miss Froud (handwritten in pencil and undated) about Miss Wood in Manchester who she thinks is an opportunist:'[She] never spoke for equal pay at a single conference, but now, when it is in the air, comes out and "leads" *again* to get votes. But the Manchester women are hoodwinked. It is a ruse, against the Federation' (original emphasis; members' correspondence file, NUWT archive).
127 The first secretary of the EPL was a man, Joseph Tate, from Birmingham. The

Birmingham feminists were wary of this and declined for a number of years to affiliate to the Federation nationally (NFWT report in *The Schoolmistress*, 14 March 1912, p. 430). For his early efforts Mr Tate was victimized by the education authorities. According to Miss Cooper, Mr Tate had felt let down by the NUT because of his support for women. He had left a teaching post in a secondary school to teach technical classes at the BSA. Due to bad trade classes were transferred to a trade school and he was told he would have a place there. A fortnight before he was to commence work the headmaster informed him that there was no longer a post. He was out of work with two or three sons to educate. He managed to secure a post at an elementary school and expected the maximum salary but received the minimum. The NUT refused to assist him in this matter. His colleagues told him: 'Well, you shouldn't have helped the women.' The women were unaware of his situation, apparently, until they were debating whether to invite him to the 1928 celebration dinner but concluded: 'He has certainly had a very uphill fight. I can't think how he has managed.' Mr Tate, for his part, was delighted to attend (correspondence from Miss Cooper to Miss Froud in orange file (unnumbered) in tea chest, NUWT archive).

128 *The Schoolmistress*, 11 April 1912, p. 12.
129 *The Schoolmistress*, 3 October 1912, p. 8.
130 'Women's suffrage and the LTA', WTFU, n.d.
131 *Ibid.* This refers to the behaviour of the men in breaking up the LTA meeting on 26 June (*The London Teacher*, 28 June 1912, pp. 4–5).
132 *Ladies' Committee Minutes*, NUT, 19 November 1910, records a letter which had been sent by an unnamed teacher to WSPU members in the NUT alerting them to the fact that women paid two shillings a year to maintain the parliamentary representatives and that three-fifths of the salaries of Dr MacNamara and Sir James Yoxall (the sponsored MPs) were paid by women yet neither of them were members of the Conciliation Committee on the franchise (*The Schoolmistress*, 5 April 1911, p. 84).
133 *The Schoolmaster*, 19 July 1913, p. 124, contains letters criticizing the NFWT council for having passed a motion (*The Schoolmaster*, 12 July 1913, p. 73) in support of Mrs Pankhurst and against the 'Cat and Mouse Bill'. In response there is a reply in *The Schoolmaster*, 26 July 1913, p. 168, from one of the NFWT council members: 'Since our history shows that political unrest cannot be cured by coercion without the redress of grievance, the remedy for the present unrest is indicated — viz., a government measure for the enfranchisement of women.'
134 There is lengthy debate in *The Schoolmaster* on the situation in Manchester, the founding city of the WSPU. Although women teachers were active in suffrage politics in the city they were unable to secure the support of the Manchester NUT in their demands. Our reason for this was the strong organization of anti-suffragists in the area, led by Arthur Gronno, who issued several pamphlets nationally warning members of the threat posed to the NUT by a feminist take-over. In particular see letters page in *The Schoolmaster*, 1 July 1911; 29 July 1911; 30 September 1911; 7 October 1911; 16 December 1911; 23 December 1911. See leaflets produced by Arthur Gronno: 'The Attempt to Capture the NUT by Women Suffragists', n.d.; 'Some Facts Concerning the Conference of the NUT and the Woman Suffrage Resolution', n.d.; 'The Fourth Attempt by Suffragists to capture the NUT Conference', n.d. (1914?), in NUWT archive.
135 *The Schoolmaster*, 5 April 1913, pp. 714–16, for debate at 1913 conference.
136 Raeburn, *op. cit.*, p. 264. Conference took place a couple of weeks after the national census boycott on 2 April and a couple of months before the June demonstration of over 40,000 supporters of the suffrage.
137 The first NUT woman president, Miss Cleghorn, took office in 1911; Miss Phillips, the first woman president of the NFCT, took up office in 1910 (*The Schoolmaster*, 1

October 1910, p. 559) and in London Miss A. K. Williams, a NFWT member, was elected president (*The Schoolmaster*, 22 April 1911, p. 804). In the NFWT Miss Fannie Thomas was elected vice-president. She specifically mentioned her support for the franchise in her election platform (*The Schoolmistress*, 16 February 1911, p. 398).

138 *The Schoolmaster*, 13 January 1912, pp. 35 and 90.

139 For example, see *The Woman Teacher*, 5 December 1911, p, 273, about discussion in Lewisham Teachers' Association. A motion supporting the franchise was passed at a meeting by one vote, and subsequently rescinded by three votes on the grounds that it wasn't an educational question. Associations such as Greenwich (which contained NFWT members) prioritized the motion while others, such as Wimbledon, rejected this (*The Woman Teacher*, 6 February 1912, pp. 383–4).

140 'Everywhere one had evidence of their ceaseless activities and of course the "antis" were in evidence also...' (*The London Teacher*, 4 April 1913, p. 244). In the following year *The London Teacher* (24 April 1914, pp. 317–18) reported: 'Five organizations were "in the field"... Most of these bodies had opened rooms, so that Lowestoft seemed to be in the throes of an election... Miss Nancy Lightman held forth persuasively and eloquently at the entrance to the South Pier. Processions of placarded ladies patrolled the streets. The most impressive and bravest to our mind, was that arranged by the Women Teachers' Franchise League [sic], in which several London ladies took part... The Lowestoft conference brought into strong relief the rise of the woman teacher orator... *the Woman's Movement is destined to affect powerfully the future of the NUT*' (original emphasis). At the 1914 conference the WFL held open air meetings each night. They reported that the area they used held from 8,000 to 10,000 people, and it was packed: 'The inhabitants of Lowestoft say it is much more like a suffrage than a NUT conference' (*The Vote*, 17 April 1914, p. 412). The WFL also organized an indoor meeting, preceded by a poster parade through the town, and nearly 1,000 copies of *The Vote* were sold (*The Vote*, 24 April 1914, pp. 3–4). Christabel Pankhurst, *op. cit.*, pp. 269–70, describes how her mother evaded the police to attend the 1914 WSPU meeting. See Kean and Oram, *op. cit.*, p. 52, for a photograph of the parades at the conference. See *The Vote*, 5 May 1916, p. 1025, for details of the meetings of the WFL and IWSPU at 1916 NUT conference.

141 *The Vote*, 24 April 1914, p. 3. A similar prayer given at the non-conformist service was listened to in 'reverent silence' (*ibid.*).

142 *The London Teacher*, 4 April 1913, p. 244. Apparently Haldane was persuaded to see a deputation by Bentliff, an executive member, who said that for every one woman thrown out of the conference there would be twenty if he didn't (*Bristol Times and Mirror*, 26 March 1913, cutting in NUWT archive).

143 Mr Cook asked them to do this in the interests of the women themselves, '"because so long as the question was before them, so long would the members be divided on great principles where they wanted unity" (cheers)' (*The London Teacher*, 20 September 1912, p. 701: account of adjourned meeting of LTA on the question attended by 1,200 teachers). Shortly after the officers of the LTA altered the rules so that such mass meetings could no longer be called by the membership and substituted committee meetings of the LTA.

144 *The Schoolmaster*, 13 April 1912, p. 719; 5 April 1913, p. 714. The same tactic was used to great effect in the NUT during the 1980s when executive opponents of unilateralism used the same device on the grounds that unilateralism, though apparently not multilateralism, was against the non-political aims of the NUT.

145 *Ladies' Committee Minutes*, NUT, special conference meeting 20 May 1911 (verbatim account).

146 *Ibid.*

147 *Ibid.*

148 The WTFU accused the men teachers of resorting to 'uproar and rowdyism'. See 'Woman's suffrage and the NUT', *op. cit.*, *The London Teacher*, 28 June 1912, p. 544, 20 December 1912, pp. 1022–3. Kean, *State Education* (1988), *op. cit.*, pp. 259–60; Kean, *Deeds not Words*, (1990), *op. cit.*, Chapters 2 and 4.

149 Phipps (1928), *op. cit.*, pp. 1–5.

150 *Votes for Women*, 19 April 1912, p. 450.

151 Helena F. Normanton, 'Sex differentiation in salary', NFWT, 1914, p. 14. The question of equal pay was linked to the way in which education was structured within the schools. Mixed schools denied promotion prospects as well as reinforcing the view that the work of women teachers with girls was regarded as less important than the role performed by men teachers with boys. By advocating separate departments, as the EPL and NFWT had done for a number of years, the feminists were also debating their own working conditions.

152 *Ibid.*, p. 21. Normanton refers to the work of the Fabian Women's Group. It had surveyed over seven hundred women teachers, nearly 40 per cent of whom had financial responsibility for dependents. Miss Townsend, secretary of the WTFU and a WSPU member, dealt with this question of pay for dependants succinctly in a letter to *The Schoolmaster*: 'If love, services, and companionship of women are not sufficient inducement to marry without extra salary, men had better remain single' (letter to *The Schoolmaster*, 18 January 1912, p. 129). A similar point was also made by Nancy Lightman at a meeting of the London Certificated Class Teachers Association: it was absurd to say that pay was related to the size of family (*The Schoolmistress*, 17 October 1912, p. 48).

153 Emily Phipps, 'Equal pay', NUWT, n.d. (1924?); editorial and an article by R. H. Roberts in *London Class Teacher*, December 1912; *The Schoolmaster*, 11 November 1911, p. 807.

154 Editorial, *The Woman Teacher*, 12 September 1911, p. 39.

155 This was as an amendment lost by 9,000 to 42,000 on a card vote (*The Schoolmistress*, 3 April 1913, p. 6).

156 After two adjourned annual general meetings (*The Schoolmaster*, 1 February 1913, p. 204).

157 *The Schoolmaster*, 8 February 1913, p. 258. The questions, worded by the officers, counterposed equal pay to existing and past policy of the association which was presently being negotiated with the LCC. Thus equal pay was seen as being in counterposition to immediate improved pay for *all* teachers.

158 Letter in *The Schoolmaster*, 10 March 1917, p. 310. Miss Phipps argued the separatist position for some time. See the correspondence with Miss Froud on this question in the members' correspondence file, 1918, NUWT archive.

159 *The Schoolmaster*, 6 April 1918, pp. 430–31, carried by 42,757 votes to 26,040. The feminists had decided not to intervene inside the conference.

160 This was also the line of the Women's Labour League. In an article on 'the claims of mothers and children' in Marion Phillips, *Women and the Labour Party*, Headley Brothers, 1918, p. 32, Margaret Llewelyn Davies advocated the endowment of motherhood as 'we should expect to see the withdrawal of most married women from the wage market. This would tend to keep up the standard rate, which will be perilously inclined to drop; while in any industrial struggle, the position of men would be greatly strengthened by the fear of starvation of the family being particularly removed.' The London Schoolmasters' Association and National Association of Schoolmasters vehemently opposed equal pay arguing that it would make teaching a wholly women's profession which would adversely affect the national character (open letter from press secretary in *The Schoolmasters' Review*, 1, 1, September 1919). The association argued that motherhood was the noblest profession and that 'the best women find in motherhood, and prefer to find in it, their chief work' (LSA, *Equal Pay and the Teaching Profession*, LSA, 1921, p. 21). Women, the LSA

argued, regarded teaching as 'a kind of interregnum to marriage . . . it is probably quite true to say that every woman in the silence of her own soul thinks and hopes she will escape from the classroom through the door of marriage' (LSA, *ibid.*, p. 49). See Kean, *Deeds not Words*, (1990), *op. cit.*, Chapter 6.

161 See Alison Oram, 'Serving two masters? The introduction of a marriage bar in teaching in the 1920s', *op. cit.*, pp. 134–48.

162 *The Schoolmaster*, 29 May 1909, p. 989, records three thousand teachers at a meeting of protest.

163 *Ladies' Committee Minutes*, NUT, 28 December 1906. At the annual meeting of women delegates at NUT conference in 1910, the delegates discussed the retention of married women after marriage and defeated by 69 votes to 54 the motion that such teachers should be retained. These meetings were called separately from those organized by the NFWT (*The Schoolmaster*, 2 April 1910, p. 626). In London the feminists had argued against this same position when it was advocated — by women colleagues — and had been successful (*The Schoolmaster*, 29 May 1909, p. 949). A debate was organized between Mrs Read, a NFWT supporter from Hackney, and Miss Clara Grant from East London. The meeting overwhelmingly backed Mrs Read's view that: 'No obstacle should be placed in the way of a married woman teacher continuing her service after marriage, as long as she renders efficient service' (*The London Teacher*, 1 June 1909, p. 184).

164 *Central Council Minutes*, NFWT, 12 June 1915, indicate that there was no official opinion on married women.

165 A. S. Byett, 'The married woman teacher', NUWT, n.d.

166 This is also true of unmarried women who were not NFWT supporters. For example, in a portrait of Miss Cleghorn (*The Woman Teacher*, 26 September 1911, p. 11): 'She considers home to be woman's supreme sphere, and woman's first duty to fit herself to motherhood . . .'.

167 'Equal pay for equal work', NFWT, July 1919.

168 *Ibid.*

169 Comments made by Miss McKenzie during the debate at central council on Whitley committees (*Central Committee Minutes*, NFWT, 7 June 1919).

170 Presidential address to annual conference of NFWT (*The Schoolmaster*, 14 June 1919, p. 950).

171 *Central Council Minutes*, NFWT, 6 September 1919. The council backed a decision already taken by the London Unit on the instigation of Agnes Dawson. She had moved that if there was not a satisfactory conclusion to the London salaries question that there should, if necessary, be a London strike. This had been agreed by a mass meeting of women teachers in Kingsway Hall. The central council meeting, again on Agnes Dawson's recommendation, agreed immediately to set up a sustentation fund from a voluntary levy, which could only be used in conjunction with a 'strike policy'. They agreed to be prepared 'at any time direct action becomes necessary'.

172 *Central Council Minutes*, NFWT, 5 October 1918; *The Schoolmaster*, 9 November 1918, p. 511.

173 *The Vote*, 5 April 1918, p. 206. This latter action had resulted in only a handful of LCC members voting for the 'discredited sale of salaries' (*ibid.*).

174 *The Times*, 11 March 1918, p. 5. A meeting called by the NFWT rejected the new salary scales being discussed by the LCC, although these were supported by the LTA.

175 *The London Teacher*, 22 March 1918, p. 121, Editorial: 'Betrayed'; *The London Teacher*, Editorial 'A salaries homiletic': *The London Teacher*, 26 April 1918, p. 149; 'The LTA conference', 10 May 1918, pp. 171–2; 'A Bitter Struggle', *The London Teacher*, 23 August 1918, p. 1.

176 A subsequent issue of *The London Teacher* (22 March 1918) contains an appeal from William Hurden to the feminists not to leave the union. William Hurden, it should

be pointed out, had always supported the franchise, although he rigorously opposed equal pay arguing that men 'as a class' had greater responsibilities. Such an appeal was doomed to failure; he started it by stating 'equal pay for equal work is not a good programme. It might be granted by our enemies in such as way as to do good to no-one, and do great injury to large numbers of teachers.' (*The London Teacher*, 19 July 1918, p. 226). William Hurden was an old member of the LTA committee, having joined the Metropolitan Board Teachers Association in 1875, and had been elected president in 1892–3.

177 *Central Council Minutes*, NFWT, 15 November 1919, moved by Agnes Dawson. Subsequently the council meeting of 30 January 1920 agreed that the council would put a resolution to the annual conference to withdraw from the NUT 'and concentrate their energies on the Federation' (moved by Misses Hewitt and Croxson).

178 First Annual Report of the NFWT, 1918. Kean, *State Education*, (1988), p. 263.

179 See correspondence from Miss Phipps to Miss Froud on the situation in Swansea (members' correspondence file, 1918, NUWT archive). William Hurden's appeal (*The London Teacher*, 19 July 1918, p. 226) also occurs *before* the decision of the central council.

180 As early as 1915 the central council took the decision not to produce a leaflet encouraging women to join the NUT as it was 'a matter for the NUT to do' (*Central Council Minutes*, NFWT, 13 February 1915 and 28 April 1916). The central council agreed to Miss Neal and Miss Wood (Newcastle) writing a letter of protest to *The Schoolmaster* about the way in which the president had dealt with amendments on the salary scales of headteachers (*Central Council Minutes*, NFWT, 28 April 1916). Referring to the union salary scale the central council agreed: 'The national union scale was passed in a conference consisting mostly of men. On every occasion when the scale was discussed amendments in favour of equal pay were on the agenda, and, when permitted, were moved by women members. At meetings of women representatives, held at the same time and place a resolution in favour of equal pay was passed unanimously' (*Central Council Minutes*, NFWT, 3 March 1917). When Mrs Chester wrote a letter to the central council complaining that the council meeting dates coincided with those of the NUT executive (thus ensuring that the loyalties of would be women members of the central council and executive were divided) Miss Woodhouse protested against the time of the council being wasted on trivial matters (*Central Council Minutes*, NFWT, 27 April 1918). The same meeting held a significant discussion on the desirability, or not, of the NFWT participating in the referendum in the NUT. A motion was moved by Misses Hewitt and Bale: 'That to prevent the dual direction of the forward women movement within the teaching profession, the NFWT officially assume the direction of the efforts of the women in the NUT to secure a favourable result in the referendum on equal pay.' This was defeated and the following members voted against: Misses Byett, Dawson, Grinter, Jones, McKenzie, Woodhouse. This is documented more fully than usual discussions of the council indicating the importance of the decision. At the meeting of 15 March 1919 they agreed to hold no official NFWT meetings at the NUT annual conference and on 17 May 1919 they agreed to publish their own official paper.

181 See n. 171.

182 The first *Annual Report* of the newly merged NFWT and WFTU for 1918 reports a London membership rising from 101 to thousands within weeks. By the end of the year the figure was 7,369 (*Annual Report*, NFWT, 1918, NUWT archive).

183 Letter from Miss Goodwin concerning the lack of an NUT presence on the National Council for Women: 'I think the NUWT should not be the only voice of the elementary school . . .'; and reporting that Mrs Tidswell (of the NUWT) had suggested to the National Council a deputation to the Board of Education against the Geddes Cuts and against the raising of the school entrance age to 6 (*Ladies' Committee Minutes*, NUT, 20 October 1922).

184 *Ladies' Committee Minutes*, NUT, 18 May 1923. These include a discussion of a letter from the Six Point Group saying they are ineligible for affiliation as they include men in their membership: 'The Ladies' Committee is of the opinion that the question as to the eligibility of the union for affiliation has been raised out of antagonism to the union.' Nevertheless the Ladies' Committee did send a representative to a Six Point Group meeting on child assault (*Ladies' Committee Minutes*, 21 September 1923) and gave half-hearted support to the Six Point Group demonstration on equal franchise. That is it gave, but then withdrew, national support for the demonstration in favour of asking the LTA's Ladies' Committee to consider the question (*Ladies' Committee Minutes*, 20 November 1925 and 15 January 1926).

185 In response to a letter from the Women's Freedom League asking them to support their resolutions to the National Council for Women they declined to support one calling for equal numbers of men and women to be present on juries (*Ladies' Committee Minutes*, NUT, 15 July 1921). On the occasion on which it recommended to the NUT the adoption of a motion passed by the Consultative Committee of Women's Organizations supporting equal pay and status for men and women police officers this was turned down on the grounds that the duties of the police officers were not comparable and they accepted this decision (*Ladies Committee Minutes*, NUT, 18 November 1921 and 16 December 1921). For the refusal to hold women's meetings at NUT conference see, for example, *Ladies' Committee Minutes*, NUT, 18 November 1921 and 17 November 1922. Initially in this period the Ladies' Committee seems to have tried to ignore the existence of the NFWT/NUWT. There are no references to their activities in the minutes from 1917 to 1921, for example. Yet by 1924 the committee was obliged to recommend the appointment of the women's organizer, and Miss Susan Griffiths, of South Wales, was subsequently appointed (*Ladies Committee Minutes*, NUT, 18 December 1924).

186 *The Woman Teacher*, 28 December 1921, p. 36.

187 *The Woman Teacher*, 28 January 1927, p. 134.

188 *Central Council Minutes*, NFWT, 10 June 1919.

189 *Central Council Minutes*, NUWT, 6 March 1920. The NFWT also faced difficulties in distributing and producing *The Woman Teacher* despite the confident tone projected by the publication. Kean, *State Education*, 1988, p. 265.

190 See n. 160.

191 These were regularly printed on the front page of *The Woman Teacher*. They included: To secure equal pay and equal increments for men and women teachers of the same professional status; to secure the maintenance of each girls' and infants' department under its own headmistress; to secure that the headships of all mixed schools should be open to women equally with men; to secure that all higher educational posts shall be open equally to women and men with equal remuneration; to secure the representation of women teachers on all education authorities; to secure direct effective representation of women teachers on all local governing bodies and in parliament (as printed, for example, in *The Woman Teacher*, 5 October 1928, front page).

192 The NFWT central council agreed to affiliate to the Consultative Committee for Equal Citizenship (*Central Council Minutes*, NFWT, 5 October 1918). It subsequently agreed to affiliate to NUSEC (*Central Council Minutes*, NFWT, 6 September 1919). The object of the NUSEC was 'to obtain all such reforms as are necessary to secure a real equality of liberties, status, and opportunities between men and women, and also such reforms as are necessary to make it possible for women adequately to discharge their functions as citizens'. Their immediate programme included equal franchise, equal moral standards, the right for married women to work, equal pay, the right to birth control for married women. The

NUSEC opposed protective legislation for women, since this was not based on equality between men and women (*Annual Report 1927-28*, NUSEC, 1928). In 1927 the equal rights supporters on the NUSEC resigned and in 1928 the organization split into the National Council for Equal Citizenship (which the NFWT supported) and the Union of Townswomen's Guilds.

193 This was an 'umbrella group' which supported the following: equal political rights; equal occupational rights (that is, every industry open to any woman individually competent); equal pay for women and men teachers; equal pay for men and women in the civil service; better legislation for unmarried mothers and their children, and against child assault (*The Woman Teacher*, 12 November 1926, p. 55).

194 See, for example, *The Woman Teacher*, 20 May 1921, p. 247 for an account of the deputation to the Prime Minister on equal pay; *Minutes* of NUWT equal political rights demonstration committee in NUWT parliamentary file in NUWT archive for details of the July 1926 demonstration; *The Vote*, 28 January 1927, pp. 25-6, and 11 February 1927, pp. 41-2, for an account of the equal political rights campaign and its meeting on the King's speech; PRO: Ed 24/1783 and Ed 24/1784 for details of campaigns on equal pay, involving the Six Point Group; *The Woman Teacher*, 22 July 1927, pp. 317-18, for an account of the equal political rights demonstration jointly organized by the Six Point Group, WFL, NUWT, and Association of Women Clerks and Secretaries.

195 It was also affiliated to the British Social Hygiene Council (formerly the National Council for Combatting Venereal Diseases), an umbrella group to which the AMSH and teachers' organizations, including the NUT, were affiliated. Kean, *State Education, op. cit.*, p. 266.

196 See, for example, the account by Miss Froud of the members' experiences inside the NUT as contained in 'Harrogate, 1918' in *The Woman Teacher*, 6 November 1936, p. 40: 'The fact was that, under the cloak of "unity", women organised in a mixed union were exploited in the interests of men, and the repeated experience of the would be reformers had proved that, owing to the power of the man controlled machine, it was utterly impossible to secure any redress of the major social grievances or to establish the idea that men and women had equal rights in the teaching profession and in their professional organisation...'

197 Miss Burls, past president of the NUWT, moving a motion on equal pay at 1931 conference, as reported in *Southend Pictorial*, 2 January 1932, in NUWT archive.

198 Report of the view taken at a meeting of the WTFU, 22 March 1917, to discuss the LTA possible affiliation to the Labour Party (*Annual Report*, WTFU, 1917).

199 *Central Council Minutes*, NUWT, 15 January 1921. See Kean, *State Education*, (1988), *op. cit.*, pp. 267-8; Kean, *Deeds not Words*, (1990), *op. cit.*, Chapter 5.

200 Kean and Oram, *op. cit.* She also faced difficulty dealing with NUT representatives on the education committee at the LCC: 'At present the "party" is depending on her tremendously for information etc. on education and she is really doing a great deal behind the scenes, and in the "party" on educational matters connected with the LCC. She says she receives little or no support from men who are supposed to be representing education, even on academic questions' (letter from Miss Froud (also a Labour Party member) to Miss Turner, 7 May 1925, in file 51 box 71, NUWT archive).

201 Kean and Oram, *Ibid.* Kean, *Deeds not words* (1990), op. cit., Chapter 5.

202 Jeffreys, *op. cit.*, pp. 153-4. The glorification of motherhood was not confined to the men of the NAMT. Eleanor Rathbone dropped the concept of equal pay in favour of the endowment of motherhood and in so doing turned her back on the feminists' call for equality between men and women on the same terms as men. This same position had been advocated some years before by the leading women in the Labour Party. Margaret Llewelyn Davies, 'The claims of mothers and children', pp. 29-39, in *Women and the Labour Party*, ed. Marion Phillips (n.d. 1918?) argued

that the progress of the race would best be served by raising motherhood to a position of power and equality (sic) and advocated the endowment of motherhood and children. As noted in Chapter 4, n. 211, this was also the NUT's position. Kean, *Deeds not Words*, (1990), *op. cit.*, Chapter 6.

203 This arrangement applied because neither the NUT nor the NUWT were affiliated to the Labour Party. Miss Savage of the Leytonstone Branch, and Leyton Labour Party, and Miss Turner from the Penge Labour Party, acted in a representative way on the ACE, and Miss Turner filed regular reports. They were subsequently joined by Mrs Key, NUWT elementary teacher, mayoress of Poplar, and wife of the Poplar mayor, Charles Key (file 51, Labour ACE in box 71, NUWT archive).

204 When Trevelyan, as President of the Board of Education, paid one visit to the committee the men on the committee prevented him being tackled about his intentions on equal pay. Equal pay had been omitted from the agenda of items of 'utmost importance' to be raised with Trevelyan. The NUT (male) members on the ACE joked that the Labour Government would give women twice as much pay as men, thus ensuring that Trevelyan was able to avoid commenting on equal pay (note by Miss Savage on the ACE meeting of 6 July 1929, file 51 in box 71, NUWT archive). The NUWT members were increasingly jaundiced about their work on the committee because of the presence of so many NUT members: 'It is like attending a meeting of the NUT now', commented Miss Savage (12 March 1928, file 51 box 71 in NUWT archive) as five out of the eleven members were NUT (male) members: Chuter Ede, Marshall Jackman, S. B. Lucas, W. K. Spikes, and G. S. M. Ellis (Goldstone's secretary). Cove, by now an MP, was also in attendance. Mrs Key commented: 'I find this job the hardest I have ever undertaken for the union because of the NUT atmosphere and the House of Commons ditto is too deadly for words...' (undated handwritten note in same file).

205 *The Woman Teacher*, 14 January 1927, 'Annual Report', pp. 109–16; Pethick-Lawrence, *op. cit.*, p. 316; Helena M. Swanwick, *I Have Been Young*, Victor Gollancz, 1935; Kamester and Vellacott, *op. cit.*, Introduction.

206 See Marion Phillips, *Women and the Miners' Lock-Out*, Labour Party, 1927, for a full account of the fundraising activities inititiated by the women, which included a specific mothers and babies scheme. See, for example, *The Woman Teacher*, 19 November 1926, p. 58, which lists the amounts of money collected by individual schools for the relief fund.

207 The 1927 NUWT conference carried a motion moved by Miss Bonwick and Miss Phipps protesting against 'the inhumane treatment of animals in sport, in public entertainment, and in the methods of their slaughter for human consumption, as such practices form a continual contradiction to much of the teaching given to children. This conference therefore calls upon the government and local associations to pass such laws and regulations as are needed for the abolition of such practices' (*The Woman Teacher*, 21 January 1927, p. 126).

208 'Annual Report', *The Woman Teacher*, 14 January 1927, pp. 106–16.

209 *The Woman Teacher*, 14 January 1927, p. 110.

210 E. F. Phipps, 'Why we do not work through the NUT', NUWT leaflet, 1927.

211 'Why I left the NUT', by members of the central council, NUWT, n.d. (1924?).

212 A dinner was held in February 1925 to celebrate Miss Phipps' success in qualifying as a barrister (file 68 in box 94, NUWT archive). A complimentary dinner was held by the Swansea NUWT in honour of Miss Neal becoming national president in 1927 (orange file in tea chest in NUWT archive). In the same folder are details of the dinner held on the achievement of the full franchise in 1928. See Kean, *Deeds not Words*, (1990), *op. cit.*, Chapter 7, for details of the feminists' cultural activities.

213 'They are waking, they are waking,
In the East and in the West,
They are throwing wide their windows to the sun;

And they see the dawn is breaking,
And they quiver with unrest,
For they know their work is waiting to be done,
They know their work is waiting to be done.'
(Chorus of 'The Awakening', as printed in the menu of the complimentary dinner to
Miss Phipps; orange file in tea chest, NUWT archive.)

214 *The Woman Teacher*, 12 November 1821.
215 *The Woman Teacher*, 22 July 1927, p. 318.
216 Minutes of NUWT equal political rights demonstration committee 1926 in NUWT parliamentary file, NUWT archive. As part of its organizing for the demonstration, local women's Labour groups were approached and leaflets were given to waitresses in Lyon's cafés by sympathetic men.
217 Letter to Miss Pierotti, 1 January 1962, in unnumbered brown box file, NUWT archive.
218 Letter from Miss Knapton to Miss Pierotti, written on the decision to wind up the NUWT in the early 60s. Dated 25 February 1961 in unnumbered brown box file.
219 See Kean, *Deeds not Words*, (1990), *op. cit.*, especially Chapters 7 and 8, for an account of the feminists' close friendships.
220 As previously stated membership figures of the NUWT were not published. However a perusal of the votes cast for the TRC elections in 1927 gives some indication of the relative weight of the NUT/NUWT.
For example:

Headmistresses:

NUT:	Miss Conway	3,948
	Miss Winfield	3,296
	Miss Scorrer	2,924
NUWT:	Miss Crosby	1,125
	Miss Hewitt	1,010
	Miss Titleboam	520

Class Mistresses:

NUT:	Miss Organ	5,710
	Miss Dunn	5,298
	Miss Gardner	5,110
NUWT:	Miss Nixon	2,000
	Miss Wainwright	1,878
	Miss Kenyon	1,437

(*The Woman Teacher*, 29 April 1927, p. 233)

Chapter 6

Socialist Organizations within the Teacher Unions

In Chapter 4 I drew the conclusion that within this period the NUT did not adopt an anti-statist position but rather that its strategies were within a statist framework. In the last chapter I drew a distinction between the statist views of the NUT and those of the NUWT/NFWT while also concluding that the feminists' critical stance could not be defined as anti-statist. Having made these points it is also important to note that socialists did organize within the teacher trades unions throughout this period. In stating this it is not suggested that there was at any time a significant Marxist current, or a socialist one which adopted anti-statist perspectives. The role of socialist organizations was primarily to make propaganda about socialist ideas rather than to *organize* teachers in industrial action against the educational state apparatus.

The Strategies of the Teachers' Socialist Association (TSA)

The first socialist teachers' group to be formed this century was the TSA in 1907.[1] H. J. Lowe, a member of the TSA, stated that the organization had been formed of Fabian, ILP and SDF members.[2] However, as I noted in Chapter 4, I have scant evidence of teachers belonging to the SDF.[3] The TSA was not a campaigning body of the ILP — or any other socialist organization — within the NUT. It was a propaganda body formed to 'propagate the gospel [of socialism] amongst teachers'.[4] This was what TSA members did; they carried out their task primarily through the meetings held at the NUT annual conference. At such meetings ILP members, like Kier Hardie or Philip Snowden, or the Fabian Dr Haden Guest, or SDF member Herbert Burrows, addressed large numbers of teachers.[5]

Apart from this, TSA and ILP supporters,[6] made propaganda about the need for teachers to become class conscious and for the NUT to build up a sustentation fund and organize itself as a trade union. I stress the point that this was propaganda because of the way in which such demands were raised and the arguments used in their favour. Speakers appealed to teachers to convert to socialism, and their appeals were based on experience: 'He had now got inside the labour movement and urged teachers to drop their snobbishness and class consciousness and ally themselves with the workers.'[7] When they moved motions at the conference of the National Federation of Class Teachers (NFCT) socialist speakers pointed to the working-class backgrounds of teachers and evoked these as an argument in support of progressive policies: 'We forget our parentage as soon as we leave college. We must come away from the side of the employers who exploit child labour and take the side of those who would make a real heaven here on earth.'[8] Such socialists did not spell out the alternative policies on salaries or on the relationship between the central and local state to those advocated by the union leadership. The bulk of socialists inside the NUT were supporters of the ILP and Fabians. As previously stated, such organizations were not desirous of creating alternatives to the state's framework for education in this period. Instead they were anxious to extend the state's parameters in the area of welfare reform and to create increased provision.[9] As Roger Seifert has argued,[10] teachers did not hold the view that the NUT executive had different interests from its members. He has developed this argument to say that there was (and is) no material basis to suggest a different interest between the rank and file and the executive. However, it is clear that *politically* there was not a sharp divide between the two, because of the nature of the political allegiances of socialist teachers. The desirability of the state extending welfare reforms, as advocated by Labour Party members, was a view broadly endorsed by the whole NUT. Such demands were not a minority opinion.

Thus when one looks for indications of organized activity inside the NUT, such as standing for office or coordinating conference motions, there is little to suggest that this was undertaken on any basis designed to change in all respects the character of the NUT itself.[11] In discussing the NUT I indicated the lack of opposition to political and ideological positions which had a statist orientation. And, as stated above, there is little to suggest that, although teachers did define themselves as socialists, they saw socialism as antagonistic to the existing state and to the dominant ideologies in education. There is not the evidence to suggest, for example, that alternative strategies were developed to the position of support for Empire Day at this time.[12] Nor is there evidence to suggest that in the area of educational philosophy there was a distinct socialist position. Indeed, Walter Sharman, a TSA supporter, and member of the LTA education committee, was the author of some particularly scathing attacks on Montessori which complemented the assault in the editorial pages of *The Schoolmaster*.[13]

Labour supporters inside the NUT did advocate free education from elementary school to university and the implementation of welfare legislation, such as the Provision of Meals Act.[14] But, as indicated in Chapter

4, such policies were compatible with those adopted by the TUC as this time and were often acceptable to the membership at large. Having said that such welfare policies were generally seen as non-contentious it is important to note the issues which *divided* socialists. Although ILP men supported the call for parliamentary franchise — as did the NUT executive, it must be remembered, and the union's Liberal general secretary – such support was less forthcoming on equal pay. The feminists received support from socialists such as W. Nefydd Roberts, William Harris and C. Hicks Bolton; but were denounced by other ILP members such as G. D. Bell.[15] Membership of the ILP was certainly no guarantee of sympathy for feminism: the first national president of the NAS, A. E. Warren, a long-time Labour supporter, had been one of the first socialists to campaign to make the NUT a trade union. Nevertheless he vehemently opposed the feminists' trade union demand of equal pay.[16] This suggests an inability to situate discussion of teachers' relationships to the state in a context which went beyond the confines of the educational state apparatus. It also indicates why the feminists remained so wary of aligning themselves as a union with the Labour Party.

Socialist Organizations at the End of the War

In the last chapter I highlighted the political divisions inside the NUT in the years immediately before the 1914–18 war. The polarization which occurred was focused on attitudes to feminism, the franchise and neutrality of the NUT with respect to political discussion. In fact, socialist organization foundered after 1911 and it may be the case that the differences between socialists on the franchise within the NUT caused this disintegration. It was not until the end of the war that references again appear in the union press to a socialist organization, the Teachers' Labour League or Group.[17]

The Teachers' Labour League was organized from an unofficial conference held during the Christmas holidays of 1916–17.[18] Based on the call by two hundred and thirty local association secretaries for the executive to hold a special salaries conference, the meeting agreed to send a deputation to the NUT executive to demand, amongst other things, that the union affiliate to the TUC and Labour Party.[19] The TLL seems to have had a short-lived existence from Christmas 1916 to April 1918 when the referendum to affiliate to the Labour Party was lost.[20] This issue was not subsequently pursued within the membership at large.[21]

The Activities and Strategies of Socialists during the 1920s

It is not without significance that the better known Teachers' Labour League, which was formed at the start of 1923,[22] took its name from this grouping which had come together on the issue of TUC/Labour Party affiliation. While it is true that in the 1920s the TLL had, albeit for a short period, a greater influence within the teaching milieu than its predecessors, in many respects it continued the practice of these earlier socialist organizations. To imply, as Martin Lawn has done in a recent article,[23] that the TLL of 1923 was the first socialist organization of its kind is to suggest that a new type of radicalism had arisen among teachers. In fact, the TLL represented less a dramatic break or reorientation in socialist education practice than a continuation of earlier ideas and activities.

In the early years of the TLL from 1923 to 1926 Communist and Labour party teachers alike were members. These years reveal a continuity with propaganda of the ILP expounded through the TSA. Likewise the Communist Party's contributions to the League's ideas parallel the kind of propaganda issued by its predessor the BSP: the focus was on the exposure of the capitalist nature of the educational system. In 1923 and 1924 policy was formulated on the extension of educational provision and the nature of imperialist teaching. An emphasis on electoralism went alongside an attempt to turn the NUT towards the working-class in other trade unions.[24] What occurred inside the TLL was not so much a coalescence of different political currents and their fusion into a new political force but a coexistence of different strategies.

The TLL saw itself as 'expressing the Labour teacher's point of view within the labour movement, and especially in submitting to the movement an educational programme drafted by Labour teachers'.[25] This aim was interpreted in different ways by the different political currents inside the TLL. For the mainstream Labour Party supporter interested in education, such as Mrs Harrison Bell, this meant 'bring[ing] into the Labour party those teachers whom the ordinary Labour propaganda has not reached' with the aim of producing threefold results: on parents, education authorities, and the Department itself.[26] This was to be achieved through contributing towards the electoral success of the Labour Party; great emphasis was placed upon teachers in local TLL branches canvassing for the Labour Party.[27]

The Communist current within the TLL interpreted the alliance between teachers and Labour in a different way. They developed two strategies. The first was to make propaganda about the need for a class conscious education aimed at challenging the state: 'The capitalist conception of education is largely that of vocational training; the manufacture of this commodity so as to make it more effective for the profit making purpose of its purchasers and owners. Capitalism looks upon the teacher merely as an instrument to such means....'[28] The second area of propaganda was aimed at creating an alliance with the trades unions, to complement the work of the Communist Party organizing within the Minority Movement.[29]

Neither the Labour nor the Communist current, for different reasons, saw the TLL in this period as an *agitational* trade union body challenging the dominant positions within the teacher unions. The Labour supporters' view of working 'in a spirit of closest co-operation and sympathy with the national Labour Party' meant that a close rapport was to be established with the educationalists within the party, including MPs interested in education.[30] They were keen to build on the existing involvement of teachers in the ACE where they had an opportunity to air their concerns alongside leading party educationalists, such as Tawney.[31]

Despite the Communists' intention of creating a movement within education comparable to that organized by the National Minority Movement in industrial unions they were reluctant to undertake agitational campaigns. There was no attempt to organize teachers in their unions around the immediate practical problems of the mid 1920s, for example, against the Geddes cuts or against unequal pay for women. In response to a letter from Ethel Froud, as general secretary of the NUWT, David Capper, the TLL secretary and Communist Party member, replied that the League accepted the Labour Party programme on equal pay for equal work, adding the following caveat: 'Further the League as a *political* organisation, cannot and does not assume to itself the function of undertaking propaganda in matters of salary.'[32] This comment, taken at face value, suggests an inability to see the interrelation between political and economic strategies. It also indicates an inability to see why the NUWT attached so much importance to this question.[33] Like the Labour members of the TLL, the Communists favoured one union for the whole of the teaching profession. This was in line with the Educational Workers' International (EWI)[34] and was advocated to combat divisions in working-class organizations. Yet they seemed unable to put forward practical proposals to assist in the reunification of the NUT and NUWT because of their inability to see the importance of the feminists' positions.

The Labour and Communist Currents in the TLL

That there were two strands of opinion in the TLL from its inception is borne out by the facts surrounding the formation of the League in early 1923. A rather simplistic explanation of this founding was given by Mrs Harrison Bell: 'It began on two sides concurrently. A group of elementary school teachers and a group of secondary school people both conceived the idea of forming a teachers' society which should definitely be in and of the Labour Party and fortunately the two groups discovered each other in time to prevent any overlapping.'[35] In fact, as I explained in Chapter 2, the Communist Party had taken a decision at the conference of October 1922 to make a determined orientation towards 'bring[ing] increasing numbers of workers under the direct leadership of the party'.[36] Such sentiments had already been expressed a few months before in *The Communist*: 'Genuine

Communist teachers should get together and organise themselves into a determined body of agitators and propagandists. The Party should give a lead . . .'[37] At the same time the Labour Pary was discussing its attitude towards teachers. Although Labour teachers such as G. D. Bell and W. G. Cove had been coopted members of the Labour Party's Advisory Committee for Education for several years,[38] there was little discussion of the role of teachers by this body until Autumn 1922. A conscious decision was taken to appeal to teachers to join the Labour Party and a leaflet was issued outlining a dozen reasons why teachers should join, on the grounds that 'Labour is the only political party with an educational programme and policy adequate to the nation's needs.'[39] The leaflet stated: 'Labour believes that a generous and liberal education for everyone is essential, as the problems that confront us can only be solved by an educated democracy.'[40] This national appeal was echoed in the London Party. Herbert Morrison wrote his own special plea to teachers to join the Labour Party in the pages of the *London Labour Party Chronicle* in the following Spring.[41]

A review of the early officers of the TLL indicates the breadth of political opinions. It also may give some indication of the way different political positions could apparently be accommodated. The first president of the League was E. W. Wilton, a teacher, who had been the Labour parliamentary candidate in Lewisham East in 1922 and 1923, and who would subsequently become the chair of the National Association of Labour Teachers.[42] The two vice chairs were Labour JPs, Alderman Conway from Bradford, who was also on the NUT executive, and Mrs T. LaChard of Kennington.[43] Only one known Communist Party member was in office, but he, David Capper, held the key post of secretary. His initial responsibilities included those of membership secretary.[44] In subsequent years there was also a large preponderance of Labour members, particularly 'moderate' members, among the officers, but Communist Party members such as A. (Sandy) Duncan of Hackney held the important position of secretary of the press and publications committee.[45] Given such a 'division of labour' within the officers of the TLL it was possible for the two currents to develop their different political positions through the respective offices they held. Local groups were free to organize their own political activities. These included electoral work canvassing on behalf of Labour Party candidates, organizing meetings on a range of educational issues and discussing resolutions for the annual TLL and Labour Party conferences.[46]

The Split between the Two Currents

The split which occurred at the TLL's December 1926 conference between 'moderate' Labour Party members and Communist and left socialist members had it origins in the different policies of these two currents, present since the organization's inception. But it was also a culmination of internal disputes which focused on the relationship between the TLL on the one hand and Communist organization and policy on the other. These internal disputes took place within the context of increasingly hostile moves inside the Labour Party and TUC nationally against the Communist Party and Minority Movement.

In line with the Communist Party policy of creating close links with Communist workers' organizations internationally, Communist members had argued that the TLL affiliate to the EWI.[47] This had been rejected at the 1924 conference.[48] Nevertheless, it was agreed to explore further the international position. Subsequently, affiliation was agreed at the 1925 conference and delegates, including those opposed to the Communist Party, had attended the EWI's Vienna conference of 1926.[49] This affiliation was to provide an opportunity for the national Labour Party to intervene in the affairs of the TLL and cause it to be disaffiliated.

A further dispute centred on the motion passed on education policy at the 1926 conference. Opposition was expressed within the Labour Party ACE and within the TLL executive committee to the motion on education at the 1926 Labour Party conference.[50] The motions submitted previously to the Labour Party conference in 1925 had sought to get the Labour Party to tackle the questions of curriculum content and control of education in addition to policies advocating the expansion of educational provision.[51] The Communist current had apparently achieved acceptance of this approach by interpreting democratic civic rights for teachers, a demand having wide support, as the first stage in full democratic control of education.[52] The pages of *Educational Worker*, the TLL journal,[53] were used to debate workers' control in education and the issue identified as 'class conscious versus neutral education'. This was a way of developing the issues raised by the presidental speech of Redgrove and the change in aims agreed at the TLL conference of 1925. Redgrove's address linked the needs of the individual child – which featured prominently in the educational provision arguments of the moderate Labour Party current – with those of the Communists as a way of raising the questions about the nature of the curriculum:

> In defining the aim of education, they should as socialists, consider not only the child but also the community. Education should, on the one hand, have as its sole object the opening up to the child of every channel of happiness and enjoyment...As an adult...it should equip the child in such a way that he might prove a useful member of the community...citizenship, seeing as it served both aims...should come first in the list of school subjects. The child when he left school should realise his true place in society, he should thoroughly understand his rights and privileges and...what the community exacted from him. This meant, of course, that he must understand the principles of socialism.[54]

Debating such policy at TLL conference or within the pages of *Educational Worker* seemed to be an uncontentious method. What proved unacceptable to the 'moderate' members of the TLL was the way in which policy on workers' control and the content of education — which had been rejected by the moderate-dominated executive as too left-wing — nevertheless appeared on the agenda of the Labour Party conference. The policy called for a workers' committee of inquiry into education to cover a definite scheme of self government with democratic control and, on the curriculum, an investigation of the pedagogy and content which fostered a 'bourgeois psychology' and 'militarism and imperialism'. Recommendations were to be made about 'how far, under a workers' administration, this might be counteracted and a proletarian attitude towards an outlook on life be cultivated'.[55] This motion was not moved by the TLL but by H. Weate, a councillor from Manchester, and the Liverpool Trades Council. It was carried by the Labour Party conference.[56] Nevertheless the president, Redgrove, a left Labour Party member and delegate to the conference from Croydon Labour Party, was censured by the TLL executive for his actions at the Labour Party conference.[57]

The motion, which challenged both state education policy and the framework within which the Labour Party conducted educational debate, was given short shrift by the Labour Party nationally. The ACE declared itself to be a competent workers' committee of inquiry and then proceeded to come out in favour of 'neutral' education; that is, it accepted the existing framework of debate, and this was endorsed by the 1927 Labour Party conference.[58]

The 'moderate' Labour Party members inside the TLL seized the opportunity provided by national Labour Party (and TUC) policy passed at the 1926 conference against Communist Party involvement in the Labour Party to launch an offensive against the Communist current inside the TLL.[59] In December 1926 these members issued a circular to all TLL members in support of a full slate of moderate Labour Party members of officers and executive of the TLL. This totally excluded Communist Party members and left socialists alike, including David Capper, Sandy Duncan, and H. Redgrove. Their leaflet stated:

> Recent activities of the League show considerable divergence in spirit from the original plans of its founders. The primary function of the League should be to provide, for teachers with socialist and Labour views, a medium whereby they, as pioneers of educational advance, may be associated in devising the best methods of hastening that advance.[60]

The leaflet also criticized the involvement of the EWI,[61] and stated that there was a 'definite organized attempt' to return members with a communist bias.[62]

The method Labour Party members chose for disseminating and

organizing their dissent is not without irony. Such methods of canvassing for support had already been barred in unions such as the AEU and condemned as disruptive in an attempt to stop *Communists* organizing.[63] Nor was this irony lost on branches under Communist Party or left socialist control. The Merseyside Branch, in response, sent copies to all branches nationally of a motion of protest against the machinery of the League being used for circulating an election appeal of misleading character, and noted 'that nine out of thirteen of those endeavouring to secure their election have formed the majority on the NEC which has conducted those activities of the League throughout the present year'.[64] The Hackney branch, the largest in the country with over fifty members,[65] issued a response to the circular to all its own members, and those in other branches. Refuting the allegations that the fall in the TLL's membership was due to communist bias, Sandy Duncan, the Hackney TLL secretary and Communist Party member, wrote: 'The chief [reasons for membership loss] are the fall of the Labour Government, the General Strike, and the restriction of propaganda arising from financial difficulties.'[66]

The 1926 TLL conference took place on Wednesday and Thursday 29 and 30 December and was attended, according to *The Schoolmaster* and *Educational Worker* alike, by about one hundred and fifty members.[67] On the Wednesday, after Redgrove's address to conference, in which he provocatively acclaimed the EWI as 'a living model of the spirit of unity for the rest of the workers to copy',[68] a telegram was received from Henderson, the Labour Party general secretary, conveying the best wishes of the Labour Party National Executive Committee.[69] On the following day, after the 'moderates' had been defeated by a large majority, leading Labour Party members walked out of the conference and the TLL.[70]

The press statement issued by those Labour Party members who walked out to form the NALT centred not on policy divisions as such but on organizational questions of the relationship of the TLL to the Communist Party and Minority Movement.[71] That is, their argument focused on debate within the wider labour movement rather than on policy differences as such within the TLL. This line of argument, albeit from a different standpoint, was continued by Redgrove in his own press statement. For him, also, it was not a question of dissension amongst the membership on policy but rather a question of the individual actions of a number of executive members seeking to raise 'the communist bogy': 'The League is not a communist body. It is, has been and will continue to be loyal to the Labour Party to which it is affiliated.'[72]

Such a split gave the Labour Party national executive committee the opportunity to expel the TLL, withdrawing the 'special concession' granted to it as 'an organisation of Labour teachers who were prepared to advocate the principles and social policy of the Labour Party in general, and educational policy in particular, among the teachers of the country'.[73] This summary removal meant that the TLL delegate was unable even to attend the Labour Party conference to argue against disaffiliation and that motions already on the conference preliminary agenda in the name of the TLL were removed from the final agenda.[74]

I have dealt with the split at some length for two main reasons. The first is to challenge the methodology of analyzing debates amongst teachers in the TLL without reference to broader political allegiances. Such an approach can suggest that the politics adopted by socialists in the TLL was formed simply by their experiences as teachers. On the contrary, it is clear from a detailed reading of the debates in a broader framework that it is the politics of the different labour movement currents which informed politics inside the TLL. The second reason is to draw parallels with the feminists' own differences, which also came not from their experiences as teachers, but from their political allegiance to different suffrage organizations.

The Effect of the Split

That there was an organization at all of socialist teachers inside the NUT in a period of political and economic downturn in the 1920s owed much to the positions of the Labour Party ACE and the Communist Party congress alike, albeit for different reasons. The subsequent split, too, owed more to the changing positions of the Labour Party and Communist Party nationally than to internal policy differences within the TLL. To underestimate the effect of the TLL's organizational links with the Communist Party and Labour Party,[75] is to suggest a distinctive political line of Labour Party and Communist teachers alike inside the teacher's unions. Such a methodology leads Martin Lawn, for example, to look for explanations based on union and teacher militancy as a rationale for the formation of the TLL.[76] To continue with such a line of argument after the 1926 split Martin Lawn focuses upon the state in isolating socialist teachers from the mass of teachers without, in turn, exploring the background to this in the labour movement. It was the actions taken by the Labour Party and TUC nationally in isolating communist militants which made direct intervention against communist and left socialist teachers unnecessary.

James Hinton has described the Cabinet's intervention to provoke the General Strike, through publicly proclaiming a revolutionary conspiracy which had no basis in fact in order to frighten the TUC into submission. He concluded that this was: 'An indication of ruling class confidence . . . such tactics could only be pursued . . . because, as they well understood, the danger of social revolution was very much more remote in 1926 than it had been seven years earlier.'[77]

It was this selfsame lack of danger of social revolution, coupled with the intervention of the Labour Party and TUC against their own socialist membership, which made any direct intervention against the TLL, other than constant surveillance and monitoring, unnecessary.[78] The consequences of the split within the education arena were that again there were two broad progressive positions advocated: that of the Labour Party and that of the Communist Party. Only now there was no interaction between the two perspectives in a single socialist organization.

Labour 'moderates', who had left the TLL, formed themselves shortly afterwards into the NALT, organized their own meetings at NUT conferences, and by 1929 had issued a policy pamphlet on education.[79] These were the members who had been keen on working within the existing Labour Party policy of extending educational provision and this they continued to do. The emphasis in their policy pamphlet was upon a common school to provide educational opportunities and to eradicate class differences. The curriculum of the school was to 'aim to develop the individuality of the child while keeping in view his future responsibilities as a citizen'.[80] Despite this line of argument which was within the framework of the ACE's discussions the NALT was not an affiliated body of the Labour Party at this time.[81] It had not become the 'accredited educational wing of the party',[82] which it had aspired to be. An effect of the Labour Party 'moderates' secession from the TLL was that the NALT did not have to defend its positions against those to the left of it, but rather had to promulgate its particular line among those teachers to the right of it, outside the Labour Party.

It was not just the NALT from which the TLL was now effectively excluded. Avenues which had been opened to create dialogue within the Labour Party nationally at conference and ACE on the nature of state education and 'class conscious' alternatives were now closed.[83] Locally, TLL branches were also excluded from membership of Labour Parties. In areas where the Communist Party or Minority Movement was strong, Labour Parties were disbanded and Communist-influenced bodies were prevented from reaffiliating to the newly constituted parties. In Hackney, for example, the Hackney Borough Labour Party was disbanded because its secretary was a Communist and the executive committees of the three constituency Labour Parties took it upon themselves to dissolve the management committees. The Hackney TLL continued its support for the disaffiliated party.[84]

Difficulties faced by the TLL from 1926 were closely linked with those faced by communists and left socialists in this period. However, unlike their counterparts in, say, the South Wales Miners' Federation, the TLL did not have a strong trade union base from which to organize its activities. The emphasis which had existed at the TLL's formation on propaganda for socialist politics, as opposed to *organizing* teachers on these lines within the teachers' unions, continued. The TLL continued to debate the need for class conscious education within the pages of the *Educational Worker*.[85] The constraint of working with *teachers* to effect educational change, as had been recognized by some teachers in 1922,[86] meant that there was an orientation towards organizing and supporting parents' councils to campaign, for example, against Empire Day celebrations: 'We believe that we are developing an educated opinion on educational questions, and by so doing, helping working-class parents to demand the best of their children.'[87] To continue the debate on the nature of education the TLL organized a deputation to the USSR which was supported by the NUWT.[88] The NUWT representatives, Ethel Froud and V. E. C. Hunt, addressed many meetings in enthusiastic terms on their return.[89]

I have previously mentioned the isolation of the TLL caused by the political balances of forces in the labour movement. I have also made clear the difficulties faced by left socialists and communists attempting to organize on socialist policies in an arena which, while containing progressive currents, did not contain large groups of teachers responsive to anti-statist policies. But, in addition, the policies of the TLL *itself*, under the influence not only of the British Communist Party, but also the EWI and, indirectly, the Communist International, led to its increased isolation. It had been the EWI which had initiated the debate within its affiliated organizations about the nature of state education and the desirability or not of class conscious education,[90] which had been taken up by the TLL. However the suggestions from Vernochet about the future direction of the TLL after the split seemed to have conflicted with the direction of debates inside the Communist International and the Communist Party. Vernochet is reported to have said that the TLL should either rebuild itself on a trades union basis and affiliate to the TUC or reaffiliate to the Labour Party by working closely with ILP member James Maxton MP.[91] The first option is similar to that discussed by the Minority Movement at its 1927 conference when it called for one union for each industry on a militant basis.[92] However, the second option which suggests a closer working with the Labour Party was one which was to be at variance with the policies of the Communist International and the Communist Party. Although the 1927 British Communist Party Congress had adopted a policy in favour of a Labour government pursuing working-class policy under working-class control, shortly afterwards the Communist International backed up by Harry Pollitt, the future Communist Party secretary, changed its attitude towards reformist parties such as the Labour Party. A debate waged inside the Communist Party on the attitude to take towards the Labour Party.[93]

In these circumstances the TLL veered toward the course of action being advocated within the Communist Party by Harry Pollitt. The TLL rejected the view that socialist revolution was unlikely in the post general strike period.[94] On the contrary, as David Capper indicated in his speech to the TLL conference on January 1929, the possibilities for socialist change were optimistic: 'For the first time since its inception the League has really settled down to the most important part of its work, namely, trade union activity inside the professional organisations . . . Our influence is being felt, to an increasing extent, both in the local branches and the executives of the teachers' association.'[95] Referring to the doubled circulation of the

Educational Worker, he confidently argued: 'Let our motto be: A ten thousand circulation for the *Educational Worker*'.[96] Throughout his address he emphasized a strategy based on 'exposure' of Labour and NUT leaders: 'The TLL is the only body of teachers which is exposing capitalist mismanagement of education and is formulating a working-class education policy.'[97] Despite David Capper's rhetoric, it is undoubtably true that exposing state education *was* what the TLL was doing. Whether it was capable of doing anything more is debatable, particularly given the direction of Communist Party policy. By the following year's conference, the Communist Party had adopted its 'class against class' policy. This defined the Labour Party as a third capitalist party and as social fascist. It was therefore to be opposed as much as all other reactionary forces.[98]

By then David Capper, reporting on the TLL conference, attended by just forty-five members, could proudly assert that 'the League definitely turned aside from the Labour Party, which it condemned as the third and most dangerous of the British capitalist parties and openly declared for the closest alliance with the revolutionary work-class movement.'[99] He concluded: 'Thus ended the most memorable conference in the history of the League . . . [it] did not hesitate to condemn weakness or mistakes in organisation and policy . . . the foundations of the future Educational Workers' Trades Union are being well but truly laid in this country.'[100] At the 1929 conference the TLL had made the decisive step of tightly and explicitly linking its policy to that of the Communist Party. In so doing it had differentiated itself sharply from other progressive currents within the teachers' unions.

While not disputing the socialist nature of the TLL's analyses, its strategy added to the difficulties of those arising from the political conjuncture. In Chapter 4 I argued that teachers' trade union consciousness was not matched by a socialist political consciousness. Ironically, in the TLL one sees a political analysis which bears little connection to an understanding of the economic position faced by teachers and thus of their particular political development. Although the Home Office and the TLL admitted that very few teachers in the TLL were Communist Party members,[101] nevertheless the politics adopted by the left-wing current within the TLL were both before and after the split in line with the policies of the Communist Party.

The Importance of the TLL

Martin Lawn has argued the TLL is important as a study of its activities 'reveals the strength of the programme of a group of socialists teachers, it reveals something of the divisions between radical teachers and between them and other teachers, and it illustrates a particular response by government in dealing with them, all in one historcal period'.[102] The importance in *this* study of including an analysis of the TLL is to illustrate the importance of discussing teacher trade unionism within a political context *outside* its own parameters. I have stressed previously the need for an analysis of teachers' economic, ideological and political role and teachers' perception of this role. In order to establish and identify the mode of existence of radical socialist current inside the teachers' unions there had to be exploration both of the nature of 'trade union activity' and teachers' political attitudes.

The NUT in general and the feminists and socialists in particular all perceived their relationship with the state as important, albeit from different stances. What distinguishes the TLL in the late 1920s is its radical socialist analysis of the role of the state. However the positions adopted by the TLL, which were essentially propagandist, did little to promote an oppositional *strategy* which could relate to the material needs of teachers. Its strategies were unable to challenge state education policy.

Notes and References

1 *Labour Leader*, 19 April 1907, p. 763.
2 H. J. Lowe, 'Socialism for schoolteachers', *Pass on Pamphlets*, no. 20, 1909, Clarion Press.
3 See Chapter 4, nn. 39–44.
4 Lowe, *op. cit.* The founding meeting of the TSA 'was strongly in favour of confining the activity of the Association to propaganda amongst teachers, and opposed to any rivalry with existing socialist organisations' (*Labour Leader*, 19 April 1907, p. 763).
5 *Labour Leader*, 19 April 1907, p. 763; *The Schoolmaster*, 3 April 1908, p. 766; *The London Teacher*, 1 May 1909, p. 151; *The London Teacher*, 1 May 1911, p.190.
6 Teachers tended to define themselves as ILP members, rather than as TSA supporters. Three motions on increasing the sustentation fund were sent in for the 1909 NUT conference from Swansea, Bolton and East Ham. At the NUT conference G. D. Bell spoke in favour of increasing the sustentation fund. He cited his experience during the West Ham dispute which had led him to join the ILP and to carry the motion for increased sustentation fund through West Ham association: 'If the members voted against the increase, then he was done with the union, and he was going to make one of his own. And when he had made it, it would be a trade union, and would be affiliated to the Labour Party' (*The Schoolmaster*, 17 April 1909, p. 713). He lost. Bell continued to pursue his career inside the NUT. In 1908 West Ham submitted a motion for NUT conference arguing it should become a trade union (*The Schoolmaster*, 11 January 1908, p. 67). In 1909 Staffordshire North submitted a similar motion (*The Schoolmaster*, 9 January 1909, p. 62).
7 G. D. Bell, speaking at NFCT conference 1908 (*The Schoolmaster*, 5 October 1908, p.551).
8 William Harris, ILP member, speaking in debate at NFCT conference 1907 arguing that the NUT should become a trade union (*The Schoolmaster*, 5 October 1907, p. 580).

Challenging the State?

9 However, there were attempts to raise the question of secular education. For example, one motion was submitted on this from West Lambeth in 1909 (*The Schoolmaster*, 9 January, p. 47) but this was not taken up consistently.

10 Seifert, *op. cit.*, p. 35.

11 For example William Harris, who referred to himself as an 'ILP-er' at NFCT conference (*The Schoolmaster*, 5 October 1907, p. 580) was a federal committee member of the NFCT for South Wales; J. T. Boulter, the unopposed secretary of the NFCT from 1906, was a member of the Co-op, and a local WEA president and lecturer (*The Schoolmaster*, 4 July 1924, obituary); W. G. S. Coad was a delegate to the NFCT conference and president of West Ham CTA in 1906–07. His father was a dock labourer. He spoke for trade union affiliation and secular education at NFCT conferences (*The Schoolmaster*, 6 October 1906, p. 604; and 5 October 1907, p. 580). William Steer was president of the NFAT in 1907 and made explicit his political sympathies (*The Schoolmaster*, 5 October 1907, p. 577 and 14 September 1907, p. 448: 'Since the Liberal Party is disappointing, the new rising power in parliament should be looked to, and teachers must unite with working men to get reforms'). He was Labour candidate in Dudley in 1918. Although the 1907 NFCT conference defeated policy put forward by G. D. Bell and J. Buckley in favour of reorganizing the NUT as a trade union by only 1,000 votes this was not pursued in subsequent years (*The Schoolmaster*, 5 October 1907, p. 558). This was also the case concerning secular education which was moved by Leyton in 1907 (*The Schoolmaster*, 14 September 1907, p. 438). However, Leyton did not resubmit its policy in future years.

12 See Chapter 4, nn. 111–15.

13 Paper on Montessori in *The London Teacher*, 3 April 1914, pp. 292–3. Walter Sharman chaired the overflow meeting of the TSA at 1911 NUT conference (*The London Teacher*, 1 May 1911, p. 190).

14 For example, Sharman and Lowe spoke in favour of implementing the Provision of Meals Act at the 1908 NFCT conference (*The Schoolmaster*, 3 October 1908, p. 551).

15 G. D. Bell intervened at 1913 NUT conference using the device of 'previous question' to ensure that parliamentary franchise as such was not lost (*The Schoolmaster*, 5 April 1913, p. 716). Within the LTA C. Hicks Bolton supported equal pay and attempted to take legal action to stop G. D. Bell and other officers restricting discussion in the association by banning quarterly meetings open to all members (*The London Teacher*, 20 December 1912, p. 1022; *The Schoolmaster*, 1 February 1913, p. 204; *The London Teacher*, 31 January 1913, p. 86, 90–91; 3 October 1913, supplement, pp. v–vi; 17 October 1913, pp. 846–7; Phipps, *op. cit.*, pp. 17–18. W. Nefydd Roberts, the unemployed teachers' leader, seconded a motion at NFCT conference 1912 on equal pay and won the support of the NFWT for this (*The Schoolmaster*, 5 October 1912, p. 576). He also backed them in their dispute over procedures in the LTA (*The London Teacher*, 13 November 1914, p. 878). William Harris spoke in favour of equal pay at the 1918 NUT conference (*The Schoolmaster*, 6 April 1918, p. 436).

17 Letter in *The Schoolmaster*, 8 December 1917, p. 648, from Corlett of Stretford refers to 'we of the Teachers' Labour League'; Crook in a letter to *The Schoolmaster*, 10 November 1917, refers to the 'Teachers' Labour Party'; letter of G. D. Bell in *The Schoolmaster*, 17 November 1917, p. 552, also refers to the Teachers' Labour League.

18 'Mr Maskelyne, a life long Conservative first publicly raised this matter [Labour Party affiliation] at a joint meeting of the London, Middlesex, and Essex committees convened to discuss the salaries campaign. To his surprise, he was supported by a member of the executive, G.D. Bell. The motion advocating alliance with the trades unions was carried, and that marked the beginning of the movement. The next step

was taken at the Birmingham 'ginger' conference, where a resolution advocating the affiliation of the NUT with the great national labour organisation was carried on Mr Maskelyne's motion with two dissensions out of a conference of at least 140 persons. The notion of an organization (i.e. the Teachers' Labour League) within the union to advocate this policy was mine . . . This movement has been quite spontaneous . . .' (G. D. Bell to *The Schoolmaster*, 17 November 1917, p. 552).

19 Of the 150 teachers present at the Birmingham conference only eight or nine were women. The deputation to the executive was led by Tasker of West Lambeth, president of the London CTA and chair of the LTA finance committee. The unofficial conference was called because of the failure of the NUT executive to do this. A sub-committee of the executive was set up to look at the group's demands which included that union scales should be obligatory on all local authorities, that the sustentation fund be increased and that if the local authorities did not concede, the union should affiliate to the Labour Party (*The Schoolmaster*, 10 February 1917, pp. 170–74 and 178).

20 *The Schoolmaster*, 6 April 1918. The motion was defeated in a referendum by 29, 743 to 15, 434. I have found no records of the TLL in this period.

21 It was raised again on the executive when TUC affiliation was discussed (*The Schoolmaster*, 10 July 1920, pp. 57–9) but there were no motions for annual conference, even though a significant number had supported affiliation.

22 A provisional organization was set up at the beginning of 1923 (undated recruitment leaflet of TLL in file 51 box 70 NUWT archive); E. W. Wilton, 'Formation of the Teachers' Labour Group' in *London Labour Chronicle*, May 1923, states that the first conference was being organized for Whitsun 1923, although prior to that the TLL was already affiliated to the Labour Party; Florence Harrison Bell, 'Teachers for Labour', *The Clarion*, 25 April 1924, says the provisional committee was set up and a constitution and rules drafted before the first conference: 'Eighteen months have elapsed since the inauguration of the League at a meeting of a dozen or so Labour teachers in a little cafe in Southampton Row' (*TLL Newsletter*, 1, Summer 1924).

23 Martin Lawn, 'Deeply tainted with socialism: the activities of the teachers' Labour League in England and Wales in the 1920s' in *History of Education Review*, 14, 2, 1985, pp. 25–35. There are no references to earlier socialist organizations in the NUT.

24 'The first meeting in the last election campaign in London was the first public meeting of the Teachers' Labour League' (Florence Harrison Bell, *op. cit.*). The TLL newsletter of Summer Term 1924, no. 1, reported the following branches having engaged in canvassing: Leyton, Mitcham, Tottenham. The Cambridge branch had affiliated to the local trades council as had Hackney. The West Ham branch was affiliated to the borough Labour Party. Norwich branch had organized classes to study economics and sociology from the socialist point of view; St Pancras had discussed 'The Teacher as Slave' and passed a motion calling on the President of the Board of Education to establish two experimental schools on the socialist principles of workers' control. At the third conference held in December 1924 several motions were passed including those calling for the raising of the school leaving age, reduction in class size in elementary schools, adequate transport facilities for children in rural areas, a widening of the curriculum in secondary schools. The reference back in the name of the TLL at Labour Party conference 1925 raised questions about the type of education offered in schools and said that education should bring about the establishment of a socialist operative commonwealth (*Annual Report*, Labour Party, 1925, p. 214).

25 Undated recruitment leaflet, TLL, in file 51 box 70, NUWT archive.

26 F. Harrison Bell, *op. cit.*

27 See n. 24 and *TLL Newsletter*, no. 3, Spring 1925: reports from branches.

28 'Is the Teacher's Work a Failure?', leaflet no. 1, TLL (n.d., 1924?). Produced for the NEC by the Norwich branch (*TLL Newsletter*, Summer 1924). The Press and Publications Committee in 1924 was convened by A. Duncan, Communist Party member from Hackney.

29 Brian Pearce, 'Early years of the CPGB', in Woodhouse and Pearce, *Essays on the History of Communism in Britain*, pp. 149–78, New Park Publications, London, 1975; Roderick Martin, *Communism and the British Trade Unions 1924–33*, Clarendon, 1969, esp. pp. 37–54; Noreen Branson, *History of the Communist Party of Great Britain 1927–1941*, London, Lawrence and Wishart, 1985, pp. 11–15.

30 Letter, December 1926, from Labour Party candidates for TLL election to all members of the TLL (in file 51 box 70 NUWT archive). MPs involved with the TLL in this period included J. Marley, MP for St Pancras North (TLL leaflet, n.d.); W. G. Cove, Morgan Jones, former parliamentary secretary to the Board of Education in the Labour government (*Daily Herald*, 31 December 1924, cutting in file 51 box 70, NUWT archive). Vice-presidents, honorary positions, included: Professor J. Findlay, F. Soddy, Sidney Webb, H. G. Wells, Bertrand Russell and Tawney (TLL leaflet n.d.).

31 Wilton, the TLL's first president, reported to the ACE meeting of June 1923 on the aims and methods of the newly formed TLL (*ACE minutes*, 19 June 1923, Labour Party) though it was not until 1925 that the TLL specifically asked for representatives on the ACE (*ACE Minutes*, 16 March 1925 and 30 March 1925, Labour Party). Before then individual members of the TLL were members of the ACE, for example G. D. Bell (*ACE Minutes*, 29 March 1920, Labour Party) and Cove (*ACE Minutes*, 25 July 1922, Labour Party).

32 Letter from David Capper to Ethel Froud, 16 July 1924, in file 51, box 70, NUWT archive.

33 In an article in *TLL Newsletter*, no. 1, Summer 1924, E. W. Wilton argued for unity of the teaching profession, seeing the TLL as a mechanism for achieving this aim.

34 For a detailed account of the discussions inside the EWI see Daniel Lindberg, *L'Internationale Communiste et l'Ecole de Classe*, Paris, 1972; *Teachers' International*, official bulletin of the EWI; Ken Jones, *Beyond Progressive Education*, London, Macmillan Education, 1983, pp. 96–7, 103, 118–19.

35 F. Harrison Bell, *op. cit.*

36 *Report on Organization* (presented by the party commission to annual conference), CPGB, 7 October 1922, p. 36.

37 School Drudge, 'The no-more warriors', *The Communist*, 19 August 1922, p. 7.

38 See n. 31.

39 *ACE Minutes*, 12 September 1922, Labour Party; Memorandum 69, ACE, 'An Appeal to Teachers', quotation taken from text of released leaflet, Labour Party, 1922.

40 *Ibid.*

41 Herbert Morrison, 'Plain words to the teachers', *London Labour Party Chronicle*, April 1923.

42 TLL leaflet, n.d. (1924?).

43 *Ibid.*

44 *Ibid.*

45 TLL Newsletter, no. 1, Spring 1924.

46 See n. 24. National Executive report 1924, in Newsletter no. 1, *op. cit.*, reports a membership approaching seven hundred and includes reports of meetings: 'It is no exaggeration to say that during the greater part of this term a League public meeting has been held at least twice a week in various parts of England and Wales . . . Special mention should however be made of the magnificent public meeting called by the League at the Scarborough Conference of the NUT last Easter . . . an audience of three hundred enthusiastic teachers attended . . .' The National Executive Report to

the 1924 conference in *TLL Newsletter*, Spring 1925, stated membership now numbered eight hundred. The NEC had organized a Labour House Party at Scarborough at Easter (NUT conference) and a weekend Summer School at Easton Lodge. Fourteen new branches had been formed.

47 *TLL Newsletter*, Spring 1925, no. 3. The following resolution was finally carried: 'This conference decides that at the present stage of the growth of the Teachers' Labour League, we are not in a position to affiliate internationally and empowers the National Executive Committee to investigate further the international position.'

48 Cove, Morgan Jones, and E. W. Wilton, argued against. Wilton put the view that the EWI was a Communist body and it would be unwise to affiliate given the Labour Party position on Communists (*Daily Herald*, 31 December 1924, cutting in file 51, box 71, NUWT archive). The Labour Party conference of 1924 stated (and reiterated in 1925) that Communists were not entitled to individual membership of the Labour Party and unions were asked not to nominate Communists as delegates to Labour organizations (Branson, *op. cit.*, p. 5).

49 Special Branch report forwarded via Home Office to Board of Education. E. P. Bell, Capper and Williams had attended the EWI conference in Vienna in 1926 (PRO: Ed 24/1757, 4 September 1926). The Foreign Office refused a visa to Korostelev and Romm to attend the TLL conference in 1926 on the advice of Percy at the Board of Education (PRO: Ed 24/1757, 23 December 1926); Jones, *op. cit.*, p. 96.

50 *ACE Minutes*, Labour Party, 4 April 1927 and 6 May 1929. At this latter meeting the report of the sub-committee's recommendations on the motion was carried (*Educational Worker*, November 1926, 1, 1; *Annual Conference Report*, Labour Party, 1927, p. 52).

51 *Annual Conference Report*, 1925, Labour Party, p. 293.

52 *TLL Newsletter*, Spring 1925, no. 3.

53 First issued in November 1926.

54 Report of TLL conference in *The Schoolmaster*, 1 January 1926, p. 20. On a card vote it was agreed by 371 to 123 to amend the aims of the TLL to include 'to enable teachers to identify themselves with other workers in the struggle to replace the capitalist state by a socialist commonwealth'.

55 *Annual Conference Report*, 1926, Labour Party, p. 264.

56 *Ibid.*

57 The motion was carried by eight votes to seven (*Educational Worker*, 1, 3, January 1927).

58 *Annual Conference Report*, Labour Party, 1927, p. 52.

59 Branson, *op. cit.*, p. 5. *Annual Conference Report*, Labour Party, 1926.

60 Letter to all members of the TLL, December 1926, in file 51, box 70 in NUWT archive.

61 However the attempt to withdraw from the EWI, which had been agreed at the 1925 conference by 291 to 211 votes (*The Schoolmaster*, 1 January 1925, p. 20), received only four votes (*The Educational Worker*, January 1927). Presumably this vote took place after the walk-out.

62 Letter to all members of the TLL, *op. cit.*

63 Martin, *op. cit*, pp. 82–3.

64 Resolution from Merseyside branch in file 51 box 70, NUWT archive.

65 Letter from A. Duncan, local TLL secretary, to all members of the Hackney Branch, 16 December 1926, file 51, *op. cit.*

66 *Ibid.*

67 *Educational Worker*, January 1927; *The Schoolmaster*, 6 January 1927, p. 26.

68 *The Schoolmaster*, 6 January 1927, *ibid.*

69 *Ibid.*

70 *Ibid.* They included Morgan Jones MP, Leah Manning, C. W. Hale, A. B. Coleman, E. P. Bell (then general secretary), and Dr O'Brien Harris, the Fabian headteacher

from Hackney. This was after Leah Manning had complained that the ideas of the TLL's founders were not being carried out, which were, she said, to win teachers for Labour 'by the mildest and quietest methods' (*Educational Worker*, January 1927).

71 *The Schoolmaster* 6 January 1927; Press statement: 'For over twelve months it has been clear that a definite division of opinion has existed inside the TLL and within the NEC on the question of loyalty to the policy of the Labour Party or adherence to the policy and methods of the Communist and Minority Movements...'

72 *Ibid.*

73 Letter from Egerton P. Wake, national agent of the Labour Party (*Educational Worker*, August 1927, special number). Apparently such conditions had not been adhered to in the past year.

74 *Ibid.* The motions covered the organization of teachers into one trades union affiliated to the TUC and Labour Party 'in order to remove the capitalist control over the educational machine'; for the NEC to call a conference before May to consider the best means of locally organizing against Empire Day celebrations; to extend the terms of reference of the workers' inquiry, established by Conference 1926 to investigate parents' councils and the remit of the Board of Education (*Annual Conference Report*, Labour Party, 1927, p. 173). Although the TLL was not present to argue against its disaffiliation, since it had already been disaffiliated, Redgrove, in his capacity as a Croydon delegate, moved the reference back. Amongst other things he stated that membership did not include more than 3 per cent Communists, and that Communist Party members had never been sent to conferences to represent the TLL (in line with the 1924 Labour Party conference decision). Morgan Jones, speaking against, said that the TLL had 'only' 525 individual members.

75 Lawn (1985), *op. cit.*, especially p. 32.

76 *Ibid.*

77 Hinton *op. cit.*, p. 140.

78 PRO: Ed 24/1757 contains Special Branch and Home Office reports on the activities of the TLL.

79 *Education — A Policy*, NALT, Labour Party, 1929; NALT organized a meeting at NUT conference 1927 addressed by Alderman Conway, Leah Manning and Morgan Jones (*Daily Herald*, 19 April 1927); the first secretary was W. E Rowlands (*Daily Herald*, 17 October 1927, cuttings in file 51 box 70, NUWT archive).

80 NALT, *op. cit.*

81 Note dated 20 March 1931 in PRO: Ed 24/1757.

82 From a letter sent to all branches of the TLL by those about to leave in December 1926, in file 51 box 70, NUWT archive.

83 As stated above, the TLL had had the right to submit motions to Labour Party annual conference, even though the teachers' unions were not affiliated to the Party. Similarly the TLL had been able to send representatives to the ACE, albeit in an individual capacity (*ACE Minutes*, Labour Party, 16 March 1925 and 30 March 1925).

84 Branson, *op. cit*, p. 5. Letter from A. Duncan to all members of the Hackney TLL branch, 16 December 1926, in file 51 box 70, NUWT archive.

85 See, for example, *Educational Worker*, 1, 3, January 1927, article by A. S. Neill; 1, 7, May 1927, article by Redgrove on propaganda in the schools; a reply to this by Professor Findlay in 1, 3, June 1927; *Educational Worker*, 1, 9, July 1927, article on neutral or class conscious education by the Esperanto Pedagogical Services; *Educational Worker*, 2, 14, December 1927, concerning debate on this issue at TLL conference 1927.

86 Letter in *The Communist*, 9 September 1922; article 'The no more warriors', 19 August 1922, *The Communist*.

87 *Educational Worker*, 1, 9, July 1927, article on parents' councils. See also *Educational Worker*, 2, 17, April 1928; 2, 18, May 1928; 2, 19, June 1928 for accounts of anti-Empire Day activities organized by parents in Leyton.

88 *Educational Worker*, January and February 1928, 2, 15; a book was published by the TLL on this, *School Teachers and Scholars in Soviet Russia*, TLL, 1929 (*The Women Teacher*, 14 January 1927, p. 106). However, Miss Froud refused to write a foreword for the book, when asked by David Capper, on the grounds that this 'would be sufficient [for many branches of the NUWT] to sever connection with the NUWT. This would serve you no useful purpose and do much harm.' Nevertheless she 'thought it one of the most interesting experiences in my life' (letter from Miss Froud to David Capper, 7 February 1929, in file 51 box 70, NUWT archive).

89 Letter from Ethel Froud, *ibid.*; *The Women Teacher*, 14 January 1927, pp. 106ff.

90 Daniel Lindberg, *op. cit.*, pp. 61ff. He reports the different positions of the different sections.

91 Note dated 24 January 1928, in PRO: Ed 24/1757.

92 Branson, *op. cit.*, p. 11.

93 *Ibid.*, pp. 19–38.

94 *Ibid.*, p. 24.

95 Presidential address by David Capper at TLL conference, January 1929, pp. 17–18 in *The Teachers' International*, April–June 1929.

96 *Ibid.*, p. 18.

97 *Ibid.*

98 Branson, *op. cit.*, pp. 31–51; 'Class against class' (General Election Programme of the CPGB), Communist Party, 1929.

99 Presidential address by David Capper in 'The Teachers' Labour League at work', *The Teachers' International*, January–March 1930 p. 3.

100 *Ibid.*, p. 7.

101 Letter from A. Duncan to Hackney TLL members, 16 December 1926, describes a handful of Communist Party members (in file 51, box 70, NUWT Archive). Note from the Home Office, from Special Branch to Board of Education, 12 September 1925: 'The number of English teachers who are definitely communists is very small: seven are known to this department and it is doubtful if there are many more' (PRO: Ed 24/1757).

102 Lawn (1985), *op. cit.*, p. 25.

Conclusion

Between 1900 and 1930 there existed distinctive groupings — outside the mainstream of trade union and political organization — which centred their concerns on education. These groupings — feminist teachers, socialist teachers and Marxists outside teaching — had developed their own distinctive policies and strategies for state education. Although there appeared at the time to be little common ground between these currents, with the benefit of hindsight it is possible to identify some shared concerns. All those I have described saw education as an important, and possibly decisive, factor in determining the occupational destinies of young people. In different ways they also saw education as a major influence on political attitudes. For the socialists working in the socialist sunday schools, access to education would bring enlightenment and a changed society. For feminist teachers, politicized by the suffrage movement, education was a means by which they would obtain full emancipation, through the education of men in their cause. Marxists saw their own political education for young people as a way of equipping a new generation of activists to campaign against the iniquities of capitalism.

There was a common optimism, too, which ran through these different attitudes towards education. For some this meant a confidence in a benign state, which would respond to progressive demands for change. For others it was reflected in the energy they brought to challenge the state on education. Some socialists — despite protestations to the contrary — accepted a social democratic and statist framework for education policy. This acceptance was based upon the concept of equality of opportunity for individual children within a neutral educational system. It entailed demanding access to state provision, albeit in an expanded form, rather than creating an alternative structure to the state system, under workers' control. Others advocated an instrumentalist view of state education as a weapon of capitalism, based on wider analysis of class forces in society. Such positions, as stated, for example, by the SLP, or the CP in the late 1920s, had little resonance. The political practice of the groups which held positions like these was such as to prevent their view from being incorporated within the broader labour movement.

Despite these differences between socialist groups, there was a general conclusion that teachers were unlikely to oppose the state's educational policies. This was true. Despite the trade union militancy evident on questions of pay and conditions, and the general sympathy expressed for the extension of state welfare reform measures, on similar lines to those of the Labour Party and TUC, most teachers lacked any degree of political and ideological autonomy from the policies of the state. This was reflected both in the general acceptance of the state's ideology within the educational state apparatus and in enthusiasm for the state's authority outside education. The fact that women teachers had a different relationship to the state, which was structured by political factors outside the educational state apparatus, and in particular by the lack of parliamentary franchise, helped create a different relationship between women and the state within the educational state apparatus. Feminist politics outside education structured the way in which feminist teachers argued for an alternative perspective within education.

I now wish to turn to the state in this period: as I have stressed, to assess the strategies of self-styled oppositionists without also discussing the state itself as a dynamic participant in the formulation of educational strategies is to draw certain — mistaken — conclusions about the role of the state and socialists and teacher trade unionists alike. The state did not simply respond to pressure from working-class organizations: it actively promoted its own strategies to incorporate them into its own frameworks. These years saw an increasing number of social welfare reforms, reforms which have been interpreted as a state concession to well organized socialist forces. They can also be seen, however, as a strengthening of capitalism brought about by the state's successful incorporation of the working class. The state's strategies were successful in the sense that they were accepted as the framework of educational debate by different class forces, including teachers, as state employees. Their success can be attributed to the inter-relation of political, economic, and ideological strategies both inside and *outside* the educational state apparatus.

This suggests that future research into state education policy may be usefully conducted outside a narrowly educational discourse. The academic distinctions between history, political science and education have permeated the way in which issues of state education policy have been approached. Working outside such rigid distinctions has raised a number of questions worthy of future study. The nature of teachers' politicization, for instance, needs to be considered outside narrow educational parameters. As I have indicated in my references to feminist teachers, an understanding of their educational views is unproductive unless one looks also to their politicization in the suffrage movement. Teachers are (still) state employees and although this does have an influence on ideological and political commitments, it is not the only factor in determining teachers' views.

A second area worthy of greater attention is the educational work carried out by socialist and Marxists with their own children. Alternatives to state educational curriculum and pedagogy were developed in socialist children's and youth organizations. These were seen as part of the cultural practice of socialists. A study of such cultural practices indicates the way in which theoretical concepts of childhood and the socialist movement's attitude towards children were developed in practice.

The third area of study this book had indicated is the interelationship between different aspects of state ideology in different state institutions. The state used the mere existence of socialist teachers — as well as of socialist youth organizations — to create a climate of opinion opposed to socialist ideas in education. The very numbers of radical socialist teachers (and members of youth organizations) thus contributed to their increasing isolation at the same time as providing a convenient focus for statist ideologies designed to promote the concept of 'neutral education'. Concurrently, while teachers were ineffective in organizing alternatives to the state's ideology within the educational state apparatus they also, unwittingly, aided those currents keen to create 'red scares' as a way of strengthening the state. Such scare strategies had a general effect outside the educational system. Today, education is still being used with success by the state for functions outside the educational state apparatus. This is exemplified most vividly by 'section 28' of the Local Government Act. Here, state education policy is being constructed to mobilize currents *outside* education in order to create a homophobic ideological climate in society at large.

Much of this book has dealt with the shattering of the days of hope at the end of the 1914–18 war when feminists hoped that enfranchisement would herald economic equality, when teachers thought Burnham would change significantly their standing and remuneration within the state, when socialist activists inspired by the Bolshevik Revolution longed for and organized for such changes in Britain. I am conscious that my account of their activity concludes at the time of their decisive defeat: the aftermath of the general strike, successive impositions of pay cuts, growing unemployment, and the advent of the National government. Even in these days of despair, though, there still remained a small core of socialist and feminist activists campaigning for their educational views. By the 1930s the Communist Party had reorganized its teachers' work. By 1939 Nan McMillan had become the first (and only) communist president of the NUWT; by the 1940s G. C. T. Giles was elected as the first communist president of the NUT.

It is hoped that the same tenacity and conviction which led these earlier socialists and feminists will encourage their latter-day counterparts to analyze the errors of their predecessors while recognizing their contribution to socialist and feminist ideas in education. Perhaps, in the same spirit, we will be able to respond to the problems of our day.

Bibliography

(Unless otherwise stated place of publication is London.)

Contemporary Book, Pamphlets and Articles

ANDERSON, T. (1919) *The Fat Bourgeois or from Message Boy to Merchant Prince.*, Glasgow.

ANDERSON, T. (1922) *Down and Out etc: A Model Lesson for Proletarian Schools*, Glasgow, Proletarian Bookstall.

ANDERSON, T. (1923) *A Few Pearls*, Glasgow, Proletarian Bookstall.

APPLETON, W. A. (1921) *What We Want and Where We Are*, Hodder and Stoughton.

BULKLEY, M. E. (1914) *The Feeding of Schoolchildren*, Ratan Tara Foundation, George Bell & Sons Ltd.

BYETT, A. S. (n.d.) *The Married Woman Teacher*, NUWT.

COLE, G. D. H. (1921) *The Future of Local Government*, Cassell & Co.

DAWSON, A. (n.d.) *Nursery Schools*, NUWT.

DRAKE, B. (1920) *Women in Trades Unions*, Labour Research Department.

ENGELS, F. (1975) 'May 4th in London', in Marx, K. and Engels, F. *Articles on Britain*, Moscow, Progress Publishers, pp. 400–06.

FISHER, H. A. L. (1923) 'Education and the Empire', *Empire Review*, 37, June.

FORD, I. O. (1904) *Women and Socialism*, ILP.

GLASIER, J. B. (1919) *The Meaning of Socialism*, Manchester, National Labour Press.

GOULD, F. J. (1923) *The Life Story of a Humanist*, Watts & Co.

GOULD, F. J. (1918) *A Socialist Plan of Education* (paper read at the annual conference of the National Socialist Party, 1918), Twentieth Century Press.

GREVILLE, F. (Countess of Warwick) (1906) *A Nation's Youth*, Cassell.

GRIFFITHS, D. (1923) *The Real Enemy*, Grant Richards Ltd.

GUEST, L. H. (1915) *The Next Steps in Educational Progress*, Theosophical Publications Society.

HAMILTON, C. (1912) 'Women in the Great State', *The Great State, Essays in Reconstruction* (preface by H. G. Wells), Harper & Brothers, pp. 219–47.

HAWARD, H. E. (1911) *Imperial Subventions in Aid of Local Taxation*, Institute of Municipal Treasurers.

HAY, W. F. (1920) *Education and the Working Class*, Liverpool, Liverpool and District Council for Independent Working Class Education.

HENDERSON, A. (1917) *The Aims of Labour*, Headley Bros.

HORRABIN, J. F. and W. (1924) *Working Class Education*, Labour Publishing Co.

HUNTER-WATTS, J. (1904) *State Maintenance for Children*, Twentieth Century Press.
HYLTON DALE, Mrs (1908) *Child Labor Under Capitalism*, Fabion Tracts no. 140.
KEELING, F. (1914) *Child Labour in the United Kingdom*, P. S. King.
LEES-SMITH, H. B. (1928) *The Encyclopedia of the Labour Movement*, 3 vols, Caxton.
LLOYD, C. M. (1919) *The Reorganisation of Local Government*, Labour Research Department.
LONDON SCHOOLMASTERS' ASSOCIATION (1921) *Equal Pay and the Teaching Profession*, LSA.
LOWE, H. J. (1909) *Socialism for Schoolteachers*, Pass on Pamphlets no. 20, Clarion Press.
MACDONALD, J. RAMSAY (1919) *Parliament and Revolution*, Manchester, National Labour Press.
MACDONALD, J. RAMSAY (1920) *A Policy for the Labour Party*, Leonard Parsons.
MACDONALD, J. RAMSAY (1924) *Why Socialism Must Come*, ILP.
MACTAVISH, J. M. (1916) *What Labour Wants from Education*, WEA.
MANSBRIDGE, A. (1918) *Education and the Working Classes* (reprinted from the *Contemporary Review*, June 1918), Contemporary Review Co.
MANSBRIDGE, A. (1920) *An Adventure in Working Class Education, Being the Story of the Workers' Educational Association 1903–1925*, Longman & Co.
MACMILLAN, M. (1911) *The Child and the State*, Manchester, National Labour Press.
MILLAR, J. P. M. and WOODBURN, A. (1936) *Bias in the Schools*, NCLC.
MURPHY, J. T. (1972) *Preparing for Power: A Critical Study of the History of the British Working Class Movement*, Pluto Press (first published 1934).
NALT (1929) *Education — A Policy*, Labour Party.
NEVINSON, M. (1923) *The Legal Wrongs of Married Women*, WFL.
PAUL, E. and C. (1921) *Proletcult*, Leonard Parsons.
PAUL, W. (1917) *The State: Its Origin and Function*, Glasgow, Socialist Labour Press.
PAUL, W. (1918) *Scientific Socialism*, Glasgow, Socialist Labour Press.
PEMBER REEVES, M. (1979) *Round About a Pound a Week*, Virago (first published 1913).
PHILLIPS, M. (Ed.) (1918) *Women and the Labour Party*, Headley Bros.
PHILLIPS, M. *Women and the Miners' Lockout: The Story of the Women's Committee for the Relief of the Miners' Wives and Children*, Labour Publishing Co.
PHILPOT, B. (1904) *London at School, The Story of the School Board 1870–1904*, T. Fisher Unwin.
PHIPPS, E. (n.d.) *Equality of Opportunity*, NUWT.
PHIPPS, E. (1928) *The History of the NUWT*, NUWT.
PLEBS LEAGUE (1910) *The Burning Question of Education . . . Being an Account of the Ruskin College Dispute, its Cause and Consequences*, Plebs League.
PLEBS LEAGUE (1923) *What to Read: A Guide for Worker Students*, Southwark Press.
A. J. R. (Ed.) (1913) *The Suffrage Annual and Women's Who's Who*, Stanley Paul & Co.
RUST, W. (n.d.) *After Twenty Years — The History of the Youth International*, YCL.
RUST, W. (n.d.) *The Case for the YCL*, YCL.
RUST, W. (1925) *What the YCL Stands For*, YCL.
SHEARS, H. C. (1919) *Socialist Policy: Reform or Revolution*, ILP New Series 17.
SNOWDEN, P. (1906) *A Straight Talk to the Ratepayers*.
SNOWDEN, P. (1920) *Labour and National Finance*, Leonard Parsons.
SNOWDEN, P. (1924) *Twenty Objections to Socialism, Answered by Philip Snowden*, ILP.
STARR, M. (1929) *Lies and Hate in Education*, Hogarth Press.
STEWART, J. (1920) *An Appeal to the Young*, WSF.
TEACHERS' LABOUR LEAGUE (1929) *Schoolteachers and Scholars in Soviet Russia*, TLL.
TEACHERS' LABOUR LEAGUE (1923–26) *Newsletters*, TLL.
TOWNSHEND, Mrs (1909) *The Case for School Nurseries*, Fabian Tract no. 145.
TREVELYAN, C. (1924) *The Broad High Road in Education*, Labour Party.

WEBB, S. (1913) *What About the Rates?*, Fabian Tracts no. 172.
WOMEN TEACHERS' FRANCHISE UNION (WTFU) (1913) *The Spirit of Citizenship*.
WTFU (n.d., 1913?) *Women's Suffrage and the LTA*.
WTFU (n.d.) *The NUT and the Women's Suffrage Resolution*.
WTFU (n.d.) *Why the Women's Suffrage Resolution is Legitimate NUT Business*.
WTFU (n.d.) *Pamphlet 1: The Referendum*.
YOUNG COMMUNIST LEAGUE (n.d.) *League Training Syllabus*.
YOUNG COMMUNIST LEAGUE (1923) *The Child of the Worker*, E.C. of Young Communist International.

Secondary Books, Pamphlets and Articles

ABRAMOVITZ, M. and ELLIASBERG, (1957) *The Growth of Public employment in Great Britain*, New York, Princeton.
ALDRED, G. (1943) *Communism — The Story of the Communist Party*, Glasgow, Strickland Press.
ALDRED, G. (1955–63) *No Traitor's Gait!*, 3 volumes in monthly parts, Glasgow, Strickland Press.
ALLEN, M. (1934) *Sir Robert Morant*, Macmillan.
ALTHUSSER, L. (1971) *Lenin and Philosophy and Other Essays*, NLB.
ANDERSON, P. (1964) 'Origins of the present crisis', *New Left Review*, 23, January/February, pp. 41–68.
ANDERSON, P. (1976) 'The antinomies of Antonio Gramsci', *New Left Review*, 100, November, pp. 5–78.
ANDREWS, L. (1976) *The Education Act 1918*, Routledge and Kegan Paul.
APPLE, M. (1982) *Education and Power*, Routledge and Kegan Paul.
APPLE, M. (1982) *Cultural and Economic Reproduction in Education: Essays on Class, Ideology and the State*, Routledge and Kegan Paul.
ARNOT, R. (1975) *South Wales Miners: A History of the South Wales Miners' Federation, 1914–1926*, Cardiff, Cymric Federation Press.
BALLARD, P. (1937) *Things I Cannot Forget*, University of London Press.
BARKER, R. (1972) *Education and Politics 1900–51: A Study of the Labour Party*, Oxford, Clarendon Press.
BELL, T. (1937) *The British Communist Party: A Short History*, Lawrence and Wishart.
BELL, T. (1941) *Pioneering Days*, Lawrence and Wishart.
BERNSTEIN, E. (1921) *My Years of Exile: Reminiscences of a Socialist*, Leonard Press.
BIRRELL, A. (1937) *Things Past Redress*, Faber.
BLUNDEN, M. (1967) *The Countess of Warwick*, Cassell.
BRACHER, S. W. (1923) *The Herald Book of Labour Members 1923–4*, Labour Publishing Co.
BRANSON, N. (1979) *Poplarism 1919–25*, Lawrence and Wishart.
BRANSON, N. (1985) *History of the Communist Party of Great Britain 1927–41*, Lawrence and Wishart.
BROCKWAY, A. FENNER (1942) *Inside the Left, Thirty Years of Platform, Press, Prison and Parliament*, George Allen and Unwin.
BROCKWAY, A. FENNER, (1946) *Socialism over Sixty Years. The Life of Jowett of Bradford 1864–1944*, George Allen and Unwin.
BRUCE, M. (1965) *The Coming of the Welfare State*, Batsford.
BUCI-GLUCKSMANN, C. (1980) *Gramsci and the State*, Lawrence and Wishart.
BUNYAN, T. (1977) *The History and Practice of the Political Police in Britain*, Quartet.
BURKE, B. (1975) *Rebels with a Cause: The History of Hackney Trades Council 1900–1975*, Centerprise Publishing Project.

BUSSEY, G. and TIMS, M. (1965) *Women's International League for Peace and Freedom*, George Allen & Unwin.

CARNOY, M. (1983/4) 'Education and theories of the State', *Education in Society*, 2, 1, pp. 3–25; and 2, pp. 3–19.

CASTELLS, M. (1978) *City Class and Power*, Macmillan.

CHALLINOR, R. (1977) *John S. Clarke: Parliamentarian, Poet, Lion-Tamer*, Pluto Press.

CLUNIE, J. (1954) *Labour is my Faith: The Autobiography of a House Painter*, Dunfermline.

CLYNES, J. R. (1937) *Memoirs*, Hutchinson.

COATES, D. J(1975) *The Labour Party and the Struggle for Socialism*, Cambridge University Press.

COLE, G. D. H. (1941) *British Working Class Politics 1832–1914*, George Routledge & Sons.

COLLINS, H. (1971) 'The marxism of the SDF', in Briggs, Asa and Saville, John (Eds.) *Essays in Labour History 1886–1923*, Macmillan, pp. 47–69.

COURTNEY, J. (1934) *The Women of my Time*, Lovat Dickinson.

COWLING, M. (1971) *The Impact of Labour 1920–24*, Cambridge University Press.

DAVIES, B. (1961) *Pages from a Worker's Life 1916*, Our History Series, Communist Party.

DONOGHUE, B. and JONES, G. W. (1973) *Herbert Morrison, Portrait of a Politician*, Weidenfeld and Nicolson.

EVANS, P. REUSCHEMEYER, D. and SKOLPOL, T. (Eds.) (1985) *Bringing the State back In*, Cambridge University Press.

FINE, B. and HARRIS, L. (1976) 'State expenditure in advanced capitalism: A critique', *New Left Review*, 98, July/August, pp. 97–112.

FINER, H. (1950) *English Local Government*, 4th ed, Methuen.

FISHER, H. A. L. (1940) *An Unfinished Autobiography*, Oxford University Press.

FRANCHINI, S. (1980) *Sylvia Pankhurst 1912–1924: Dal Suffragismo Alla Revoluzione Sociale*, Pisa, ETS University.

FRANCIS, H. and SMITH, D. (1980) *The Fed: A History of the South Wales Miners in the Twentieth Century*, Lawrence and Wishart.

FRASER, D. (1976) *Urban Politics in Victorian England: The Structure of Politics in Victorian Cities*, Leicester, Leicester University Press.

FROW, E. and R. (1970) *A Survey of the Half-Time System in Education*, Manchester, E. J. Morten.

FROW, R. and E. (n.d., 1978?) *The Communist Party in Manchester 1920–1926*, Manchester.

GAMBLE, A. (1981) *Britain in Decline*, Macmillan papermac.

GARNER, L. (1984) *Stepping Stones to Women's Liberty*, Heinemann.

GILBERT, BB. (1966) *The Evolution of National Insurance in Great Britain*, Michael Joseph.

GILBERT, B. B. (1970) *British Social Policy 1914–39*, Batsford.

GILL, A. (1968) 'The Leicestershire School Board 1879–1903', in Simon, B. (Ed.) *Education in Leciestershire 1840–1940*, Leciester, Leicester University Press, pp. 156–77.

GLENDAY, M. and PRICE, M. (1974) *Reluctant Revolutionaries: A Century of Headmistresses 1874–1974*, Pitman.

GOSDEN, P. H. (1977) 'The origins of co-optation to membership of local education committees', *British Journal of Educational Studies*, 25, 3, October, pp. 258–67.

GOUGH, I. (1975) 'State expenditure in advanced capitalism', *New Left Review*, 92, July/August, pp. 53–92.

GOUGH, I. (1979) *The Political Economy of the Welfare State*, Macmillan.

GRAMSCI, A. (1971) *Selections from the Prison Notebooks*, Ed. Hoare, Q. and Smith, G. N. Lawrence and Wishart.

GRIGGS, C. (1983) *The Trades Union Congress and the Struggle for Education 1868–1925*, Lewes, Falmer Press.

HAMILTON, M. A. (1938) *Arthur Henderson, A Biography*, Heinemann.

HARLOE, M. (Ed.) (1981) *New Perspectives in Urban Change and Conflict*, Heinemann Education.

HARRIS, N. (1972) *Competition and the Corporate Society*, Methuen.

HARRISON, S. (1962) *Alex Gossip*, Lawrence and Wishart.

HAW, G. (1917) *The Life Story of Will Crooks, MP*, Cassell.

HAY, J. R. (1975) *The Origins of the Liberal Welfare Reforms 1906–1914*, Macmillan.

HINTON, J. (1983) *Labour and Socialism — A History of the British Labour Movement 1867–1974*, Wheatsheaf Books, Brighton.

HOBSON, J. A. (1938) *Confessions of an Economic Heretic*, George Allen.

HOLLOWAY, J. and PICCIOTTO, S. (1977) 'Crisis and the State', *Capital and Class*, 2, pp. 76–101.

HOWARD, M. (1981) *War and the Liberal Conscience*, Oxford University Press.

HOWELL, D. (1983) *British Workers and the ILP 1888–1906*, Manchester, Manchester University Press.

HUME, P. (1982) *The NUWSS 1897–1914*, New York, Garland.

HURWITZ, S. (1949) *State Intervention in Great Britain: A Study of Economic Control and Social Response 1914–1919*, New York, Columbia University Press.

JACKSON, T. A. (1953) *Solo Trumpet, Some Memories of Socialist Agitation and Propaganda*, Lawrence and Wishart.

JAMES, R. R. (1969) *Memoirs of a Conservative, J.C.C. Davidson's Memoirs and Papers 1910–1937*, Weidenfeld and Nicolson.

JEFFREYS, S. (1985) *The Spinster and Her Enemies, Feminism and Sexuality 1880–1930*, Pandora Press.

JENKINS, E. W. (1973) 'The Board of Education and the Reconstruction Committee', *The Journal of Educational Administration and History*, 5, 1, January, pp. 42–51.

JESSOP, B. (1984) *The Capitalist State*, Oxford, Basil Blackwell.

JESSOP, B. (1985) *Nicos Poulantzas — Marxist Theory and Political strategy*, MacMillan.

JONES, J. (1937) *Unfinished Journey*, Hamish Hamilton.

JONES, K., (1983) *Beyond Progressive Education*, Macmillan.

KEAN, H. (1990) *Deeds not Words: The Lives of Suffragette Teachers*, Pluto Press.

KEAN, H. and ORAM, A. (1988) 'Who would be Free herself must strike the blow: Agnes Dawson and the NUWT', *South London Record*, 3, South London History Workshop.

KEITH-LUCAS, B. and RICHARDS, P. G. (1978) *A History of Local Government in the Twentieth Century*, George Allen and Unwin.

KEKEWICH, Sir G. (1920) *The Education Department and After*, Constable.

KENDALL, W. (1969) *The Revolutionary Movement in Britain 1900–1921: The Origins of British Communism*, Weidenfeld and Nicolson.

LANGAN, M. and SCHWARZ, B. (Eds.) (1985) *Crises in the British State 1880–1930*, Hutchinson.

LANSBURY, G. (1928) *My Life*, Constable.

LAWN, M. (1985) 'Deeply tainted with socialism: The activities of the Teachers' Labour League in England and Wales in the 1920s', *History of Education Review*, 14, 2, pp. 25–35.

LAWN, M. and OZGA, J. (1986) 'Unequal partners: Teachers under direct rule', *British Journal of Sociology and Education*, 7, 2, pp. 225–37.

LAWN, M. (1987) *Servants of the State. The Contested Control of Teaching 1900–1930*, Lewes, Falmer Press.

LAWN, M. and GRACE, G. (1987) *Teachers: The Culture and Politics of work*, Lewes, Falmer Press.

LAWRENCE, B. (1972) *The Administration of Education in Britain*, Batsford.

LENIN, V. I. (1969) 'State and revolution', *Selected Works*, Lawrence and Wishart, pp. 264–351.

LIDDINGTON, J. and NORRIS, J. (1978) *One Hand Tied Behind Us: The Rise of the Women's Suffrage Movement*, Virago.,

LINKLATER, A. (1980) *An Unhusbanded Life: Charlotte Despard, Suffragette, Socialist and Sinn Feiner*, Hutchinson.

LYMAN, R. (1957) *The First Labour Government 1924*, Chapman.

McCRINDLE, J. and ROWBOTHAM, S. (1979) *Dutiful Daughters*, Harmondsworth, Penguin.

MACINTYRE, S. (1980) *A Proletarian Science. Marxism in Britain 1917–1933*, Cambridge University Press.

MACINTYRE, S. (1980) *Little Moscows: Communism and Working Class Militancy in Inter-War Britain*, Croom Helm.

McKIBBIN, R. (1974) *The Evolution of the Labour Party*, Oxford University Press.

MACLEOD, R. M. (1968) *Treasury Control and Social Administration. A Study of Establishment Growth at the Local Government Board 1871–1905*, George Bell.

McNAIR, J. (1955) *James Maxton The Beloved Rebel*, George Allen and Unwin.

McSHANE, H. (1978) *No Mean Fighter*, Pluto Press.

MANNING, L. (1970) *A Life for Education*, Victor Gollancz.

MARTIN, R. (1969) *Communism and the British Trades Unions 1924–1933. A Study of the National Minority Movement*, Oxford, Clarendon Press.

MARTINDALE, H. (1938) *Women Servants of the State 1870–1938 — A History of Women in the Civil Service*, George Allen and Unwin.

MARTLEW, C. (1983) 'The State and local government finance', *Public Administration*, 61, Summer, pp. 127–47.

MARWICK, A. (1965) *The Deluge — British Society in the First World War*, Bodley Head.

MARX, K. (1968) 'Critique of the Gotha Programme', in Marx, K. and Engels, F. *Selected Works in One Volume*, Lawrence and Wishart, pp. 315–35.

MARX, K. and ENGELS, F. (1970) *The German Ideology (Part One)*, Ed. Arthur, C. J., Lawrence and Wishart.

MIDDLEMAS, K. (1979) *Politics in Industrial Society. The Experience of the British System Since 1911*, Andre Deutsch.

MIDDLETON, L. (Ed.) (1977) *Women in the Labour Movement: The British Experience*, Croom Helm.

MILIBAND, SR. (1983) 'Poulantzas and the capitalist state', *New Left Review*, 82, November/December, pp. 83–92.

MILLIBAND, R. (1983) 'State power and class', *New Left Review*, 138, March/April, pp. 57–68.

MONTEFIORE, D. (1927) *From a Victorian to a Modern*, E. Archer.

MORTON, A. L. and TATE, G. (1956, rev. edn. 1973) *The British Labour Movement 1770–1920*, Lawrence and Wishart.

NAIRN, T. (1977) 'The twilight of the British State', *New Left Review*, 101, February/April, pp. 3–61.

NEVINSON, M. (1926) *Life's Fitful Fever*, A. and C. Black.

NEWMAN, Sir G. (1939) *The Building of a Nation's Health*, Macmillan.

NEWSOME, S. (1960) *The Women's Freedom League*, Women's Freedom League.

OFFE, C. (1984) *Contradictions of the Welfare State*, Hutchinson.

ORAM, A. (1985) 'Sex antagonism in the teaching profession: The equal pay issue 1914–1939', *History of Education Review*, 14, 2, pp. 36–48.

ORAM, A. (1983) 'Serving two masters? The introduction of a marriage bar in teaching in the 1920s', in London Feminist History Group, *The Sexual Dynamics of History*, Pluto, pp. 134–53.

OWEN, P. (1988) 'Who would be free herself must strike the blow', *History of Education Review*, 17, 1, March, pp. 83–100.

OZGA, J. and LAWN, M. (1981) *Teachers, Professionalism and Class — A Study of Organised Teachers*, Lewes, Falmer Press.

PAGE, ARNOT, R. (1975) *South Wales Miners: A History of the South Wales Miners' Federation, 1914–1926*, Cardiff, Cymric Federation Press.

PANKHURST, C. (1987) *Unshackled*, Cresset Women's Voices (first published 1959).

PANKHURST, S. (1987) *The Home Front*, Cresset Library (first published 1932).

PARTINGTON, G. (1976) *Women Teachers in the 20th Century in England and Wales*, Slough, NFER.

PATTISON, R. (1973) 'The Birrell Education Bill of 1906', *Journal of Educational Administration and History*, 5, 1, pp. 34–41.

PEACOCK, A. and WISEMAN, J. (1967) *Growth of Public Expenditure in the United Kingdom*, University of New York Studies in Economics, rev. edn. George Allen and Unwin.

PERCY, E. (1958) *Some Memories*, Eyre and Spottiswode.

PETHWICK-LAWRENCE, E. (1938) *My Part in a Changing World*, Victor Gollancz.

PIEROTTI, A. M. (1963) *The Story of the NUWT*, NUWT.

PILE, Sir W. (1979) *The Department of Education and Science*, George Allen and Unwin.

POLLARD, S. (1969) *The Development of the British Economy 1914–1967*, 2nd edn, Edward Arnold.

POLLITT, H. (1940) *Serving My Time*, Lawrence and Wishart.

POOK, E. M. (1984) *The Leysian Mission 1886–1986. A Century of Caring*, Epworth Press.

POULANTZAS, N. (1973) *Political Power and Social Classes*, New Left Books.

POULANTZAS, N. (1975) *Classes in Contemporary Capitalism*, New Left Books.

REEDER, D. (1981) 'A recurring debate: Education and industry', in Dale, England, Fergusson and Macdonald (Eds.) *Education and the State*, Vol. 1, Lewes, Falmer Press, pp. 177–204.

ROTHSTEIN, A. (1960) *An SDF Branch 1903-6*, Our History Series no. 19, Communist Party.

ROVER, C. (1967) *Women's Suffrage and Party Politics in Britain 1866–1914*, Routledge and Kegan Paul.

ROWBOTHAM, S. (1977) *A New World for Women: Stella Browne, Socialist Feminist*, Pluto Press.

ROWBOTHAM, S. (1986) *Friends of Alice Wheeldon*, Pluto Press.

ROY, W. (1968) *The Teachers' Union*, Schoolmaster Publishing Company Ltd.

SADLIER, M. (1949) *Michael Ernest Sadler*, Constable.

SAMUEL, R. (1985) 'The lost world of British Communism', *New Left Review*, 154, November/December, pp. 3–53.

SAMUEL, R. (1986) 'Staying Power: the lost world of British Communism, Part Two', *New Left Review*, 156, March/April, pp. 63–113.

SAMUEL, R. (1987) 'Class politics: The lost world of British Communism, Part Three', *New Left Review*, 165, September/October, pp. 21–52.

SANDERS, W. (1927) *Early Socialist Days*, Hogarth.

SEIFERT, R. V. (1987) *Teacher Militancy. A History of Teacher Strikes 1896–1987*, Lewes, Falmer Press.

SELLECK, R. J. W. (1972) *English Primary Education and the Progressives 1914–1939*, Routledge and Kegan Paul.

SELLECK, R. J. W. (1968) *The New Education 1870–1914*, Pitman.

SHERINGTON, G. (1981) *English Education, Social Change and the War 1911–1920*, Manchester University Press.

SIMON, B. (1974) *Education and the Labour Movement 1870–1920*, Lawrence and Wishart.

SIMON, B. (1974) *The Politics of Educational Reform 1920–40*, Lawrence and Wishart.

SIDELSKY, R. (1967) *Politicians and the Slump. The Labour Government of 1929–1931*, Macmillan.

SPOOR, A. (1967) *White Collar Union. Sixty Years of NALGO*, Heinemann.

SUTHERLAND, G. (Ed.) (1972) *Studies in the Growth of Nineteenth Century Government*, Routledge and Kegan Paul.

SWANWICK, H. M. (1935) *I Have Been Young*, Victor Gollancz.

TATE, G. (Ed.) (1950) *London Trades Council 1860–1950. A History*, Lawrence and Wishart.

TAYLOR, H. A. (1933) *Jix: Viscount Brentford*, Stanley Paul and Company.

THERBORN, G. (1977) 'The rule of capital and the rise of democracy', *New Left Review*, 103, May/June, pp. 3–41.

THOMS, D. W. (1974) 'The Education Act of 1918 and the development of central Government control of education', *The Journal of Educational Administration and History*, 6, 2, July, pp. 26–30.

THOMSON, Sir B. (1935) *The Story of Scotland Yard*, Grayson and Grayson.

THOMSON, Sir B. (1939) *The Scene Changes*, Collins.

THOMPSON, P. (1967) *Socialists, Liberals and Labour — The Struggle for London 1885–1914*, Routledge and Kegan Paul.

THORNE, W. (1925) *My Life's Battles*, George Newnes.

TILLETT, B. (1931) *Memories and Reflections*, John Long.

TILLETT, B. (1943) *Fighter and Pioneer* (speeches edited by George Light), Blandford Press.

TREVELYAN, C. (1921) *From Liberalism to Labour*, George Allen and Unwin.

TROPP, A. (1957) *The Schoolteachers*, Heinemann.

TSUZUKI, C. (1961) *H. M. Hyndman and British Socialism*, (Ed. Pelling), Oxford University press.

VERNON, B. D. (1982) *Ellen Wilkinson*, Croom Helm.

WAITES, B. (1976) 'The language and imagery of "class" in early twentieth century England 1900–1925', *Literature and History*, 4, Autumn, pp. 30–55.

WARD, L. O. (1974) 'H. A. L. Fisher and the teachers', *The British Journal of Educational Studies*, 22, 2, February, pp. 191–9.

WELLER, K. (1985) *'Don't Be A Soldier' The Radical Anti-War Movement in North London 1914–1913*, Journeyman Press.

WILLS, W. D. (1964) *Homer Lane*, George Allen and Unwin.

WOOD, E. M. (1981) 'The separation of the economic and political in capitalism', *New Left Review*, 127, May/June, pp. 86–95.

WOOD, E. M. (1986) *The Retreat from Class. A New 'True' Socialism*, Verso.

WOODHOUSE, M. and PEARCE, B. (1975) *Essays on the History of Communism in Britain*, New Park Publications.

YOUNG, J. D. (1979) *The Rousing of the Scottish Working Class*, Croom Helm.

Periodicals

British Socialist
Bulletin for Leaders of Communist Children's Groups
The Call
The Clarion
The Class Teacher
The Colliery Workers' Magazine

The Communist
Communist International
The Communist Review
The Educational Worker
Justice
Labour Leader
League Leaflet
The Link
The London Citizen (East Ham edition)
The London Class Teacher
The London Labour Party Circular/London Labour Chronicle
The London Teacher
The New World (East Ham)
Plebs
The Red Dawn
The Revolution
Rhondda Socialist
The Schoolmaster
The Schoolmasters' Review
The Schoolmistress
Social Democrat
The Socialist
Socialist Annual
Socialist Record
The South Wales Worker
Sunday Worker
Swansea Labour News
The Times
The Vote
Votes for Women
The Woman Teacher 1911–1912
The Woman Teacher (NUWT) 1919–
The Woman's Dreadnought
The Worker
Workers' Dreadnought
Workers' Life
Workers' Weekly
Young Communist
Young Comrade
The Young Socialist
Young Worker 1921
Young Worker 1926–

Parliamentary and Cabinet Papers

Unpublished papers in the Public Record office

CAB 24
Ed 24
HO 45

Cmnd. papers

Cmnd. 7315 xi: *Final Report of the Departmental Committee on Local Taxation*, HMSO, 1914.

Cmnd. 9230: *Machinery of Government*, Report of the Machinery of Government Committee of the Ministry of Reconstruction, HMSO, 1918.

Cmnd. 443: *Report of the Standing Joint Committee on a Provisional Minimum Scale of Salaries for Teachers in Public Elementary Schools*, HMSO, 1919.

Cmnd. 8666–8696: *Commission of Inquiry into Industrial Unrest*, HMSO, 1919.

Cmnd, 931: *Expenditure on Education*, Board of Education, HMSO, 1920.

Cmnd. 3134: *Proposals for Reform in Local Government and in the Financial Relations Between the Exchequer and the Local Authorities*, HMSO, 1928.

Cmnd. 2129: *Report of the Board of Education 1922–23*, HMSO, 1924.

Cmnd. 8244: *Education 1900–1950*, Ministry of Education, HMSO, 1950.

Official Papers

Education Act 1902, (2 Edw 7 ch 42), 1902.
Education Act 1918.
Reconstruction Problems 18. Industrial Councils: The Whitley Scheme, Ministry of Reconstruction, 1919.
Reconstruction Problems 19, State Regulation of Wages, Ministry of Reconstruction, 191.
Report of the Imperial Education Conference, HMSO, 1924.
Hansard.

Reports

Conference Reports:

British Socialist Party
Communist Party
Labour Party
Labour Representation Committee
London Teachers' Association (1917)
National Union of Teachers
Social Democratic Federation/Party

Annual Reports:

Association for Moral and Social Hygiene
British Social Hygiene Council
Independent Labour Party
London County Council Women Teachers' Union
London Teachers' Association
National Federation of Women Teachers (London Unit)
National Union of Societies for Equal Citizenship
National Union of Teachers
National Union of Women Teachers
Trade Union Congress
Women's Labour League
Women's Social and Political Union
Women Teachers' Franchise Union

Archive and Unpublished Material

Fawcett Library: material dealing with suffragettes and women teachers.
Labour Party Archive: memoranda and minutes of the advisory committee on Education.
Marx Memorial Library: material dealing with the Communist Party; British Socialist Party North West Ham minute book.
National Union of Teachers Library: minute books and circulars of NUT executive and sub-committees, the National Federation of Assistant Teachers, and London Members' Committee.
National Union of Women Teachers Archive (in the Institute of Education): extensive range of material including minute books; correspondence; photographs; leaflets of the Equal Pay League, National Federation of Women Teachers and National Union of Women Teachers; leaflets and unpublished correspondence of the Teachers' Labour League.

Theses

Brooks, J. R. (1974) *R. H. Tawney and the Reform of English Education*, Ph.D., University of Wales, Bangor.

Chewter, D. M. (1965) *The History of the SLP from 1902-21 With Special Reference to the Development of its Ideas*, B.Litt., University of Oxford.

Billington, R. H. C. (1976) *The Women's Education and Suffrage Movement 1850-1914: Innovation and Institutionalisation*, Ph.D., Hull University.

Hamilton, I. (1972) *Education for Revolution: The Plebs League and Labour College Movement 1908-1921*, M.A., University of Warwick.

Kean, H. (1981) *Towards a Curriculum in the Interests of the Working Class*, M.A., Institute of Education, University of London.

Kean, H. (1988) *State Education Policy 1900-1930: the Nature of the Socialist and Teacher Trade Unionist Response*, Ph.D, King's College, University of London.

Lynch, G. (1974) *Ideology and the Social Organisation of Educational Knowledge in England and Scotland 1840-1920*, M.A., Institute of Education, University of London.

McCann, W. P. (1960) *Trade Unionist, Socialist and Co-operative Organisations in Relation to Popular Education 1870-1902*, Ph.D., Manchester University.

Roberts, J. H. (1970) *The National Council of Labour Colleges: An Experiment in Workers' Education*, M.Sc., Edinburgh.

Index

British Empire Union   69n
British Socialist Party   2, 28, 41, 76n
  and the curriculum   30, 31, 32
  and the Education Act   (1918) 32
  and the LP   48n
  and parliament   28
  and the SLP   37
  and the Socialist Sunday Schools   76n
  and the state   29, 30, 33
  and the YSL   63
Brockway, Fenner A.   48n
Broome, A.   157n
Brotherton, J.   77n
Buckley, J.   118n, 182n
Bukharin, N.   51n
Bulkley, M. M.   47n, 48n
Burgess, A. C.   112n
Burls, S.   153n, 165n
Burnham   6, 15, 81, 84, 85, 92, 102–3,
  109n, 110n, 117, 121n, 130, 146, 150,
  190
Burrows,   H. 48n, 106n, 168
Burston, school strike   38, 51n
Butcher, J.   56, 68n, 70n
Byett, A.   129, 131, 143, 153n, 154n,
  155n, 158n, 162n, 163n
Buxton   149

Cabinet   177
  reports on labour situation   12, 13, 20n
  reports on revolutionary and subversive
   organisations   13, 20n, 56, 69n, 70n,
   74
  war cabinet committee   144
Campbell, A.   74n
Campbell, B.   69n
Campbell, T.   65
Camberwell   130
Cambridge   183n
Canning   Town 24
Capitalism
  and education   34, 36, 41–42, 52n, 60
  maintenance of,   26
  and schools   31, 32, 59
Capper, D.   85, 107n, 172, 173, 175, 179,
  180, 184n, 185n, 187n
Chamberlain, A.   71n
Chelsea   130
Chester, A.   163n
Chewter, D.   45n, 50n
Chew, A. Neild   153n
Children   144, 190
  becoming future socialists   59, 62, 64,
  174

  as consumers   26
  physical condition of,   8, 9, 19n
  political activity of,   60, 61, 62
  and SLP   36
  state maintenance of,   24, 25, 26, 29,
   35, 50n, 111n
Churchill, Lord R.   4
Churchill, W.   70n
Chuter Ede, J.   166
Cinema Positions of:
  London County Council   114n–115n
  London Teachers' Association   93,
   114n, 115
  National Federation of Women
   Teachers   93–94
  National Union of Teachers   93, 114n
  National Union of Women
   Teachers   93–94
  Victoria Leage   114n, 115n
Citizenship
  and BSP   30
  and curriculum   174
  and feminist teachers   129, 138, 143,
   184, 152n, 164n
  and teachers   88, 94, 96
Clarke, M.   107n
Clarion clubs   28
Class conscious education   32, 33–34, 41,
  42, 58, 60, 65, 171, 174, 175, 178,
  183n, 186n
Class size   91, 110, 111n
Cleghorn, I.   99, 126, 135, 140, 152n,
  159n
Clementson, G.   118n
Clerks Union 98
Clunie, J.   34, 50n, 46n
Clynes, J. R.   27
Coad, G. S.   111n, 118n, 182n
Coates, F.   58, 76n
Cockerton judgment   5
Cocksedge, Mrs   156n
Cole, G. D. H.   106n
Coleman, A. B.   185n
Collins, H.   45n, 46n
Committee on Physical Deterioration   9,
  19n
Communist children's groups   1, 53, 57,
  68n, 70n, 72n, 74n
Communist International   179
Communist Party   22, 34, 40–43, 46n,
  52n 60, 63, 174, 178, 188, 190
  class against class policy   42, 52n, 179,
  180
  conference 1922,   40–41